Cuneiform Texts and the Writing of History

History does not begin in classical antiquity. Several cultures in the Near East predate Greek historical tradition by many centuries. To understand the history of one of the main ancient Near Eastern cultures, that of Mesopotamia, the scholar has to rely on cuneiform texts, which represent the oldest tradition of writing in human history, in use for nearly 3,000 years. The number and variety of texts written in the cuneiform script are enormous, and present a unique source for the study of history. This book describes the possibilities and challenges the material presents to the modern historian.

Cuneiform Texts and the Writing of History discusses how the abundant Mesopotamian sources can be used for the study of various aspects of history: political, social, economic and gender. Marc Van De Mieroop:

- criticizes disciplinary methodologies which are often informed by a desire to write a history of events;
- scrutinizes the intellectual background of historical writings;
- examines how Mesopotamia's position as the 'other' in classical and biblical writings has influenced scholarship;
- suggests how the cuneiform texts can be used in innovative ways;
- illustrates approaches with examples taken from the entirety of Mesopotamian history.

Cuneiform Texts and the Writing of History provides a challenging introduction to the written sources from Mesopotamia which will be useful to academics and students.

Marc Van De Mieroop is Professor of Ancient Near East History at Columbia University in New York. His previous publications include *The Ancient Mesopotamian City* (1997).

Approaching the Ancient World
Series editor: Richard Stoneman

The sources for the study of the Greek and Roman world are diffuse, diverse, and often complex, and special training is needed in order to use them to the best advantage in constructing a historical picture.

The books in this series provide an introduction to the problems and methods involved in the study of ancient history. The topics covered will range from the use of literary sources for Greek history and for Roman history, through numismatics, epigraphy, and dirt archaeology, to the use of legal evidence and of art and artefacts in chronology. There will also be books on statistical and comparative method, and on feminist approaches.

The Uses of Greek Mythology
Ken Dowden

Art, Artefacts, and Chronology in Classical Archaeology
William R. Biers

Reading Papyri, Writing Ancient History
Roger S. Bagnall

Ancient History from Coins
Christopher Howgego

The Sources of Roman Law
Olivia Robinson

Cuneiform Texts and the Writing of History
Marc Van De Mieroop

Cuneiform Texts and the Writing of History

Marc Van De Mieroop

London and New York

First published 1999
by Routledge
11 New Fetter Lane, London EC4P 4EE

Simultaneously published in the USA and Canada
by Routledge
29 West 35th Street, New York, NY 10001

Routledge is an imprint of the Taylor & Francis Group

The right of Marc Van De Mieroop to be identified as the
Author of this Work has been asserted by him in accordance
with the Copyright, Designs and Patents Act 1988

Typeset in Baskerville by Keystroke, Jacaranda Lodge, Wolverhampton
Printed and bound in Great Britain by TJ International Ltd,
Padstow, Cornwall

British Library Cataloguing in Publication Data
A catalogue record for this book is available from the British Library

Library of Congress Cataloguing in Publication Data
Van De Mieroop, Marc.
    Cuneiform texts and the writing of history / Marc Van De Mieroop.
        (Approaching the ancient world)
    Includes bibliographical references and index.
    1. Iraq – History – To 643 – Sources. 2. Iraq – History – To 643 –
Historiography. 3. Cuneiform tablets. 4. Cuneiform inscriptions.
I. Title. II. Series.
DS71.V35 1999
    935 – dc21   98–49057

ISBN 0–415–19532–2 (hbk)
ISBN 0–415–19533–0 (pbk)

Contents

Illustrations

Acknowledgements

The idea for writing a book of this type was first suggested to me by my colleague Roger S. Bagnall, whose own discussion of the use of papyri in the writing of ancient history inspired me when it was still in manuscript form. Richard Stoneman, editor of the series Approaching the Ancient World, welcomed the suggestion that ancient Mesopotamia would be considered as well, and skillfully guided the proposal through its evaluation process.

While writing the book, I could rely on the advice of Peter Machinist and Kazuya Maekawa, who each carefully read part of the manuscript. My student Seth Richardson once more was greatly helpful with his editorial skills. I thank them all. My greatest debt is owed to Zainab Bahrani, with whom I was able to discuss every aspect of the book, and whose thoughtful comments on the entire manuscript have radically influenced the final result.

Plate 1 Date-list with abbreviated year names of Kings Hammurabi and Samsu-iluna of Babylon after the conquest of Larsa. For instance, lines 1–4 read: "year: army of Elam; year: the land Jamutbalum; year: army of Mankisum; year: canal Hammurabi-is-the-abundance-of-the-people."
Source: Clay (1915: no. 33). Photograph courtesy of Yale Babylonian Collection.

Plate 2 Obverse of an Old Babylonian letter from Sirum to his sister Elmeshum complaining about her stinginess.

Source: Lutz (1917: no. 15). Photograph courtesy of Yale Babylonian Collection.

Plate 3 Building inscription of King Sargon II of Assyria, written on a clay cylinder. The text commemorates the restoration of the Eanna-temple at Uruk for the goddess Ishtar.

Source: Clay (1915: no. 38). Photograph courtesy of Yale Babylonian Collection.

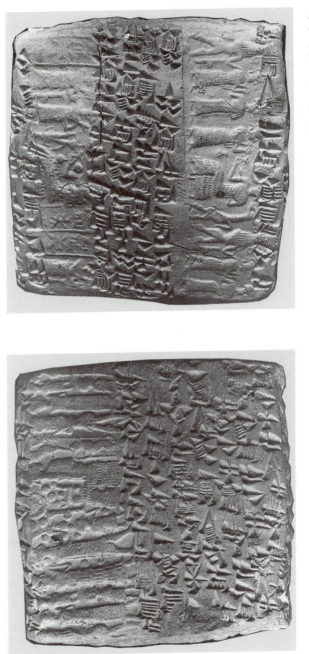

Plate 4 Old Assyrian legal statement that several debts of three men have been settled. The photographs show the original clay envelope.

Source: Clay (1927: no. 206). Photograph courtesy of Yale Babylonian Collection.

Plate 5 Old Babylonian tablet containing birth omina, including some "historical omens." For instance, col. III, lines 8–9: "If the foetus is like a lion, it is the omen of Naram-Sin, who subdued the world."
Source: Goetze (1947b: no. 56). Photograph courtesy of Yale Babylonian Collection.

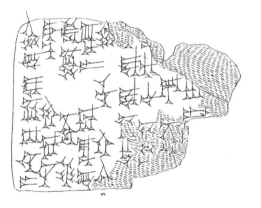

Plate 6 Hand-copy and photograph of the so-called Sargon autobiography. The fragmentary texts reads: "I am Sargon, the beloved of Ishtar, who roamed the four quarters (of the earth). The radiance of Shamash. . . ." Hand-copies are the usual way in which cuneiform tablets are reproduced for their primary publication.

Source: Clay (1923: no. 4). Photograph courtesy of Yale Babylonian Collection.

Introduction

Numerous are the books and articles that seek to address the problem of how we write history. The extent of this literature reflects the anxiety historians feel about their work as it becomes the voice of authority, the lens through which the reader sees a particular moment of the past. Epistemology can rouse passions rarely seen otherwise in the historical profession. The awareness that the scholar of the present is the interpreter of the past, that his or her words guide the reader in an alien world, leads to a self-conscious wondering about the questions that are being asked, the ways in which they are addressed, and the form in which they are answered. The nineteenth-century idea that the past could be represented "as it really happened," that the scholar can stand back and let the source material speak for itself, unfortunately may not be dead. However, rather than being the ideal method, it can now only be regarded as one paradigm in historical research, the validity of which needs to be argued (Novick 1988). From the outset I can state that this book is written with the conviction that the scholar's own historical condition determines the account that is being written, that objectivity is an elusive ideal, and that the questions asked and models and interpretative frameworks employed are determined by the scholar's contemporary concerns rather than by the sources investigated.

One might argue that the further removed from us the historical culture we study, the greater the role of the historian in its representation. While the Western readers of a book on modern European history can grasp concepts and contexts of the events described as their own, they feel less familiar when being introduced to cultures more distant in space and time. Their points of reference become more vague, their separation from that which they are to discover greater. The guidance provided then by the historian is more important to them, more crucial for their understanding. Paradoxically, introspection by the practitioners of history seems greater for those dealing with more recent periods, than for those studying the more distant past.

This book's aim is to investigate the practices of historians of a culture very removed in time, actually the first textually recorded culture in human history: ancient Mesopotamia. If we take the historian's work to begin when textual remains appear, as opposed to the prehistorian who interprets the material culture of pre-literate societies, then the earliest historical sources available derive from the Middle East in antiquity, where already around 3000 BC writing was invented. What is perhaps most remarkable is that this script, called cuneiform today, formed the basis of a continuous tradition that lasted for more than three millennia. It was adapted to record numerous languages, and spread from its place of invention, southern Iraq, to distant places like Egypt and central Anatolia. Its resilience was astonishing, and it became only gradually replaced by other, alphabetic, scripts due to reasons we do not fully comprehend yet. The cuneiform text, impressed by a reed stylus on a pillow-shaped clay tablet or carved on stone, remains one of the prime characteristics of ancient Mesopotamia. Although it is not easy to delineate the chronological boundaries of ancient Mesopotamian history exactly (Van De Mieroop 1997c: 229–31), the presence of cuneiform writing for a variety of textual genres, indicates at the least its cultural *floruit*.

The quantity and variety of cuneiform texts are enormous, something not always recognized by people not initiated in their study. This book is intended to show the riches of source material available to the historian provided by this record. In many respects it is richer than what is found in the rest of the ancient world; it includes, for instance, numerous documents of economic and legal praxis that are rarely found in Greece or Rome. On the other hand, it has its limitations. One crucial historical source available for, amongst others, most periods of European history, the investigative historical narrative, is lacking. This absence led in the past to an attitude that Mesopotamia, and ancient Egypt for that matter, were outside the historical tradition. The lack of a proper historiography made it impossible to write a history of these cultures. The modern practice of incorporating in historical sources archival materials and the like, should long have eliminated such an attitude, yet remnants of it persist and many books still see the pre-Greek Near East as a proto-historical period, on the verge of history but not yet there. Every historian should be aware of the type of data available in ancient Mesopotamia, at the least for the purpose of comparative studies. The lack of acquaintance of most historians with these data, even those specializing in antiquity, is partly due to the fact that specialists have not bothered to make such information available to a wider public. The present book hopes to rectify this omission.

In addition, the book aims to demonstrate how the cuneiform textual sources can be used in various aspects of historical research. Scholars of Mesopotamia often are so wrapped up with the philological difficulties that their sources present, that the historical usage of them becomes an afterthought, mostly informed by ideas of common sense. The discipline is exceedingly empirical in its approach. Since it deals with a very long period of time, some 3,000 years, and is relatively young, having been only firmly established since the second half of the nineteenth century, there is still a profusion of facts that can be discovered: sequences of reigns, battles, areas controlled, names of kings and queens, and so on. Any newly edited text can yield this type of information, and so many texts are still unpublished that the potential for new factual data is infinite. Just amassing facts is, however, not the goal of history. The greatest task lies in interpreting them. The scholar is guided there by ideas and biases on all aspects of the field of study. Even simple translations are interpretations. So every scholar of Mesopotamia interprets, and here it is useful to look at the practices in other areas of history, that are more developed and have a firmer grasp on the primary material. General trends in historical research are informative, as they can open new avenues of research by providing new angles with which to approach the material, or can warn us about the naïve and improper use of certain sets of data. In the following chapters, I will demonstrate some of the methodologies that are available, and provide examples from Mesopotamian history to show the applicability of such methodologies. If the book sounds critical at times, it is because the discipline seems often stuck in a nineteenth-century approach that does not properly credit, in my opinion, what Mesopotamia has to offer us.

It is not my intent to give a historiography of the discipline, or a complete survey of its current practices. Such an exercise of modern intellectual history would be useful, to show the discipline's affinities to such areas as biblical studies, Egyptology, Classics and the like, and to demonstrate beyond a doubt that it is not exempt from contemporary influences. Instead, I will take various areas of historical research, point out some of the current approaches to them, and indicate what ways of investigation seem promising to me in yielding historical insight. The choice of areas and of approaches is obviously influenced by my own interests and concerns, and by definition cannot be all-encompassing. I have focused on four aspects of history only. Political history will receive a great deal of attention, as it still dominates the study of history in general, and especially that of ancient Mesopotamia where royal acts provide the framework in which almost all other data are placed. It is also an area where the positivistic search for factual information is very great, due to a general sense of ignorance in such matters. Second, I will discuss "history from below," the examination of non-elite members of society, who cannot be studied as individuals due to lack of relevant data but only as members of groups, usually interacting with large institutions. They are mostly non-literate, hence outside our direct ken, but even the texts of those who could read and write provide highly restricted access to their daily concerns. Third, the models employed in economic history will be discussed, since this area is extremely popular in the study of ancient Mesopotamia, because of the numerous records available to us. Despite this apparent abundance of sources, economic history is still faced with a great deal of uncertainty, or scholarly interpretation, due to the existence of undocumented activity, the importance of which is impossible to gauge. Finally, I will discuss gendered approaches to Mesopotamian history, as this relatively recent discipline demonstrates how new methodologies can substantially broaden our historical understanding. Again, models are used here that need to be examined within the ancient Mesopotamian context.

It is clear that there are several aspects of historiographical research that I do not address, even obliquely. Some, such as biographical history, are set aside because of the almost complete lack of data, although the reasons for such a shortage would be an interesting question to investigate. My main regret is the absence of intellectual history. Despite long scholarly interest in Mesopotamian religious and scientific practices, work in this area has been very ahistorical. It is very hard to place systems of belief within a historical context, primarily because we cannot attach them to individual thinkers, and see them reflected in a textual tradition that seems to merge the new with the old, that does not discard but modifies. It would have been an enormous task to try to present even an outline of the difficulties involved, so I have not attempted to do so.

I will concentrate here almost exclusively on written sources, disregarding what archaeology and art history, among other sciences, have to tell us about ancient Mesopotamia. This is not because I consider those disciplines to be inferior to historical work with texts. It is because I do not regard them simply as hand-maiden to the discipline of history that I have left them aside. They have their own problems of interpretation, which require the skills of a specialist to explain. Art history is not merely providing illustrative pictures of facts or people described in texts, archae-ology is not just demonstrating what a textually attested place looked like. They investigate the products of a culture in ways different from text-based scholarship, and come to conclusions using their own methodologies. Obviously, the historian should be aware of what they do and what information they can provide, just as art historians and archaeologists should of be aware what texts can contribute to their work, and in many ways these disciplines overlap. In the end, multi-disciplinary approaches to research questions are most promising of yielding results. Methodological discussions of art history and archaeology with specific focus on ancient Mesopotamia are not available, but it is to be hoped that they will appear in the near future.

For non-specialists I should address some issues of terminology. I use the term Mesopotamia to refer to the area of the Middle East encompassed by modern Iraq and north-eastern Syria, with some adjacent regions, as it existed in antiquity. The term also acts as an umbrella for the cultures that existed in that area. Both geographically and chronologically the definition of this term is difficult, and in practice it refers to the region and time-periods when texts written in cuneiform are available. The term has many problems, as it is a colonial designation that presents this area of the world in a temporal and regional vacuum without con-temporary connections (Bahrani 1998a), but since it is still the best-known name for the area of study investigated here, I will use it. Within Mesopotamia, we distinguish between two broad cultural areas, Babylonian and Assyria, each with their own histories, which

Table 1 Chronological chart of Mesopotamian history

Babylonia		BC	Assyria	
Historical period	Selected rulers		Historical period	Selected rulers
Seleucid	Seleucus I (305–281)	300	Seleucid	
Achaemenid		400	Achaemenid	
		500		
Neo-Babylonian	Nabonidus (555–39) Nebuchadnezar II (604–562)	600		
		700	Neo-Assyrian	Sennacherib (704–681) Sargon II (721–05)
		800		
		900		Assurnasirpal (883–59)
Middle Babylonian		1000		
		1100		
		1200		Tiglath-Pileser I (1114–1076) Tukulti-Ninurta I (1243–07)
Kassite	Kurigalzu II (1332–08)	1300	Middle Assyrian	
		1400		
		1500		
		1600		
Old Babylonian		1700		

Table 1 continued

Babylonia		BC	Assyria	
Historical period	Selected rulers		Historical period	Selected rulers
	Hammurabi (1792–50)	1800	Old Assyrian	Shamshi-Adad I (1813–1781)
Isin/Larsa	Rim-Sin (1822–1763)	1900		
		2000		
Ur III	Shulgi (2094–47)	2100		
		2200		
	Naram-Sin (2254–18)	2300		
Agade	Sargon (2334–2279)	2400		
	Uru'inimgina	2500		
		2600		
Early Dynastic		2700		
		2800		
		2900		
		3000		

Note: All dates are according to J. A. Brinkman's appendix in Oppenheim (1977: 335–46).

often were intertwined due to the close proximity to one another and many shared cultural elements. Specialists studying the texts of ancient Mesopotamia are often called Assyriologist, and they do not study only the Assyrian language, but also at least Babylonian and Sumerian, if not also Hittite, Eblaic, Hurrian, and other languages written in cuneiform. Specific terms such as Sumerologist, etc., are also used but I have avoided those in this book.

The ancient history of Mesopotamia is complex, due to its length, its variety of peoples and cultures. I will not even attempt to summarize it here in a short narrative, but refer the reader to some recent treatments.[1] A chart indicating the traditionally used period designations is provided (Table 1), so that these terms can be placed in time when found in the text. I hope this book will demonstrate to the reader the enormous potential for historical research, the wealth of varied sources, the diversity of possible approaches, and the great interest of this still relatively unexplored ancient civilization.

Chapter 1

The First Half of History[1]

A long time ago in a far-away land history was made when people – one or more, man or woman – invented writing. As far as we know this happened around the year 3000 BC in the city of Uruk in southern Iraq,[2] where a truly urban culture had developed independently from any outside influence or inspiration. Uruk was an enormous city, perhaps some 5.5 square kilometers in size, with majestic temples, monumental art, a society with unprecedented complexity and social hierarchy, which required a method of record keeping that was sufficiently flexible to represent the spoken language. The exact definition of "writing" is not so easily established, but it has to be distinguished from marks and signs that convey information without a connection to the phonetic form of the language spoken by the writer. "Writing is *written language*" (Gelb 1952: 13). Thus in many non-literate or prehistoric cultures marks of ownership exist, but these do not represent the pronunciation of the owner's name; they are only symbols recognized by more than one person as the identification of individuals. When, however, a name is phonetically rendered we can speak of writing. For the first 600 years at least the script remained limited in its ability to render language, and texts written are barely intelligible to us, because they were primarily mnemonic devices (Bottéro 1992: 67–86). They differ, however, from the record-keeping devices that preceded them in that they show that the concept of representing the sounds of words was understood. This was a Mesopotamian invention, or more precisely one made in Sumer, the southernmost region of Mesopotamia. Thus "history begins at Sumer" as the title of a popular book proclaims (Kramer 1959), if we accept the dictum that writing is the characteristic that separates history from prehistory. And since the present book deals with cuneiform writing and history I will take the invention of writing in Sumer as its starting point.

The writing system invented or developed around 3000 BC was of a pictographic character; its signs were drawings. But quite soon it evolved into a script now called cuneiform, wedge-shaped writing, probably as a result of the materials used: upon a pillow-shaped tablet of moist clay signs were traced with a sharp reed stylus. It soon became clear that it was more convenient and faster to impress the stylus upon the clay surface thereby forming box-shaped characters rather than rounded ones. This evolution was completed by 2400 BC. The cuneiform signs were made up of straight lines, with a broader head where the, now blunt, stylus was pressed into the clay, which led to the wedge-shaped look. In later periods when inscriptions were carved on stone, these wedges were imitated by the stone-cutters, and they have become characteristic of the writing system. The evolution of the script is of little importance here.[3] The spread of the use of this script, both for the type of subject matters that were recorded and for its geographical extent and the length of its use, will be further discussed, however, in order to establish a basis for an evaluation of its uses to the historian.

Cuneiform is a script, not a language. It can be used to render any language, even though it was developed, most likely, to write Sumerian. Already in the twenty-fifth century it also recorded Akkadian, a Semitic language very different in character from the Sumerian one. And, although it did have difficulties representing the phonetic differences between certain consonants in Akkadian, it functioned as well as any writing system in rendering that language. Cuneiform was used throughout the centuries to write a large variety of languages, some Semitic like Eblaic and Aramaic, some Indo-European, like Hittite, and some without any known linguistic affiliation, like Hurrian, Urartean, or Elamite.

The region of modern-day Iraq and north-eastern Syria, traditionally called Mesopotamia among scholars of its ancient history, has always been the heartland of the use of the cuneiform writing system. Here the script was invented; here it was adapted for the rendering of various languages; from here it spread over the rest of the Middle East due to political and cultural expansion; and here it remained in use the longest until it died out completely in the first century AD. The total number of published texts so far easily surpasses 50,000, and even larger quantities remain unpublished in museums, while the numbers still to be excavated cannot be fathomed. The materials used to write, clay and reed, were abundantly available and cheap, and the archaeological conditions of the region promoted the preservation of the tablets. When the building in which they were kept was burned down, the clay was baked and became almost indestructible. When no burning took place, a more common occurrence, the building collapse, also of clay, protected them. Moreover, often in antiquity itself disused tablets were employed to fill benches or underneath floors, where they remained sealed. The climatic conditions of the region with its great aridity have preserved these objects quite well. Only when the water table has risen above the levels where tablets are to be found, as in Babylon of the early second millennium BC, did the humidity dissolve them. It is clear that other writing materials were in use at times in the region, certainly parchment and wax tables, but these have almost all disappeared.

A recent detailed survey of the cuneiform textual material from Mesopotamia is not available, although it would be of great value to specialist and layman alike. I will not provide one here either, but hope to delineate in broad outlines what a historian has to work with, based on knowledge of published, and if available unpublished, texts. In Table 2 an estimate is given of the numbers of various types of texts available in the periods we traditionally distinguish in the histories of Babylonia and Assyria. I include there all texts, not just those that have historical relevance. These periods are in my opinion of little historical value as they are based on philological criteria rather than historical ones, in that dynasties with extensive textual remains (e.g. Ur III) are assigned separate periods, while those with little written evidence are lumped together into a long period (e.g. Middle Babylonian; Van De Mieroop 1997a). But since the abundance or scarcity of textual records are of concern here, this periodization of history will suffice. Admittedly the distinctions I rely on, abundant, common, and few, are extremely imprecise, but they are often the result of the lack of information provided by specialists working on particular periods of time. Obviously, the situation constantly changes in that new excavations can yield thousands of documents overnight but, in general, recent finds in the Mesopotamian heartland have not changed the distribution of well and poorly documented time-periods.

Table 2 Approximate numbers of various text types in the periods of Babylonian and Assyrian history. A = abundant, more than 5,000; C = common, more than 100; F = few, less than 100.

Periods	Babylonia									Assyria		
Dates	Uruk-JN 3000–2900	ED 2900–2350	OAkk 2350–2100	Ur III 2100–2000	OB 2000–1595	Kass 1595–1157	MB 1157–625	NB 625–539	LB 539–AD 75	OAss 1900–1600	MAss 1400–1200	NAss 1200–612
Text type												
Admin doc (public)	C	C	C	A	C	C	F	A	C	C	C?	C
Legal doc (private)		F	F	F	C	F?	F	A	C	C	C?	C
Letters (public + private)		F	F	F	C	C	F?	C	F	C	C?	C
Historiographic texts		F	F	F	C	F	F	F	F	F	F	C
Literary texts		F	F	F	C			C	C		F	C
Scholarly texts	F	F	F	F	C				C			C

In Table 3 are listed the historical periods of Babylonia and Assyria, with the names of the cities where the most important text finds for that period were made. It can be easily seen that certain places, such as Nippur and Uruk, have yielded texts from most historical periods, while others, such as Kanesh, are known in one period only. This can be the result of historical circumstances, in that a place was only occupied for a short period of time, or of the excavation history. Certain sites, such as Uruk, have been extensively excavated for close to a century now, while others, like Dur-Kurigalzu, were only explored for a short while. The politics of the Middle East often influence the possibilities for excavation. For instance, since the 1970s Syria has been the focus of much archaeological work, partly due to the political circumstances in Iraq. Consequently, many new textual remains from that country have been uncovered, fundamentally changing the geographical coverage of documentation available to us. Future excavations may cause new shifts in the focus of the documentation at hand.

The types of text available to the historian are very varied in nature, each "genre" presenting its own challenges. In what follows I will discuss the categories used in Table 2 with special concern for their historical use. This discussion cannot be exhaustive, as the typology employed here is rather crude and as all sorts of ways exist in which to analyze these textual remains, but I hope it will become clear how rich the documentation at hand is.

ADMINISTRATIVE DOCUMENTS

Cuneiform was invented for the purpose of record-keeping by the public institutions and for its entire history this remained one of its primary purposes. Public administrative documents are common in almost all periods, produced by bureaucracies of palaces and temples. The complexity of their economies required records of transfers of goods: for instance, in the archive of a craft workshop attached to the palace, we find evidence of deliveries of materials, of internal transfers from one department to another, and of issues of finished products. The materials were tracked in order to ascertain that no unauthorized deductions were made, and in this spirit it was irrelevant whether the amounts involved were large or small, even nil. Thus an office that had to account for its receipts on a daily basis could provide the information that no activity took place. Some short examples of records from

Table 3 Chronology of Mesopotamian history with selected text finds

Babylonia	Historical periods — Assyria	BC	Selected archives — South	North and West
		100	Babylon, Kutha, Borsippa	
Parthian				
		200		
Seleucid		300	Babylon, Borsippa, Uruk, Ur	
		400	Babylon, Sippar, Uruk, Nippur	
Achaemenid		500		
		600	Babylon, Borsippa, Dilbat, Sippar, Nippur, Uruk, Ur	
Neo-Babylonian		700		
	Neo-Assyrian	800	Babylon, Borsippa, Nippur, Uruk	Nineveh, Nimrud, Assur, Tell Halaf
		900		
Middle Babylonian		1000		
		1100		
		1200		
		1300		Hattusas, Ugarit, Amarna, Dur-Katlimmu

Table 3 continued

| Historical periods | | Selected archives | | |
Babylonia	Assyria	BC	South	North and West
Kassite	Middle Assyrian	1400	Dur-Kurigalzu, Nippur	Assur, Tell Billa, Nuzi, Alalakh
		1500		
		1600		Terqa
Old Babylonian		1700	Sippar, Kish, Dilbat	Mari, Qattara, Shehna
	Old Assyrian	1800	Nippur	Kanesh
Isin/Larsa		1900	Isin, Larsa, Uruk, Ur, Kutalla	
		2000	Nippur	
Ur III		2100	Ur, Umma, Girsu, Puzrish-Dagan	
		2200		
		2300	Adab, Umma, Girsu	Gasur
Agade		2400		Ebla, Tell Beydar, Mari
		2500	Girsu	
		2600	Abu-Salabikh, Fara	
Early Dynastic		2700		
		2800	Ur	
		2900		
Jemdet Nasr		3000	Jemdet Nasr, Uruk	
Uruk		3100	Uruk	

the royal workshop at Isin of the twentieth century BC will illustrate this point.

1 Delivery of material to workshop officials: 180 liters of bitumen from the storage house, Shu-Ninkarak received. Copy, sealed by Nanna-kiag. Date (month, year, day) (Van De Mieroop 1987a: no. 19).

2 Issue of material to craftsmen: 2 liters bitumen, first time; 2 liters bitumen, second time; to Lu-Ninshubur, the barber; 2 liters bitumen, first time; 2 liters bitumen, second time; to Ipqusha, the reedworker; via Nur-Eshtar; 20 liters bitumen to Ili-usrani, the scribe; via Kurrub-Erra, the accountant. Date (month, year). From Nanna-kiag (ibid.: no. 62).

3 Issues of finished products by workshop officials: [ ] flutes, the bitumen used for them was 2.5 liters, offerings for Enlil, via Ur-Shulpa'e; 4 waterskins for double-mouthed water-proofed drinking vessels for the king, via Lu-Ninshubur; [2 lines broken], via Libur-beli. Issued by Shu-Ninkarak. Date (month, year, day) (ibid.: no. 133).

4 Record of no activity: On day 10 there was no activity. Date (month, year) (ibid.: no. 199).

Administrative archives are to be found in almost all periods of Mesopotamian history, almost everywhere where cuneiform writing was used. They predominate in our textual record because the public institutions were commonly the most prominent economic units in a city or district, and because archaeological exploration, both scientific and illicit, has concentrated on the monumental buildings in which they were stored. The records continue to serve the same purposes, although there are many variations in their structures and subject matters. Since many of them are dated to the day, they allow us to reconstruct activities of certain palace or temple bureaux in a good chronological framework. Their value as historical sources lies in different areas: they enable the study of economic activity; they can illustrate the deeds of rulers or institutions known from other sources; and their dates can demonstrate the control of a dynasty over a particular town.

The study of economic activities is an obvious goal for those scholars working with administrative documents and will be discussed in Chapter 4. Since the archives derive from temples and palaces whose elites are known from other sources as well, we can sometimes find evidence about the activities of kings, princesses, and the like in them, or we can reconstruct part of the careers of higher administrators. Finally, because of the dating practices in Mesopotamia, to be discussed presently, administrative records, as well as private legal texts, can provide information on the political control of a particular town. Since each dynasty had its own system of year names, eponyms, or regnal years, the find of a dated tablet at a site identifies who was politically in control there. For instance, in early second-millennium Babylonia various city-based dynasties fought for hegemony over the region, including Uruk, Larsa, Isin, and Babylon. If a tablet dated to a king of Larsa is found in the city of Nippur, we know that the latter was controlled by Larsa at that time. In the later second millennium the presence of Assyrian eponym dated tablets at northern Syrian sites shows how the Assyrian state had expanded in the west at that time. Such information is more accurate, temporally and geographically, and less biased by propagandistic tendencies than statements to that effect in royal annals, for instance. Hence, administrative documents provide valuable information in various areas of history.

PRIVATE LEGAL DOCUMENTS

In the private economic sphere certain individuals and families were engaged in sufficiently complex economic activities to necessitate detailed record keeping. Moreover, legal transactions resulting in the transfer of property where ownership could be contested in the future also required a document that testified to the owner's rights. The majority of these records were kept in the houses of the individuals involved and hence are to be found in the residential areas of towns. These are, unfortunately, still sparsely investigated. We know from certain chance finds that the extent of these archives could be enormous: for instance, in the northern Babylonian city of Sippar-Amnanum (modern Tell ed-Der), the house of a lamentation priest of the goddess Annunitum, named Ur-Utu, was discovered containing 1,985 tablets and fragments. These include private loan contracts, sales, and rentals, letters, religious texts (prayers, omens), and school texts. The archive also contained administrative documents such as ration lists for military and religious personnel, and it was not an unusual occurrence that temple or palace officials kept some of their work-related documents at home. The archive covers a period of some 250 years, and was recovered so completely because the house in which it was stored was burned down in 1729 BC (Gasche 1989: 42, 105–7).

There are also some unique documents that describe the contents of an individual's archive, which show that they were a lot more extensive than anything we have recovered so far. For instance, a Middle Assyrian text from Assur, dating to the thirteenth century, provides an inventory of a store-room belonging to a prominent family. The text has three sections detailing (i) a chariot and spare parts; (ii) tablets in a variety of containers; and (iii) various items such as furniture, utensils, weapons, etc. The second part lists a large number of tablets recording the debts of individuals or groups:

> 1 chest of (obligations) on Shamash-erish; 1 chest of clearance(s) of people and fields, of (the town of) Sharika; 1 chest of (obligations) on Assur-la-tahatti; 1 ditto (= chest) of expropriated tablets of [(obligations) on citizens of As]sur; 1 ditto of (obligations) on Assur-mushabshi [ ]; 1 ditto of (obligations) on Ishtar-erish; 1 chest [ ] of the (town of) Karana; 1 ditto of (obligations) on craftsmen; 1 [chest of] cattle and donkeys owed by the citizens of Assur; 1 ditto of (obligations) on Rish-Adad; 1 chest of herald's proclamations for houses in the Inner City (= Assur); 1 chest of sheep owed by citizens of Assur; 1 ditto of corn owed by citizens of Assur; 1 ditto of mixed silver owed by citizens of Assur; 1 di[tto of] and donkeys owed by shepherds; 1 vat of tablets of Rish-Adad; 1 chest of tablets of the palace owed by the horse-trainer; 1 chest of envelopes of Rish-Adad; 1 half-vessel of . . . of the provinces(?); 1 vat of (obligations) on Uqa-den-ili(?); 1 pot(?) of Arzuhina workmanship (of) Mannu-gir-[ ] and his brothers and Sin-sheya; 1 vat of tablets of [PN], the butler; 1 chest [ ] of . . . of clear[ances(?)]; 1 chest of . . . of [ ] of Ishtar-ummi and Shamash-lu-dayyan; 1 vat (and) 1 vessel of letters(?). Total: 24 chests of tablets.

> (Postgate 1988: no. 50)

Such an extensive archive, carefully boxed and labelled, has never been recovered by us. But it is only in numbers that our known archives are lacking, not in variety. Private citizens kept only specific sets of records, namely those that documented that something was owed to them, or that proved their ownership. Thus, of the legal documents of the Assyrian capital of Nineveh dating to the years 747 to 660 BC, 350 texts in total, 30 percent are loans and 63.7 percent are records of purchase (Kwasman and Parpola 1991: xxii).

The loan is probably the most common private business transaction we find in the textual record, because it was not solely an outright gift of goods to be returned at a later date, but also functioned as a mechanism of exchange in a society with a poorly developed market. Thus, when an artisan was hired to make a pair of sandals, a "loan" of silver was issued to be repaid with sandals at some appointed time. Of primary importance was the fact that the creditor, or customer, could demonstrate that he or she was owed something. Once the obligation of the debtor was fulfilled, the document was destroyed, so that we only have a minute fraction of the number that was written down. A typical neo-Assyrian loan document reads as follows:

> Seal of Mannu-ki-ahi, deputy (governor) of Arrapha; seal of Nabu-ashared. 10 minas of silver, capital, by the mina of Carchemish, belonging to Remanni-Adad, chief chariot driver, at their disposal. They shall pay back the capital of the silver in the month Nisan (I). [If they do not pa]y, the silver shall increase by a fourth. Witness, date (month, day, year).
> (Kwasman and Parpola 1991: no. 318)

Sale documents were kept longer. When they involved living creatures, slaves, or animals, they may have been preserved for their lifetimes. When real estate was acquired – fields, orchards, or houses – the new owner kept the sale document, together with earlier deeds that ascertained the legitimacy of ownership of the seller, and these records were passed on to the heirs (Charpin 1986). The purpose of these records was very circumscribed: they protected the owner against legal claims on property. Similarly, inheritance division records and dowry lists testified to the legality of ownership. The format of the documents reflects this concern. This is, for instance, a neo-Assyrian record of an acquisition of a house:

> Fingernail of Sharru-lu-dari, fingernail of Atar-suru, fingernail of Amat-Su'la, wife of Bel-duri, shield-bearing "third man," owners of the house being sold. A house with its

beams, doors and a yard in Nineveh, adjoining the house of Mannu-ki-ahhe, the house of Ilu-issiya, and the street, Silli-Assur, Egyptian scribe, has contracted and bought for one mina of silver (by the mina) of the king from Sharru-lu-dari, Atar-suru and Amat-Su'la, the wife of Bel-duri. The money is paid completely. That house is purchased and acquired. Any revocation, lawsuit, or litigation is void. Whoever in the future, at any time, whether these men (or anyone else), seeks a lawsuit and litigation against Silli-Assur, shall pay 10 minas of silver. Witnesses, and date (month, day, year).

(Kwasman and Parpola 1991: no 142)

I do not want to downplay the enormous variety and richness of private legal documents known to us, but it is wrong to assume that basically everything was written down in antiquity. The documents reflect very particular concerns, hence they provide very particular information to us (Van De Mieroop 1997b).

A word needs to be said about the dating systems used in Mesopotamia, which provide a boon to the historian in more than one way. The large majority of legal and administrative texts were dated by month, day, and year. Various systems of year dating were in use in Assyria and in Babylonia, the latter changing practice over time. The Assyrian system from the earliest evidence available to us in the nineteenth century to the fall of Assyria in 612 uses the name of an official to indicate every single year. That official was called in Akkadian *limmu* ("eponym") and was selected among the high dignitaries of the state, either by lot or according to a hierarchy where high officials, starting with the king, received the office in a descending order. To have value as a dating system, a list of eponyms needed to be kept, and several of those are preserved which allow the reconstruction of the sequence from the tenth to the seventh centuries (Millard 1994). Some of these lists provide very summary information about military campaigns, which can then be correlated with data from the annals. For periods without eponym lists, series of names have been established by modern scholars based on information on eponyms in other texts, or on internal information in *limmu*-dated texts. Since numerous Assyrian documents are dated "in the year of PN" we have a good chronological framework for our studies.

In Babylonia the situation varies over time, but we can say that three main systems were in use in succession: (1) from the twenty-fourth to the mid-fourteenth century a system of year names, (2) from *ca.* 1350 to 280 one where the regnal years of kings are used, and (3) the Seleucid and Arsacid eras after 280 BC. Prior to the Sargonic period in the twenty-fourth century a number of systems seem to have been used side by side, regnal years, year names, and possibly eponyms (Hallo 1988: 176–7), but the data are so slim that we can only reconstruct the chronological framework for some isolated rulers. With the Sargonic dynasty, or just before it, a system of year names came into use, which proves to be of incredible benefit to the historian. Each year is named after an important event that took place in the preceding year. The events commemorated are primarily military campaigns, buildings of temples or cult objects, appointments of high priest and priestesses, and public works such as irrigation projects or the building of city walls. Again, the sequence of these names is recorded in lists. These are not fully recovered so far, but quite well known for most of the period from the twenty-first to the seventeenth centuries. For instance, the following text lists the year names of four rulers of the dynasty of Larsa, including:

> The year that the cities Ka'idda and Nazarum were captured.
> The year that the great wall of Larsa was built.
> The year of four copper statues of Enlil in Nippur and three throne bases.
> The year of the golden statues of Utu and Shenirda.
> The year that the army of Elam was smitten.
> Five years that Sin-iqisham was king.
> The year that Silli-Adad was removed from kingship.
> The year that Warad-Sin (became) king.
> The year that the wall of Kazallu was destroyed and the army of Mutiabal was smitten in Larsa.
>
> (Sigrist 1985: 163)

Not only do these year names allow us to place dated documents exactly in time, but they also provide at least a framework for the reconstruction of certain events in a reign. Thus the relations between the Ur III state and the Hurrians to the north of Mesopotamia can be reconstructed in a chronological sequence based on the date formulae of the southern dynasty (Hallo 1978). Albeit a very biased view, we find here an account of what was considered to be important year after year by the Babylonian rulers.

After the period of political disruption that characterized the sixteenth century, the emerging Kassite dynasty started using year names but switched sometime during the fourteenth century to a system of dating by regnal year of the king (Brinkman 1976: 397–414), a system that remained in use under numerous dynasties until the early third century, e.g. "year 10 of Artaxerxes, king of Babylon." This provides a good chronological framework, as long as we know the sequence of reigns and whether the ruler is Artaxerxes I, II, or III, but it does not inform us of what was considered to have been the important event for each year.

The Hellenistic rulers of Babylonia moved from this system of dating by regnal year of each king to the use of a "Seleucid era." Seleucus I's son, Antiochus I, did not start a new sequence at his accession but continued to date his years from the moment his father had gained control over Babylon in 311. A similar system was used by the Parthians who conquered Mesopotamia in the second century BC and utilized an "Arsacid era" that started in 247.

In general we can say that the dating systems used in Mesopotamia are exceedingly accurate, providing often the day, month, and year that a text was written, which allows us to at least establish the relative chronology of many legal and administrative documents. Often the absolute chronology can be extrapolated from this, as at many points, especially in the first millennium, we can anchor the sequence we have into our reckoning of years BC. This aspect is of little consequence for the internal history of Mesopotamia, however, and will not be discussed here (see Garelli 1969: 227–39).

LETTERS

Letters on cuneiform tablets are also present in every period of Mesopotamian history except for the earliest. They have the great advantage that they are informative about subjects not treated in administrative and legal documents, and that they are more explicit, more immediate than these laconic records. But letters have several disadvantages for historical research. Most often they are not dated, and although they can be broadly assigned to a period based on stylistic or formal criteria, they can only be placed in time accurately if an individual mentioned in them is known otherwise. Moreover, since their subject matters are often unique, they are very hard to understand, especially when the correspondents know a lot of the background of the message, unfamiliar to us. Many letters are written by officials, including the king, regarding matters of state, which could involve seemingly futile matters. They do, however, also include international correspondence between various kings. Perhaps most impressive in that group are the letters of the second half of the second millennium between the Egyptian court and its peers throughout Western Asia: Babylonia, Assyria, Mitanni (northern Syria), Hatti (Anatolia), and Alashiya (Cyprus). These were written on clay tablets in the Akkadian language which functioned as the international language at that time. Such documents are obviously of great importance to the historian for they reveal, although cloaked in diplomatic parlance, how great kings interacted with one another. Also in other periods the international news of the time can be revealed by letters, such as those written to the king of Mari, Zimri-Lim, by his representatives at the court of Hammurabi of Babylon. For instance,

> Say to my Lord, thus speaks your servant Yarim-Addu. The mission of Tab-eli-matim, Sin-bel-aplim and the high dignitaries of Hammurabi, who were sent a long time ago to Mashkan-shapir, has not yet returned. [But] Rim-Sin has written to Hammurabi as follows: "My troops are assembled in my country, and I hope your troops are assembled as well in your country. If the enemy attacks you, my troops and boats will join you, and I hope that your troops and boats will join me if the enemy attacks me!" This is what Rim-Sin wrote to Hammurabi. But their troops have not yet joined up. I cannot write a more detailed report about this to my Lord.
>
> (Charpin *et al.* 1988: 170–1)

Information from such sources needs to be pieced together laboriously, but can provide unparalleled details on affairs of state.

A type of text that can be regarded as somewhat similar to international diplomatic correspondence is the treaty (cf. Barré 1992). A written version of an agreement between two states is very rare until the mid-second millennium and even then the most explicit documentation derives from Anatolia and north-western Syria. In third-millennium Babylonian texts, such as those dealing with the Umma–Lagash border conflicts, references are made to agreements on the location of borders, but we have no text of such an arrangement. It is possible that these inter-state agreements were only verbal at this time, and were put down in writing only later on. The first treaties found are indeed phrased as speeches. The earliest treaties so far known were found in the west Syrian city of Ebla, dating to the twenty-fourth century, supposedly ten pieces in total. The language of the only well-studied example, the treaty between Ebla and an unknown place named A.BAR.QA, is very opaque, however, and few conclusions can be drawn from the text (Edzard 1992). During the Old Akkadian dynasty Naram-Sin may have concluded a treaty with an unidentified ruler of Elam. The text is written in the Elamite language, still poorly understood, and besides a number of god names, frequent references to the name Naram-Sin, and a phrase that may state "the enemy of Naram-Sin is my enemy, the friend(?) of Naram-Sin is my friend" nothing in the text is clear (Carter and Stolper 1984: 14).

We have to wait until the early second millennium before any comprehensible texts of treaties are found, in Mari on the Middle Euphrates (Durand 1986: Charpin 1991) and in the northern Mesopotamian city of Shehna (Tell Leilan), (Eidem 1991).[4] The various kings of the region concluded treaties with one another, either in a military alliance or to regulate regular diplomatic interactions. From references in other texts it is clear that many other treaties were concluded all over Mesopotamia, some orally, others in writing (Charpin 1990), without any of them being preserved. It is only in the second half of the second millennium, when international diplomacy seems to have thrived, that pre-served treaties become common, but all of them derive from the Hittites (Beckman 1996) and north-western Syria (Reiner 1969: 531–2). In the first millennium, with the neo-Assyrian empire, we find a relative large corpus of actually preserved treaties, although it is clear from references in other texts that many more of them were concluded. These could be with other states regarded as equals to Assyria, with vassals of peripheral territories, and with the Assyrian subjects of the king who swore loyalty oaths (Parpola and Watanabe 1988). Thus, in general, the treaties which were a crucial tool in the international policies of the Mesopotamian states remain poorly documented, yet those available are invaluable historical sources.

Also in the private sphere correspondence was common, dealing with a wide array of private and professional concerns. When available in substantial numbers, such letters can facilitate the reconstruction of business practices, as in the case of the Old

Assyrian traders at Kanesh, for instance. The many letters found in this colony of Assyrian merchants in the middle of Anatolia show how partners back home provided them with the goods they needed, organized its transport in caravans, dealt with claims and complaints, and so on. The corpus permits a wholly unique view on long-distance trade in Mesopotamia, which we would never derive from other sources. But with few exceptions the letters have been used as secondary sources in historical reconstructions, adding color to sketches already drawn from other materials.

HISTORIOGRAPHIC TEXTS

I use the term "historiographic texts" with a certain reluctance, as it assumes an intent by their writers of composing a version of their past, an intent which may not have been present at all. Mesopotamian scholars have, however, used this term commonly, including therein a wide array of text genres. A primary division has to be made between commemorative records of events, written soon after their occurrence, and chronographic texts that were written for very different purposes. The first group includes annals and building accounts of Mesopotamian kings, royal inscriptions, often carved in stone on visible surfaces. They rarely mention anything before the reign of the king for whom they are composed.[5] These monumental royal inscriptions are extremely numerous, come from almost all periods of Mesopotamian history, and can be very detailed. Besides them exists a category of chronographic texts which provides records of events from the writer's past. They are primarily lists, of kings with the number of years they ruled, of year names in early Babylonia, of eponyms in Assyria. These can be accompanied by short notations of events such as what military campaign took place in a particular eponymous year. These texts were not displayed; their purpose varied from purely utilitarian – establishing the sequence of year names according to which administrative texts were dated – to propagandistic, such as promoting the cult of a certain god.

All these texts have been extensively surveyed and analyzed, and many of them are now being re-edited (see Chapter 2). Their classification is not my concern here, as earlier literature treats that subject well (e.g. Edzard 1980–83a, b; Glassner 1993; Grayson 1980; Renger 1980–83). Historiographic texts were among the first Mesopotamian texts to be discovered and translated. Indeed, the

Royal Asiatic Society in London considered Akkadian deciphered
when a prism with the annals of Tiglath-Pileser I was translated
independently by four scholars in 1857. Their usefulness is
obvious: they are often detailed in their description of, at least,
military events and they often provide information in a chronological sequence. But there are numerous chronological problems:
the number of campaigns or even of regnal years of individual
kings often differs between sources or manuscripts. Thus for the
famous Assyrian king Sennacherib, whose reign is traditionally
dated 704–681, there are three different accession dates in the
sources, 705, 704, and 703, and the exact number and dates of
his campaigns which seem beautifully laid out in his annals, is also
uncertain (Grayson 1991a: 105). Or to the well-documented
king from Larsa, Warad-Sin (ruled 1834–23), most sources assign a
twelve-year reign, with one exception, equally authoritative at first
glance, that gives him thirteen years (Stol 1976: 1–6). Still, I believe
that these are details in a general chronological structure that is
impressive for its spread and detail. Going backwards in time until
1400 BC we are confident about both the relative and absolute
chronologies of Assyrian rulers. For Babylonian history there
are huge segments where we are positive about the succession of
at least the major kings: *ca.* 2400–1600, *ca.* 1300–1000, and 747–64
BC.

The detail provided by the royal inscriptions unfortunately
relates primarily to military events. Assyrian kings in particular saw
their almost annual campaigning as the major accomplishment
to be recorded, which has certainly reinforced their biblical image
of ruthless predators. But while building activity may predominate
as the topic of Sumerian and early-Babylonian inscriptions, these
also provide a lot of information on military activity, despite the
common assertion to the opposite (e.g. Grayson 1980: 154). Quite
a few of them extensively dealt with military events, like the Stele of
Vultures of Eanatum in the twenty-fourth century or the historical
inscriptions of King Shu-Sin. Others contain such information
within building inscriptions; for instance, Samsu-iluna recounts his
conquest of the South before he commemorates the restoration
of the city walls and temple at Sippar (Frayne 1990: 374–8). Also in
Assyria, royal building inscriptions, especially starting with those
of Adad-nerari I (*ca.* 1300), provide the campaigns as a means of
dating the construction: after the king had gone on campaigns in
a sequence of years, he built a palace or a temple. What may have

been the primary purpose of the annalistic texts, the commemoration of a construction, becomes almost an appendix to a long account of annual campaigns (Grayson 1980: 151–2). Chronographic texts, such as the Babylonian Chronicle series (Grayson 1975b: nos 1–13a) can also be replete with military information.

This material may be a gold mine for the historian interested in military and international political events, but for the internal political history it is not very informative. It has, however, enabled us to write long accounts of certain periods of Mesopotamian history, especially during the neo-Assyrian period, as so much detail is available.

LITERARY TEXTS

The distinction between historiographic texts and literature is far from clear-cut, in Mesopotamia as in many other cultures. Mesopotamian scholarship distinguishes a genre of "historical–literary texts", literary in style but dealing with "historical or natural events rather than mythological or supernatural occurrences" (Grayson 1980: 183, see Grayson 1975a). Some Assyrian royal inscriptions, justifiably, have been credited with great literary merit (e.g. Dalley 1995: 83–4), but are not usually considered to be part of Mesopotamian literature. We have no simple criterion to differentiate between literary and non-literary texts, as style is a difficult concept to use in a textual tradition so alien to ours, and as the Mesopotamians themselves did not indicate a generic categorization of their writings which would help us. Several scholars have sought to avoid this difficulty by employing a category of "canonical texts", i.e. those that were copied over the generations with a set wording and sequence of component parts (e.g. Hallo 1991a). The long-term copying does indicate that the Mesopotamians saw these texts as different from archival and monumental texts, which are almost exclusively known from single manuscripts or from mass-produced copies made in a short period of time (e.g. Nebuchadnezar II bricks). Although this concept has the great advantage that it seemingly uses a categorization that existed in the minds of the Mesopotamians, it excludes almost all early literary texts, known from one manuscript only (Foster 1993: 46), as well as some later compositions,[6] and it lumps together a wide variety of text types, epics, myths, hymns, with omens, lexical lists, etc. Thus I will utilize here a vague concept of literary texts, those that have stylistic characteristics acknowledged by us as literary, such as verse, meter, word play, simile, and metaphor. Such texts are common throughout Mesopotamian history, in the Sumerian and Akkadian languages, and have been used extensively as historical sources. The legitimacy of their use as such is a thorny matter.

Among the large literary corpus scholars have distinguished various groups of texts with decreasing value to the historian: stories with known historical figures as their main characters, stories with a general historical or legendary quality, and purely mythological texts (cf. Grayson 1975a: 41). Again, the Mesopotamians themselves did not inform us of any distinction they would have made. Several literary texts have historically known figures as their main characters, or refer to dynasties that are otherwise known. There is a lot of debate about their classification (cf. J. Westenholz 1997: 16–24), but for the Akkadian material I will follow here again the outline by Grayson (1975a, 1980: 182–8). He distinguishes between prophecies, historical epics, and pseudo-autobiographies. In the first group events from the past are "prophesied" by the writer in order to establish his credibility for a real prediction. The texts do not indicate names of individual rulers, but circumstantial evidence allows us sometimes to determine who was intended. Treatment of the Babylonian god Marduk is the sole criterion by which the rulers are judged: those who treat the god well are "good," those who do not, are "bad" and will be punished. For instance, in the "Dynastic Prophecy" is stated:

> A rebel prince will arise.
> [He will establish] the dynasty of Harran.
> [He will exercise kingship] for seventeen years.
> He will oppress the land, and he will cancel[?] the festival of Esagil.
> [He will build] a fortress in Babylon.
> He will plot evil against Akkad.
> A king from Elam will arise, the scepter [ ]
> He will remove him from his throne [ ]
> He will seize the throne and of the king who arose from the throne [ ]
> The king of Elam will change his place [ ]
> He will cause him to dwell in another land [ ].
>
> (Longman 1991: 239)

We can reconstruct with certainty that this refers to Nabonidus, the last king of the neo-Babylonian dynasty, who came from Harran and ruled Babylon for seventeen years. He was removed by Cyrus of Persia, called here by its ancient name Elam, who seems to have saved Nabonidus's life and exiled him. This type of text does then contain historical information that can only be extracted with the help of knowledge derived from other sources.

The historical epics are probably the most complex sources for a Mesopotamian historian. We have at our disposal a number of texts in the Akkadian language, that have otherwise known historical figures as their main characters. These figures can be early kings: there is a substantial corpus of narratives regarding the Old Akkadian rulers Sargon and Naram-Sin (J. Westenholz 1997), which have been extensively studied and figure prominently in some reconstructions of that period. I will treat them and the problems they raise in detail in Chapter 2. Five second-millennium Assyrian or Babylonian kings, and one neo-Babylonian king figure in other epics. Almost all these texts are extremely fragmentary, and the information that can be derived from them is minor. Only the Epic of Tukulti-Ninurta I has sufficiently preserved detail to contribute to the knowledge of his reign.

A third group of Akkadian literary–historical texts consists of a small number of first-person narratives supposedly written by a Mesopotamian ruler. Grayson pointed out only a few of these compositions, but others have included many more texts (Longman 1991). Again, the heroes range from the Old Akkadian ruler Sargon to the mother of the last neo-Babylonian king, Adad-guppi, mother of Nabonidus.

The identification of Akkadian literary texts as historically valid because of the appearance of an otherwise well-attested ruler in them, breaks down, however, when we compare it with similar Sumerian material which has been given much less historical credence. In the Sumerian language there exists a set of texts that depicts the activities of rulers from a dynasty in Uruk, which perhaps did indeed exist in the mid-third millennium. The kings involved are Enmerkar, Lugalbanda, and Gilgamesh, who appear in the Sumerian King List as father, son, and great-grandson, although within the literary material Gilgamesh appears as the son of Lugalbanda. While the appearance in the Sumerian King List by itself is far from a confirmation of their existence, it can be argued in a roundabout way that they are historical figures. One of the

Gilgamesh texts, "Gilgamesh and Agga,"[7] describes a siege of the city of Uruk by the army of the city Kish, led by King Agga. The latter's father, Enmebaragesi, is known from two inscriptions from the mid-third millennium, stating his name as Mebarasi, and the title "king of Kish" (Cooper 1986: 18). Agga himself is perhaps attested as king of another city, Umma (ibid.: 92). It can thus perhaps be concluded that all characters found in these epics regarding the kings of Uruk were historical figures, some of whom became later deified (Lugalbanda and Gilgamesh). Yet, some of the tales about these men have clear mythological contents, such as the story of Gilgamesh's fight with the bull of heaven. So, how are we to evaluate such stories, except by deciding what seems humanly possible (a battle with Kish) and what seems impossible (a fight against the bull of heaven)? But there are many grey areas: was Lugalbanda's expedition to Aratta in Afghanistan possible or not? We are left to guess.

In their search for narrative sources, a topic I will explore further later on, scholars have even turned to compositions that clearly fall in the domain of fiction, "myths" dealing with gods rather than humans. As pointed out above, Grayson (1975a: 41) distinguishes between stories with a general historical or legendary quality, and purely mythological texts. In the first group he includes the stories of Gilgamesh, Etana, Atra-hasis, Erra, and Adapa, all of which can be regarded as myths (Dalley 1989). Among these texts the Erra-myth, depicting the god of fire as going on a rampage, has been most consistently interpreted as revealing historical events. A very recent statement asserts that it was composed between 854 and 819 and that it relates the terrible military events that occurred in Babylonia sometime between 1100 and 850. The author describes it as a historical text couched in theological terms (Glassner 1993: 45–7). But such an appraisal is based on circular reasoning: the text relates a terrible devastation of several Babylonian cities which could have taken place at various points in time, including the period from 1100 to 850. Yet other dates have been suggested in scholarship as well (cf. Cagni 1977: 20–1; Edzard 1976–80: 169), and the dates of the composition and of the events described can be moved in tandem to various centuries. The manuscript tradition does not help either, as all the known manuscripts derive from the eighth century, at least a century after the most recent possible date of composition. Thus, neither the events nor the composition of the text can be dated exactly. The dating of the composition is based on the assumed date of the events, which are then deemed ascertained by the text, a system which I find methodologically suspect. Even worse for a historian, the description of the devastation could be hyperbolic or even pure fantasy. The latter is not excluded, in my opinion, as the text was considered to have an apotropaic value. Its recital was supposed to keep away evil from the reciter's house (Reiner 1960), and why could this paradigmatic evil not be invented? It used to be thought actually that the composition described the ravages of pestilence rather than of war, and although I am not claiming that we should revive this idea, the fact that it was commonly accepted should warn us that there is great latitude in interpreting the text.

The final category in Grayson's account is the purely mytho-logical, including such texts as the Creation myth (Enuma elish), the myth of Anzu, and the tale of Nergal and Ereshkigal. Even stories of this nature have been included as historical sources by some scholars. Thus the famous flood story has been seen as a metaphoric remembrance of the invasion of the Mesopotamian lowlands by Amorite nomads in the twenty-eighth or twenty-seventh centuries (cf. Renger 1996: 43). Even if this tenuous connection, based on the similarity in sound between the Sumerian word for flood, a.ma.ru, and the Akkadian name of a group of nomads, Amurru, were sustainable, it would clearly tell us very little of historical value.

The use of literature, both about known humans and gods, is thus a tricky affair for the Mesopotamian historian. Although I am not averse to the idea that historical events inspired certain literary compositions or their details, I doubt very much that we today as historians can distinguish between fact and fiction, that we can identify with any degree of certainty how a historical episode was turned into a tale. In the end, much of the search for history in literature has produced little of great consequence. We know that the years 1100 to 850 were troubled times for Babylonia, and whether or not the Erra epic was inspired by these is not contributing much to the knowledge of this period. The use of the so-called historical–literary texts has had more misleading effects, however. The whole image of the Akkadian "empire," the control of much of the Middle East by a city-state in the north of Babylonia, has been modelled to a great extent by the Mesopotamian literary traditions about this period. It is true that these kings boasted of an unprecedented control over a wide area, but the data used by historians to confirm this are interpreted to fit that model. It has been stated, correctly in my opinion, that the greatest accomplishment of the Old Akkadian rulers has been their creation of the image of great glory, perpetuated throughout Mesopotamian history and picked up by modern scholars (Michalowski 1993). The propaganda machine was a great success; how truthful it was remains to be questioned.

SCHOLARLY TEXTS

The final category of texts, scholarly ones, may seem unlikely to have much historical value, but actually some of them have been acclaimed as lying "at the very root of all Mesopotamian historiography" (Finkelstein 1963: 463). What we call scholarly texts are primarily lists: of words, god names, phrases, and observations of phenomena in nature, the human body, the planetary world, and so on. The latter group contains the omen literature, the most extensive body of non-economic textual material from Mesopotamia. The Mesopotamians saw every aspect of the world that surrounded them as containing signs of the intent of the gods. If these messages were properly read and interpreted, evil could be averted by imploring the gods to change their minds. Everything was of interest: the flight of birds, the patterns smoke made, the appearance of newborns, the movements of planets and stars, to name only a few things. All observations and their outcomes were phrased in the same way, e.g.: "If a man starts a journey and a crow stands on the right and caws, that man will not go where he intends, he will be unhappy" (Guinan 1989: 230). Tens of thousands of such statements, some seemingly based on observation, others made up along patterns of good/evil, are found (see Bottéro 1992: 125–37).

Within this enormous corpus there is a small number of so-called historical omens, those that in the apodosis refer to something that happened to a historically known figure. They deal primarily with early rulers, especially those of the Old Akkadian and Ur III dynasties. Most of these apodoses are extremely vague, such as "If the liver is covered with holes and [if] they are permanent, it is an omen of Sargon who ran into darkness, but saw the light" (Goetze 1947a: 256). Some are bizarre, like "omen of Amar-Sin who died from the bite of a shoe" (ibid.: 261), and some refer to what could be considered real historical events. The latter group contains only twelve historical observations, however, often mentioned in more than one omen (Cooper 1980: 103 n. 12). There is a variety of opinions on the historical value of these statements: some scholars credit them with great accuracy (Hallo 1991b), even as being the only real accurate historical statements in Mesopotamian literature (Finkelstein 1963); others find merit only in those with a realistic historical content, while a few doubt that they contribute anything to our historical knowledge (Cooper 1980). Indeed, the last stance seems to be the proper one. Obviously one can stretch the imagination to accept that Amar-Sin died from an infected foot, but this would still only be a tidbit of knowledge of little consequence. More dangerous is to rely on these omens to ascertain that Sargon campaigned in central Iran, or that Naram-Sin conquered Apishal, location unknown. The omens stating the latter actually show how the authors often played with words to make up the connection between the observation of an ominous sign, its result, and even the formulation of that result. In several apodoses mentioning the conquest of Apishal the success is credited to a breach in the wall (Akkadian *pilshu*), a play with the consonants plsh and pshl, more obvious in a Semitic language than in English. Moreover, a breach (*pilshu*) in the exta of the sacrificial animal is said to have predicted this conquest. These word plays seem more crucial in the phrasing of the omen than the historical background.

Omens have been used to verify statements in historical–literary texts, discussed above, as if these are two independent sources. They are not: either they both derive from the same source, or one inspired the other, and we cannot determine the accuracy of any of them. So, the problems of using omens as historical sources are so great that they should be discarded as such. Again, it seems more appropriate to me to investigate why some rulers became the central characters of these omens, why they seem so accident prone, and what the benefit was of preserving these traditions.

Finally, on a more positive note, there is a type of Mesopotamian scholarly literature that contains fragments of historical information, unfortunately only for the late periods. From the mid-seventh century on until 61 BC scholars from Babylon compiled astronomical diaries, where they noted down planetary and astral events, but also the weather, prices, and some historical events they thought important (Hunger and Sachs 1988–96). The latter vary from battles and diplomatic visits to statements that "five dogs approached one bitch" (van der Spek 1993: 93–4). Yet, they contain clear statements about political history, e.g.:

> That year (274 BC), the king left his . . . , his wife and a famous official in the land Sardis to strengthen the guard. He went to Transpotamia against the troops of Egypt which were encamped in Transpotamia, and the troops of Egypt withdrew before him. Month XII, the twenty-fourth day, the satrap of Babylonia brought out much silver, cloth, goods and utensils(?) from Babylon and Seleucia, the royal city, and twenty elephants, which the satrap of Bactria had sent to the king, to Transpotamia, before the king.
>
> (Hunger and Sachs 1988–96: vol. 1: 345)

Also the indications of prices on the market are a great tool for the economic historian. The purpose of these texts was to prepare astronomical horoscopes and omens, and there is no ideological purpose in the recording of the events at all. So these notes are of pure historical value. Unfortunately, these texts start quite late in Mesopotamian history. Moreover, the observers were all in Babylon and report almost exclusively events of that city only. For other parts of the world they have to rely on hearsay. Furthermore, Babylon loses much of its political status in the Seleucid period, so it was no longer in the center of things. Still these texts can provide useful data (van der Spek 1993).

The discussion above has focused on the material from Mesopotamia itself, which indeed dominates the cuneiform record. But the writing system was exported to other regions of the Middle East through processes of political expansion and cultural influence. Most often the use of cuneiform only survived temporarily outside the periods of direct Mesopotamian contacts, but sometimes the technique was adapted for the recording of the local language, survived, and developed independently. The regions involved were western Iran, Anatolia, Syria–Palestine and Egypt.

In western Iran we see a use of cuneiform writing to record the local Elamite language that parallels what we see in Mesopotamia proper. Politically and culturally the regions were closely related, and thus it is not such a surprise that changes in the local Elamite script reflect those seen in Mesopotamia. Cuneiform was fully acknowledged as the common script in western Iran (Walker 1987:

41–2). The types of texts written there are primarily building inscriptions and economic documents. The former are very standardized in contents and contain little historical information, the latter are difficult to understand until the Persian period. Hence, much of the history of western Iran is written based on sources from Mesopotamia proper (see Carter and Stolper 1984).

In this region an alphabetic form of cuneiform developed in the late period: under the Achaemenid Persian dynasty in the sixth century a script was developed to record the Old Persian language, which looks like cuneiform, but whose signs have no relationship to the Babylonian ones. It contains only thirty-six characters, mostly of a syllabic type indicating a consonant with any of the three vowels. Furthermore it uses five signs that indicate an entire word, such as "king." It is said to have been invented under Darius or one of his immediate predecessors for prestige reasons, and only survived into the mid-fourth century (Walker 1987: 46–7). Its development did not lead to the abandonment of the Babylonian and Elamite cuneiform scripts, while also alphabetically written Aramaic was used in the Persian empire.

In Anatolia a multitude of languages was recorded in the cuneiform writing system, heavily inspired by Mesopotamian examples. The earliest evidence of script derives from the early second millennium when merchants from Assyria established colonies there, and recorded their transactions and correspondence in a highly singular form of cuneiform. A reduced number of signs was used, almost exclusively syllabic ones, and their graphic rendering is very distinct. A handful of inscriptions and a letter show that the local rulers adopted this script as their own. Soon after the disappearance of the Old Assyrian colonies Anatolians seem to have borrowed the Babylonian syllabary and sign forms for their records. The texts of the Hittites, almost exclusively from the capital Hattusas, all display southern characteristics. Numerous languages were recorded in this script: Hittite, Hurrian, Luwian, Palaic, and Hattian, which are languages with varied linguistic affiliations (Walker 1987: 42–4). The majority of texts are in Hittite and Akkadian. They include royal annals, treaties, letters, legal and administrative documents, literary compositions, and rituals. Most of the manuscripts date to the fourteenth to twelfth centuries, but probably the use of writing goes back to the seventeenth century, with the creation of the Hittite state. Cuneiform was not the only script in use among the Hittites; a type of hieroglyphic writing existed simultaneously although mostly known from isolated renderings of names until after the fall of the Hittite state around 1200. The Hittite textual record, in its various languages, is extensive and a rich ground for historical investigations on this important state in the mid- to late second millennium.

After the Hittite state's disappearance no cuneiform texts are found in Anatolia until the Urartean inscriptions from eastern Anatolia. Dating from the ninth through seventh centuries, they are very much influenced by Assyrian cuneiform of the period. Some inscriptions are written in Assyrian, but the majority is in the Urartean language. Written on clay are a small number of letters and administrative documents, that show the knowledge of cuneiform in the state's chancellery (Wilhelm 1986). Also a hieroglyphic script is found here, but it remains undecipherable so far. A history of Urartu cannot be written with the indigenous sources alone, and only through the frequent mentions of the state in Assyrian texts do we know its main outlines.

In the Syro-Palestinian area the appearance of cuneiform records is almost entirely due to the strong cultural influences of Mesopotamia. In the mid-third millennium, southern Mesopotamian writing is found as far west as Ebla near Aleppo. A large palace archive excavated there contained texts written in the Sumerian language and in the local Eblaic one. The script and syllabary used are almost exactly like what we find in northern Babylonia at the time. About 80 percent of the signs used are word-signs, which can be read in any language, while a limited number of syllabic signs is used to record the local idiom explicitly. The strong cultural connection with northern Babylonia is clear from the appearance of lexical texts found at Ebla, which parallel exactly those from sites in Babylonia (Walker 1987: 40–1). Almost all texts from Ebla are economic in character, while lexical ones make up the majority of the remainder; some isolated literary and historical texts are barely comprehensible. Other Syrian sites from Mari on the middle Euphrates to Tell Beydar in northern Syria became similarly exposed to southern Mesopotamian influences in their writings in this period.

Subsequently, cuneiform writing remained in use in the Syro-Palestinian area until the sixth century, primarily to record the Akkadian language. In certain periods and regions the documentation is abundant. North-eastern Syria, close to Mesopotamia proper and often incorporated in its political systems, has yielded large archives of the early and late second millennium. In the middle of that millennium a powerful state of Mitanni exercised control over the entire region and used cuneiform to record a variety of texts, legal, administrative, epistolary, scholarly, and religious. The languages used were Akkadian and what seems to have been the native tongue of the ruling class, Hurrian. Throughout the second millennium Akkadian seems to have been the common language of international diplomacy throughout the Middle East. The palace archives from Mari (nineteenth–eighteenth centuries) show that rulers from western Iran to Palestine communicated in Akkadian, while those of Akhetaten in Egypt (fourteenth century) contain letters from rulers from Mesopotamia to Cyprus in the same language. Small finds in Syro-Palestinian sites show that Akkadian was known throughout the region (Edzard 1985), and even the Egyptian court needed to have scribes knowledgeable in the language and script for its foreign affairs. The city of Ugarit on the north Syrian coast has an especially rich cuneiform record of the fourteenth through twelfth centuries, again in a variety of languages including Akkadian and Hurrian. An alphabetic cuneiform script was in use, as for Old Persian with sign values that are unrelated to the Babylonian syllabary (Walker 1987: 44–6). It is in fact in this area of the Middle East that the alphabet was developed throughout the second millennium with sign forms that are entirely distinct from the cuneiform ones.

Alphabetic scripts, Phoenician, Hebrew, and Aramaic, were used by local Syro-Palestinian dynasts in the first millennium, while cuneiform was only used for administrative purposes where the Assyrians or Babylonians were in control. Some rare bilingual inscriptions written in two distinct scripts appear in areas under Assyrian control. The cuneiform record of the first millennium in the Syro-Palestinian area remains small, but we know that the script was imposed by the Mesopotamian powers whenever they took over direct governance. The use of alphabetic scripts became increasingly popular and was adopted by the Assyrians and Babylonians themselves. Under the Persians Aramaic became one of the main languages of administration, and with the Hellenistic kingdoms Aramaic and Greek came to dominate the administrative record. As these languages were written on papyrus and parchment rather than on clay, the documents have almost all decayed.

Cuneiform was thus the dominant writing system of the Middle East for half of its recorded history. For thousands of years men and women recorded an enormous variety of information in numerous languages, which provides the raw data for the historian interested in the ancient history of this part of the world. The data are raw in that they most often are not filtered through a long tradition of interpretation and edition before they come to us. They sometimes contain the fingerprints of their original authors! The task of interpretation falls thus on the shoulders of the modern historian, on the one hand, faced with an abundance of records, names, facts and figures, on the other hand, grappling with a silence from these people "who wrote on clay." The challenges and opportunities facing us in various aspects of historical research on the Mesopotamians, the main writers of cuneiform texts, will be the focus of the present book.

Chapter 2

History from Above

Despite recent trends in history to search for the "common" man and woman, much of our thoughts are still structured along lines determined by the fortunes of elites, especially rulers and dynasties. Our periodizations of antiquity, both on a long-term scale and in the detailed subdivisions of short periods and individual regions, are still often based on a perception of change in rule. Poorly written, or taught, histories tend to turn into annotated king lists with battles highlighted as major events. This is still very much true for the histories of ancient Mesopotamia, where an abundance of royal names is known and where dynastic shifts determine our view of historical change almost to the absolute. When Mesopotamia was almost entirely forgotten in the west from late antiquity to the mid-nineteenth century AD, the only memory that lingered in people's minds came from the Hebrew Bible where Israel's and Judah's encounters with the Assyrian and Babylonian empires were summarily described. The focus was upon kings and battles: the Assyrians Shalmaneser, Sargon and Sennacherib, whose campaigns led to the destruction of the state of Israel and turned Judah into a puppet state; the Babylonian Nebuchadnezar, guilty of destroying Jerusalem and taking its people in captivity. Many Western writers and artists used these as characters well known to their audiences (e.g. Byron, Rembrandt). These kings, and some of their queens, colleagues, and officials, lingered as the ghosts of a forgotten civilization. Even today their biblical characters continue to dominate our perception of them. How can we see Assyrians as anything but warlike? We even continue to use the Hebraized versions of their names: Sargon instead of Sharruken, Nebuchadnezar instead of Nabu-kudurri-uṣur, etc.

It is then somewhat of an irony that some of these very same kings figured prominently in the first modern discoveries of ancient Mesopotamian material. British and French adventurer–archaeologists unearthed some of the Assyrian palaces in the mid-nineteenth century, finding inscriptions on clay and stone describing in much detail similar military exploits. The annals and building inscriptions of Assyrian kings were the first texts to be deciphered and for a long time remained the main focus of translators and historians. Rather speedily the list of known royal names became longer and continued to grow so that today several hundreds of them are known and set in time and space. How do we write the histories of these people? How do we use their own writings and those of later Mesopotamians who "remembered" them in our historical research? This chapter will outline some of the approaches of earlier scholars to these sources, and investigate some new avenues of research. At the end I will attempt an explanation of why the narrative writings available to us have dominated our thoughts on the Mesopotamian subjects they describe.

ASSYRIAN ROYAL INSCRIPTIONS

Mesopotamian kings, and a handful of queens, thought it proper to record some of their deeds in writing, as any self-respecting ruler might, in order to guarantee the survival of their memory in the minds of later generations. The Epic of Gilgamesh, now the most famous literary text from Mesopotamia, struggled with the issue of immortality and advised the reader where to find it. While it was futile for man to seek eternal life, his memory was guaranteed when his deeds were recorded in writing on stone:

> He [Gilgamesh] went on a distant journey, pushing himself
>   to exhaustion,
> but then was brought to peace.
> He carved on a stone stela all of his toils.

> (Kovacs 1989: 3)

The concept that the king required an inscription stating at least his name and title dates back to the twenty-seventh century BC and continues uninterrupted into the Hellenistic period. We do know of kings for whom no royal inscription is attested as yet, but these were mostly weak rulers, unable to commission building projects or stone monuments which could contain such texts, leaving clear traces in the archaeological record. I doubt, however, that any ruler failed to register his rule in writing and many more royal inscriptions remain to be found, in my opinion.

The purpose of the royal inscriptions was to commemorate a deed, from the offering of a small bowl to a god to the building of an enormous palace or temple, even an entire city. While early inscriptional formulae contained simply a name and title, these soon included descriptive statements of the deed itself: "I offered this," or "I built this palace/temple," and a lot of secondary information which has become of extreme interest to the historian. There is substantial variety in the types of accounts that resulted from this literary expansion, and differences existed between Babylonia and Assyria. In both regions, the titulary was expanded to include statements about control over various cities and countries and to claim special connections to numerous gods. Moreover, in Assyria, the activity commemorated in the inscription was often established in time by enumerating the military campaigns that preceded it. The latter became the bulk of text in the royal inscriptions of the neo-Assyrian kings, and therefore have been used as a primary source to study their reigns. When the military information is provided in a chronological order, detailing one or more campaigns, we call the inscriptions annalistic texts; when the military events are not ordered chronologically but according to a geographical pattern, we call them display texts. The latter appear also without references to military events in Assyria, while in Sumer and in Babylonia military accounts are often omitted from commemorative inscriptions (Grayson 1980).

The annalistic accounts are a gold mine for the historian of kings and battles. Since building activity took place throughout a king's reign, various editions of these annals are preserved written at different points in time. Moreover, numerous exemplars of the same or slightly variant editions were inscribed. For instance, more than 150 manuscripts are known relating the military activities of King Sennacherib (ruled 704–681) (Levine 1983: 64). The first scholars to deal with these texts attempted to reconstruct the most complete, i.e. most recent, version of such annals by joining together fragments and by ignoring the dates of various accounts of the same campaign. Scribal variants were noted in the critical apparatus; only when major discrepancies were found in two accounts were they published separately. The aim was to present an annalistic narrative of the entire reign enumerating campaign after campaign with the detail provided by the king's own accounts, even if they were never found together in the same ancient text, and whatever the date of the sources employed. These scholars saw the accounts as a succession of statements regarding individual campaigns and a building project, the various editions of which were considered to be mostly repetitions, with small, almost meaningless, variations (Liverani 1981: 225–7).

Such reconstructed annals became then the basis for the historian's narrative of an individual reign. An example of such procedures can be found in Sidney Smith's description of King Sennacherib in the first edition of the *Cambridge Ancient History* (Smith 1929: 61–79).[1] His study deals with three topics: Sennacherib's troubles with Babylonia which lasted his entire reign; his campaigns in Syria and Palestine; and his building activities. The discussion of the first topic often paraphrases Sennacherib's own accounts, but a selection was made by the modern author. For instance, the king's first forays in Babylonia are described in these words:

> The Assyrian then proceeded to reduce Chaldaea more thoroughly than any of his predecessors had done. In all eighty-eight fortified towns belonging to the Chaldaean clans were captured; in addition to these all the great cities of Babylonia, save Ur of the Chaldees, were besieged and taken. It is unfortunate that there are variant accounts of Sennacherib's arrangement for the government of the country at the conclusion of the campaign in Chaldaea. Undoubtedly the earlier account states that Sennacherib set up a Babylonian, Bel-ibni, who had been educated at the Assyrian court, as king of Sumer and Akkad. The variant account says that he made Bel-ibni king of Akkad and set his own officers as governors over the Chaldaean districts. It is, of course, possible that the two accounts are not so opposed as they seem; perhaps Sennacherib left his officers in Chaldaea to serve under the new Babylonian king.
>
> (Smith 1929: 64–5)

This statement is based on a mixture of sources written by Sennacherib's court. The events described took place during his first formal campaign, which started in late 703 BC, and aimed to depose the Chaldean Merodach-baladan from the throne of Babylon. As this was his first campaign, all exemplars of his annalistic texts refer to it, but they provide slightly different versions.

Smith's account here relies extensively on a text written after the first campaign and presumably before the second one, as no reference is made to the latter. Sennacherib states:

> A total of eighty-eight strong cities, fortified settlements of the Chaldeans together with 820 small settlements in their territories, I besieged and captured, and I carried away their spoils. The grain and the dates that were in their orchards, their harvests in the plain, I made my troops devour. I destroyed, devastated and burned [their towns] and turned them into forgotten tells. The Arabs, Arameans, and Chaldeans who were in Uruk, Nippur, Kish, and Hursagkalama, together with their citizens, the transgressors, I forced to come out and I counted as booty. The grain and dates that were in their orchards, the fields that they had worked, and the crops of the outlying regions and the mountain flanks, I made my troops devour. Bel-ibni, a member of the *rab bani* class, the offspring of Shu'anna [Babylon], who had grown up in my palace like a young puppy, I placed over them as king of Akkad and Sumer.
>
> (Luckenbill 1924: 54 ll. 50–4)

A substantially shorter account is found on a cylinder inscription dated to the year 702, written after the second campaign. Its contents agree with the earlier text, however, in all but two details: the statement that 89 rather than 88 walled cities were captured and the inclusion of Kutha in the list of cities whose inhabitants were deported (ibid.: 56–7). These changes are so minor that Smith does not even bother to mention them.

What does merit Smith's attention, however, is the difference in the political settlement Sennacherib imposed upon Babylonia. He quotes an arrangement by which Bel-ibni was not the king of Sumer and Akkad by himself, but had to share power with a number of Assyrian officials, appointed as governors over various Chaldean districts. The source for that situation is the so-called Rassam cylinder, actually a text found in several manuscripts dated to 700 BC and written after Sennacherib's third campaign. The king states there:

> Bel-ibni, a member of the *rab bani* class, I placed on the throne. The people of the land of Akkad I made subject to him. Over all the districts of the land of the Chaldeans I

placed my high officials as governors and the yoke of my rule I laid upon them.

(Borger 1979: 70)

What Smith omits to say is that even later accounts do not mention Bel-ibni at all. The reason for that change lies in the fact that Sennacherib returned to Babylonia in his fourth campaign, in 700 BC, to deal once more with Merodach-baladan and removed Bel-ibni, "who had been false to the Assyrian cause" (Grayson 1991a: 107), replacing him with Sennacherib's own son, Assur-nadin-shumi. We find this version from accounts written after the fourth campaign (e.g. Smith 1875: 308) through the final annalistic text of his reign, written after the eighth campaign, and dated to 691. In the latter text Sennacherib states:

Upon my return I placed Assur-nadin-shumi, my first-born son, my offspring on his throne. The wide land of Sumer and Akkad I made subject to him.

(Luckenbill 1924: 35 col. III ll. 71–4)

Several later sources, written after the sixth campaign, conflate the first campaign of Sennacherib against Merodach-baladan with the selection of his son as king of Babylonia. These are not annalistic accounts (Levine 1982: 38); but the combination in the same paragraph of the battle near Kish, an event that took place during his first campaign, and the appointment of Assur-nadin-shumi, in the fourth, is meant to suggest these events were related in time.

In a battle in the plain in the area of Kish I repelled Merodach-baladan, king of Babylonia. I took away his kingship. All the Chaldeans together with the mass of the troops of the Elamites, his allies, I slayed with my weapons. I placed Assur-nadin-shumi, my first-born son, my offspring on his throne. The wide land of Akkad I made subject to him.

(Luckenbill 1924: 76–7, ll. 7–12)

Now we know from other sources that Bel-ibni was indeed king of Babylon for three years. The Babylonian Chronicle series, a sequence of fifteen tablets that summarily lists the names of the kings of Babylon from the mid-eighth to the late third centuries BC along with some events for each year, mentions him and his successor Assur-nadin-shumi:

> When he [Sennacherib] withdrew, he placed Bel-ibni on the
> throne of Babylon . . . For three years Bel-ibni ruled Babylon,
> Sennacherib placed his son, Assur-nadin-shumi, on the
> throne in Babylon . . . For six years Assur-nadin-shumi ruled
> Babylon.
>> (Grayson 1975b: 77–8 Chron 1, col. ii ll. 23, 29–31, 43)

Moreover, Bel-ibni appears in two king lists (Babylonian King
List A: col. iv l. 15, Ptolemaic Canon l. 8; Grayson 1980–83: 93,
101), and there are a number of letters (Grayson 1975b: 213) and
documents (Brinkman and Kennedy 1983: 14–15) that are dated
to his reign, clearly demonstrating his existence as king.

The question is, then, how to deal with these various accounts
and what the changes tell the historian about the composition
of royal annals. It is obvious that we are not to take them at
face value. If only the later versions of Sennacherib's annals had
been preserved we would not have known of a Bel-ibni at all. The
first scholar to urge a source criticism was the American A. T.
Olmstead, who already in 1916 demonstrated that various versions
of annals existed which had to be evaluated for their historical
contents. His rule of thumb in this work was that the versions
closest in time to the events described were the most accurate, and
that later ones abbreviated earlier information and inflated figures
of booty and deportees. In his opinion, the annals were rewritten
after each campaign to acknowledge the king's new successes,
and in that process accounts of earlier campaigns were shortened
to accommodate the new text (Olmstead 1916). This rule of
thumb was applied by Sidney Smith to the passages quoted above;
he prefers the number of 88 captured cities to the 89 of a later
version, and he points out that Bel-ibni ruled as king of Sumer
and Akkad according to the earlier account. The principle is
still accepted as valid in more recent writings (Grayson 1980), and
it is indeed true that later versions of campaign accounts can be
substantially shorter than the older ones, although this is not necessarily the case (Levine 1981). It is also obvious that the earliest
account is the most reliable one, if we seek to find out particular
events, as we know that later versions commonly used it as a source
(Liverani 1981: 252).

But several other processes of redaction were involved as well,
some of which tell us much more about what went on in the
Assyrian court than the contents of the texts themselves, and allow

us to place the narrated events in a wider historical context. I will document only some of these processes, but many others must have been at work at different points in time and in different institutional settings. The corpus of texts involved is so enormous that even an entire monograph would be unable to deal with all of them. First, changes in the political situation can lead to changes in the description of events and even in the tone of the language used to narrate them. This is demonstrated by the various accounts dealing with Bel-ibni, as laid out above (compare Levine 1981; Liverani 1981). We have basically four different versions of his rule.

1 Bel-ibni is appointed king over Sumer and Akkad, i.e. southern and northern Babylonia, as sole ruler. This is found after Sennacherib's first campaign.
2 Bel-ibni is appointed only as king of Akkad, i.e. northern Babylonia, and the south is governed by a number of Assyrian officials. This version was written after Sennacherib's third campaign.
3 Bel-ibni is not mentioned at all and no ruler is said to be imposed on Babylon at the end of Sennacherib's first campaign. But after he returns to the region in his fourth campaign he places his son Assur-nadin-shumi on the throne. This version appears in texts written after the fourth campaign.
4 Assur-nadin-shumi is mentioned as the king of Babylon seemingly appointed at the end of the first campaign. This is found in some non-annalistic texts, which do not narrate events in a chronological sequence.

Three of these four accounts can be correlated with the particular political relations between Assyria and Babylonia at the time of their writing. When Sennacherib accomplished his first defeat of Merodach-baladan he was confident of his successful settlement of the Babylonian problem, and appointed a local man of non-royal blood as king. The latter had been educated at the Assyrian court, and Sennacherib rather mockingly refers to him as a "young puppy." Bel-ibni is "placed" over the people as king, and Sennacherib's tone is assured and boastful (Liverani 1981: 253). But matters did not work out the way he had hoped: Merodach-baladan continued to cause trouble in the south, and Bel-ibni was not able, or willing, to deal with him. Thus Sennacherib appointed Assyrian governors of more southerly territory alongside Bel-ibni, before he launched his fourth campaign. That explains the second version of the events, where the tone has also changed to one that presents Bel-ibni in a more subordinate light. There was no mention of his education at court in Assyria, and the people were "made subject to him," a statement that stresses Bel-ibni's inferior role (ibid.: 256). Finally, in his fourth campaign Sennacherib forced Merodach-baladan to flee to Elam, where he died in exile, and removed Bel-ibni from the throne, an event that was not even considered worth a mention. Upon his return home he appointed his son as king of Babylon. After these events, the official versions of the previous conditions in Babylonia omit reference to Bel-ibni, and state only that Assur-nadin-shumi was appointed after the fourth campaign. Since Bel-ibni was a non-entity when these texts were written there was no reason for him to be mentioned. Then finally, the rule of Assur-nadin-shumi seems to have become the natural state of affairs in Babylonia, so the fourth version suggests that he had been there since the first campaign. Thus the troubles with Babylonia were conflated into one account.

Narratives of campaigns were thus constantly rewritten. We can call this revisionist history, but that was probably not the intent of the writers. Of importance to them was the situation that existed at the time of the writing, not the situation of the past which had no relevance any longer. Obviously, the telling of certain events remained the same: every campaign had a victorious outcome and throughout the various versions this aspect was never neglected: it was a completed accomplishment. But other aspects of the texts were rewritten, far from a process of mere abbreviation and inflation of the amounts of booty, as Olmstead suggested. Irrelevant information could be omitted, while further developments could be included. After a military campaign by the Assyrian king the political situation in the invaded land would change, but that change was not a one-time event; further repercussions of the invasion could occur. The writers of the various versions of the annals recorded the situation that was in place when they wrote, and that was relevant to them. Thus the various stages in Sennacherib's attempts at controlling Babylonia politically were reported – not as one following the other in time, but as one replacing the previous stage ignoring situations that had existed earlier. Other examples of this process can be found in such texts as the annals of Shalmaneser III (ruled 858–824). When his annals were composed soon after his sixteenth year it was only mentioned that he had removed Marduk-mudammiq as king of Namri. But when his famous Black Obelisk was inscribed after his thirty-first year, a new king, Yanzu, had been appointed there, seemingly after a long interval. That fact was recorded as if it had taken place right away after the removal of Marduk-mudammiq (Levine 1981: 63–4). The current situation is what counted to the author, rather than a cover-up of the past.

Levine pointed out that what Olmstead called an inflation of the amounts of booty as time passed was probably a similar process of keeping track of the current situation (ibid.: 64). Booty continued to be amassed over several years, so that when the valuables taken were reported in various versions of the annalistic texts, the amounts recorded increased likewise according to the reality at the time of writing. Thus the recorded sums represented all goods collected when a particular version was written, not the actual amounts received at the conclusion of the recorded campaign.

Even the tone of the earlier accounts could be changed somewhat to reflect current thinking about a particular event. What might have seemed an accomplished fact in the past could have required re-evaluation because of subsequent developments. Again taking Sennacherib's Babylonian problems as an example, we see how the account after his first campaign sounds triumphant and confident. Merodach-baladan, in a cowardly way, abandoned his army to save his life long before Sennacherib had even reached him. The author seems assured that he will not reappear as he reports that a five-day search in the marshes failed to locate the Chaldean. It seemed that he had fled too far to be of any relevance to the situation in Babylonia. But only a year later, Merodach-baladan was credited with having waited until the heat of battle before he fled, silently acknowledging the fact that he was still a player on the Babylonian scene. The triumphalist tone has disappeared. His resurgence was indeed a fact, as we know from changes in the Bel-ibni episode. After his third campaign, Sennacherib merely mentions that Merodach-baladan fled to save his life. No reference is made to the futile search for him, and his reappearance on the Babylonian scene seems, then, no surprise. The flight was no longer very relevant, and is thus only summarily noted. Finally when Merodach-baladan did indeed flee forever as a result of Sennacherib's fourth campaign, the earlier, temporary, flight is simply ignored. The problem of Merodach-baladan had passed, and his successful removal becomes another sign of Sennacherib's greatness (Liverani 1981: 252–7).

The "rewriting" of annalistic texts does not apply only to their narrative sections, but also to the introductory titulary. This may seem a mere listing of honorific titles and epithets strung together at random to please the ruler's ego, but much thought was put into its composition. Through it a message was conveyed about the ruler's real accomplishments and an ideology of rule was reflected. A straightforward example of this can be observed in the various versions of Tiglath-Pileser I's (ruled 1114–1076) annals, which are the earliest examples of this type of text. Tiglath-Pileser campaigned extensively from the very beginning of his reign, especially in the north, east, and west of Assyria. His earlier inscriptions give him a list of titles which are vague in their geographical content. For instance, these appear in a text written after his fifth year:

> Tiglath-pileser, strong king, king of the universe without rival, king of the four quarters, king of all rulers, lord of lords, herdsman, king of kings, pious purification priest, to whom was given the pure scepter at the command of Shamash and who was given complete control over the people, subjects of Enlil, steadfast shepherd, whose name was called over the rulers, exalted high-priest, whose weapons Assur has sharpened and whose name he has called forever for the ruling of the four quarters, who captures distant regions with borders above and below, brilliant day whose shine overwhelms the quarters, splendid flame that covers the enemy land like a rain storm, who by the command of Enlil has no rival (and) defeats the enemy of Assur.
>
> (Grayson 1991b: 13, ll. 28–45)

Here, although geographical references are made to the four quarters of the world and to distant regions "above" and "below," i.e. to the north and south of Assyria, no specific places are mentioned. It is only after his campaigns in Babylonia that Tiglath-Pileser makes the geographical references in his list of titles more explicit:

> Who, by the command of Shamash, the hero, has conquered through battle and strength from Babylon in the land Akkad

to the Upper Sea in the land Amurru and the sea of the land Nairi, and became lord of all of it.

(ibid.: 41, ll. 5–8)

He has thus reached Babylon, the Mediterranean Sea in the west, and Lake Van in the north, facts commemorated in his titulary.

But sometimes the references are not that obvious. Liverani has demonstrated that the changes in Sennacherib's titles are informative of his accomplishments. While his early inscriptions use vague territorial titles that claim universal kingship, once he has campaigned in the south (campaign 1), east (campaign 2), west (campaign 3), and north (campaign 5) he can legitimately claim the ancient title "king of the four quarters." Liverani even suggests that the northern campaign was undertaken more for ideological reasons, to complete the cycle, than for military ones (1981). These examples show that to some extent kings had to *earn* their titles, and that we should not take the variations in them as meaningless.

That titles and epithets reflect a clearly defined ideology of kingship is demonstrated by a recent careful reading of the inscriptions of Esarhaddon (ruled 680–669) by B. N. Porter (1993). Esarhaddon inherited kingship of Assyria and Babylonia from his father Sennacherib, who, as seen above, had had his troubles with the southern kingdom, which had culminated in the violent destruction of Babylon. Instead of trying to subdue the region by force, Esarhaddon seems to have decided to portray his kingship there within the context of local traditions rather than as a foreign occupier of the throne. While his father had been the epitome of the destructive conqueror, none of the earlier Assyrian rulers, though more kindly disposed towards Babylonia, had undertaken major building projects there. In contrast, Esarhaddon as a proper "Babylonian" king sponsored the restoration and construction of several temples; the focus of his attention was Babylon and the sanctuary devoted to its god Marduk. Meanwhile, Esarhaddon also promoted building in Assyria, and we can compare his portrayals as king of Assyria and as king of Babylonia in the building inscriptions found in the two kingdoms. In Assyria he is portrayed as a traditional Assyrian king, using elements of the standard titulary. For instance, in this inscription from Assur dated to the second year of his reign, 679 BC, these titles are used:

> Esarhaddon, great king, strong king, king of the universe,
> king of Assyria, governor of Enlil, priest of Assur, son of
> Sennacherib, great king, strong king, king of the universe,
> king of Assyria, governor of Enlil, priest of Assur, the king
> who since his youth has feared the command of Assur,
> Shamash, Bel, and Nabu, and . . . their strength.
>
> (Borger 1956: 1, col. I ll. 1–13; Porter 1993: 97)

These are normal and very traditional titles employed by Assyrian
kings for centuries.

As king of Babylonia the new ruler portrayed himself in a
different light, however. This inscription from Babylon, dated to
his first regnal year, 680 BC, employs the following titles:

> Esarhaddon, great king, strong king, king of the universe,
> king of Assyria, governor of Babylon, king of Sumer and
> Akkad, steadfast shepherd, favorite of the lord of lords [i.e.
> Marduk], attentive prince beloved of Ṣarpanitum, the queen
> of the universe, goddess of all that is, reverent king who since
> his youth paid attention to their lordship and praised their
> strength, slave who prays, humble, submissive, who fears
> their divine power.
>
> (Borger 1956: 11–2, col. I ll. 1–18; Porter 1993: 95–6)

These titles and epithets do not obscure the fact that he is king of
Assyria, but after a summary acknowledgement of that point, they
shift the focus to Babylonia and its gods. Esarhaddon is called governor of Babylon, but king of Sumer and Akkad, ancient names
for the region. The gods mentioned are not those prominent in
the Assyrian pantheon (Enlil, Assur, Shamash, Bel, and Nabu), but
Ṣarpanitum and her husband, Marduk, the chief god of Babylon,
who is referred to here as "lord of lords." Finally, no mention is
made of the king's father Sennacherib, who must not have been
beloved by the Babylonians. It is clear that this text was written to
represent Esarhaddon as a traditional king of Babylon and that the
sentiments of a Babylonian audience were kept in mind.

An evolution in this attitude is visible, however, after the middle
of Esarhaddon's reign. Porter argues that he sought to create
a union between Assyria and Babylonia[2] and that this is reflected
in the titulary used. A number of texts from the later years of his
reign describe simultaneous building projects in Assur and Babylon.
The most complete of these texts starts with a long introductory

section, fifty-one lines long, where Esarhaddon's selection as king by the gods is stated as well as a list of titles and epithets. Among the gods mentioned we find both the supreme god of the Assyrian pantheon, Assur, and his Babylonian counterpart, Marduk. Also the titles refer to both regions:

Assyria	Babylonia
king of the universe	governor of Babylon
king of Assyria	king of Sumer and Akkad
governor of Enlil	[ ] of Tashmetum
priest of Assur	judicious prince
chosen by Ishtar of Niveveh	
selected by Ishtar of Arbela	

(Borger 1956: 79–80; Porter 1993: 122–3)

This parallelism continues throughout the list of epithets with references both to Assyrian and to Babylonian gods, cities, and temples. The audiences addressed here are, in other words, not two distinct groups, Assyrian and Babylonian, but one group only, Assyro-Babylonian. A close reading of these seemingly vapid lists of titles reveals thus a great deal about the political ideology of Esarhaddon's reign, something that is not explicitly stated within the royal inscriptions themselves.

What can we conclude then about the use of royal inscriptions in the study of Mesopotamian history? We can read these texts on at least two levels: as containing factual historical data and as being historical artefacts themselves. The first level of reading has always been, and will probably continue to be, the most immediate and popular approach. A number of seeming facts and events are disclosed about an individual's reign. These can be classified (military, political, administrative, etc.), dated, and their representation within the record can be evaluated for their truthfulness by comparison with independent sources, if these exist. Read in this way, these texts have provided the bulk of the descriptions of Mesopotamian history and they have molded our perception of the rulers or dynasties we study. Since Assyrians mention their military exploits in detail, military history dominates our accounts of them. Babylonians, on the other hand, focus upon civic projects, especially temple building, which have become the main facts known about their reigns.

Source criticism is obviously an important responsibility in this work, and has grown increasingly refined as additional sources have become available. While the logical preference for those annalistic texts closest in time to the events they describe is still a crude methodological stance, the comparison with independent accounts allows a higher degree of criticism. The availability, as well as usefulness, of such independent sources varies enormously over time. And each of these presents its own interpretive challenges, as I will demonstrate throughout the present book. To return to the example of the Assyrian empire, the historicity of data revealed by the royal inscriptions can be evaluated with sources produced either by the Assyrians themselves or by some of their victims and enemies. Among Assyrian sources, the extensive correspondence of the royal court can shed light on events left obscure in the annals. The murder of Sennacherib, for instance, is at best only hinted at in the royal inscriptions of his son Esarhaddon, whose rise to the throne was far from smooth (Borger 1956: 40–5). Non-Assyrian sources are more explicit: the Babylonian Chronicle, the Hebrew Bible, Josephus, the neo-Babylonian king Nabonidus, and the Hellenistic historian Berossus all talk of his assassination by one or two of his sons, but the names mentioned, Adramelech or Ardumuzan and Sharezer, are so altered that their original Assyrian form cannot be identified. A study of a letter from Nineveh (Parpola 1980) has revealed the name of the culprit, Arda-Mulissi, Sennacherib's eldest son at the time (Grayson 1991a: 120–1).[3] Since letters derive from the same milieu as the royal inscriptions, they can deal with the same events and talk about the same people; but their purpose is so dissimilar that they can shed a very different light on them. Legal and administrative texts, queries to the gods, and so on can similarly be used to verify data contained in the royal inscriptions.

Non-Assyrian sources concerning the Assyrian empire are abundant only in Babylonia and in Judah. The Babylonian Chronicle, seemingly a dry enumeration of events affecting Babylonia in annalistic fashion, can corroborate or amend Assyrian versions of incidents. For instance, the battle of Hallule between Sennacherib and the Elamites, described as a victory by the Assyrians, is said in the Babylonian Chronicle to have been an Elamite success (Grayson 1965: 342). Since interactions between Assyria and Babylonia were so intense, their writings necessarily treat the same facts but often from different points of view.

The use of the Hebrew Bible as a source for Assyrian history pre-dates the study of Assyrian texts themselves, and often biblical and Assyrian narratives are contrasted and combined as if they were equivalent sources, often creating problematic results. If I can refer again to Sidney Smith's description of Sennacherib's reign in the 1926 edition of *The Cambridge Ancient History* (1929), he follows his account of the Babylonian troubles with one of the campaigns in Syria and Palestine. There Sennacherib's own narration of the third campaign is padded with paraphrases of the biblical text: "Hezekiah sent three of his own officials out to parley with the Assyrians, who employed the Hebrew language, and spoke so loudly that the garrison could hear" (Smith 1929: 73; compare 2 Kings xviii 17–xix 6 // Isaiah xxxvi). The problems of biblical historiography are so complex that they cannot be addressed here, but it is clear that the Bible at least confirms the presence of Assyrians in Israel and Judah as an independent source, and that close correlations between the two sources can occur (Machinist 1983). Much ink has flowed over passages where the two narratives diverge, and it is mostly impossible to credit one source with a greater degree of accuracy than the other. Both exist within their own worlds and ideologies, and they were written for different purposes, which need to be investigated separately.

Finally, archaeology can play an important role in the evaluation of textual data, although great caution is needed when trying to combine information from these two records. Ideally destruction layers in particular sites can be dated with such a degree of accuracy that they can be related to a campaign or attack described in an annalistic or other account. Thus excavations of the city of Lachish, which was besieged and captured by Sennacherib during a raid on Judah his third campaign, have shown evidence of the battle itself and of the city's destruction (Ussishkin 1997: 320–1). Ironically, this military feat by Sennacherib is not explicitly mentioned in his annals. He does describe the attack on Judah and its capital Jerusalem, which he failed to capture, and that he sacked a number of cities in the region (Luckenbill 1924: 32–3), but he does not name Lachish. We know, however, with certainty that the city was taken by him, because of its depiction on palace reliefs in Nineveh (Russell 1991: 200–9), which in conjunction with the archaeological remains have allowed a vivid reconstruction of this event. The city involved can be identified by a short inscription next to the depiction of the king stating: "Sennacherib, king of the universe, king of Assyria, sat on his throne and the booty of Lachish passed before him" (Luckenbill 1924: 156). It is highly unusual that such an exact connection can be made between texts and archaeology. Archaeological dating techniques are often too inaccurate to distinguish clearly between various military campaigns, and the textual information is often too vague about the identification of the cities destroyed. Obviously, archaeology can provide important insights on other matters, such as the occupation of a region by the Assyrians which can be shown by the appearance of fortresses, for instance, but confirmation of precise historical data is rare.

All these issues relate to the use of Assyrian texts as sources for an *histoire événementielle*, a narrative of facts and events, ideally "as they actually happened." It is likely that the search for them will continue, through the re-analysis of known sources and the publication of new ones, as we are still very poorly informed about the factual history of Mesopotamia compared to many other, but far from all, periods of history. The desire to know what happened and when is a common curiosity, and the wealth of sources will continue to provide new data. Since we consider these texts by definition to have a propagandistic character, we may often be weary of their message, however. We know that an image of events was portrayed that perpetuated the Assyrian idea that the campaigns were always successful, so we always take the declaration of a victory with a grain of salt. In other respects as well these texts were not as truthful as we would like them to be: as the changes in the Bel-ibni account demonstrate, the situation accomplished at the time of writing was more important than an accurate description of past circumstances. Somehow we must always worry that the accounts we possess contain such a rewriting of the past. The facts that we do recover, then, are always to be questioned, evaluated, and used critically.

The texts produced by the Mesopotamian courts to commemorate their kings' deeds can also be read on another level. They are not only narratives that contain information about facts, but they are also artefacts of history that are messages in themselves. They can reveal to us some of the ideologies, preconceptions, and aims of the rulers and their courts, through their language and style, the physical shape of the object on which they are inscribed, and their original location. The reading of royal inscriptions on this level disregards the question of whether or not they contain the "truth." It submits them to a literary–critical reading that divorces contents from form and focuses on the latter. Such an approach is greatly influenced by structuralism and semiotics. It temporarily flourished in the field of Mesopotamian studies in the late 1970s and early 1980s when these methodological stances were at the tail-end of their popularity in the humanities and social sciences in general, and was primarily undertaken by a team of scholars from the University of Rome.

The texts as political messages are signs which can be analyzed as containing signifiers and signifieds. The signifiers are individual words, phrases, and combinations of sentences, which can be categorized, and placed within a lexicon and a grammar that reveal an ideological stance. Thus the analysis of the titularies of Sennacherib and Esarhaddon presented above shows how each one of them, in their choice of words and referents, signifies a particular idea of rule pertinent to the time of writing. Within the narrative sections of the inscriptions the word choices reflect an ideology of difference (Liverani 1979); the structure of passages is such that it juxtaposes "Assyria" to "the other," "good" to "evil," "us" to "them" (Zaccagnini 1981a). Literary topoi are used to depict foreign opponents to Assyria's might, hence their individual characteristics are not revealed to us except as an archetype of the "enemy" (Fales 1987). Read in this way, the royal inscriptions appear as tools in an ideological project of the Assyrian elite. Conquest and domination of foreign lands are natural; they are necessitated by their disorder and chaos, negative characteristics that need to be rectified by the Assyrian king.

These considerations lead to questions about the audience of these inscriptions and their original placement. It used to be thought that few people alive at the time of writing ever had either the possibility or the ability to read these texts. Many of the texts were written to be buried in the foundations of the buildings whose construction they commemorated, and those written on monuments, the wall-reliefs, bull-colossi, and thresholds were, if not barely legible in the dark rooms, incomprehensible to the large majority of, non-literate, people. The intended audiences were considered to be the gods themselves addressed throughout the texts, and future rulers who might unearth them when the building had collapsed (Oppenheim 1977: 146–8). The latter are commonly invoked at the end of the inscriptions. For instance, Sennacherib states as follows:

> In the future, among the kings my sons, whose name Assur and Ishtar will pronounce for the shepherding of land and

people, when this palace will become old and ruined, may
a future prince restore its ruins, may he see the stela with
my name written on it, may he pour oil, may he make an
offering over it, and may he return it to its place.

(Luckenbill 1924: 130 col. VI ll 73–9)

The issue of audience is a thorny one, as it raises questions about
access to inscriptions, literacy rates, and the comprehension of
literary Akkadian in a period when people spoke a very different
vernacular, if not another language altogether, such as Aramaic.
If the analysis of royal inscriptions as bearers of an ideological
message to a contemporary audience is correct, however, it seems
an unavoidable conclusion that such an audience had access to
them and could understand them (Porter 1993: 105–17).

The audiences of these messages included varied groups of
humans and deities: literate and non-literate speakers of Assyrian,
conquered subjects within the realm unable to speak or comprehend Assyrian, foreigners outside the borders, future kings, and
the gods. These were reached in a variety of ways. Those able to
read inscriptions might have done so, but surely were only a small
minority. Others may have listened to at least some royal statements, as a narration of Sargon II's eighth campaign (Mayer 1983)
mentions that it was to be read aloud to the citizens of the city
Assur. For those people who did not speak Assyrian, it is possible
that a spoken translation into Aramaic was provided at the time
(Machinist 1993: 98–102). The mere fact that a written text existed
might have had a great impact on those people who could see,
although not comprehend, the texts themselves (Porter 1995).

The existence of the texts themselves, in their written and oral
forms, conveys a message that goes beyond their contents. When
proclaimed, in high literary Akkadian, in vernacular Assyrian, or
in an Aramaic translation, the spectacle and pomp surrounding
these events, entirely unknown to us, probably displayed imperial
pride. When inscribed on visible surfaces within the palaces, there
must have been concerns about their placement which cannot
have been entirely arbitrary (Russell 1991). Texts could be
inscribed on reliefs depicting elements of the events they describe,
and the relationship between these two means of communication
needs to be investigated. A study of the context, in addition to the
contents, of texts is thus crucial. Research in this area has only
begun recently.

The semiotic analysis of Assyrian remains should not be a final step, however, and, in my opinion, has focused too much upon one, modern, stereotype about their creators. All too often the signified in these analyses has been one thing only: power. Studies of texts, reliefs, architecture, and so on, all have led to the conclusion that these gave a propagandistic message of might. Assyria can be seen only as an imperial war machine, its remains only as signs of an ideology of domination. Such a reading is clearly important and should not be discarded. But this exclusive reading is in itself a sign of a modern ideology: the ancient Near Eastern ruler, as his modern Middle Eastern counterpart, can be seen only as a dictator, a wanton aggressor.

A post-structuralist analysis of the signifiers as a coherent system of multiple interacting elements, leads to a deeper understanding of the Assyrian remains. The forms, placements, contents, and many other aspects of the communications we receive from the Assyrians provide access to their ways of thinking and their beliefs. For instance, a study of the mutilation of texts and images revealed an entirely different aspect of the Assyrians' perceptions of these creations: they are not only communications of imperial might, they are one with what they represent and describe, they function as an uncanny double (Bahrani 1995). The separation of text from image, something I have been guilty of myself here, is unacceptable in this reading, as both media formed a single unit in the Mesopotamian mind. Together, they held a meaning that was permeated with the ego of the subject. The image/text became the individual. Therefore its mutilation had a fundamental significance: not merely a representation was damaged, but the subject itself was subdued and destroyed. The recognition of that fact says something about the power of these royal monuments that we still have a hard time fathoming. They are not a representation of an individual, they *are* the individual. That such power was recognized by the ancient Mesopotamians is shown by what happened to the Assyrian palace reliefs when the capital Nineveh was captured by Babylonians and Medes in 612. The palaces were not put to the torch immediately, but were carefully examined for images of particularly despised people: Sennacherib who had destroyed Babylon; the soldier who had cut off the head of the Elamite king Teumman;[4] Assurbanipal who had held a banquet underneath a tree where that head had been hung for display, and so on. These men were recognized by their deeds or by short inscriptions stating their names. The act of defacement was not a *damnatio memoriae*, as the epigraphs were left intact, nor a wanton act of violence. This was an attack on these individuals, who had been long dead by then, but whose power emanated from their images.

Probably this was not just true of images, reliefs, statues, and texts, but also of monumental architectural remains, even entire cities. When Nineveh, the Assyrian capital, fell to the Babylonians and Medes, it seemingly was ritually flooded, an act of such import that its memory survived in later biblical and Greek sources (Machinist 1997). Was this merely a random act of revenge for the devastation of Babylon by Sennacherib, the Assyrian ruler who had moved his capital to Nineveh and had completely recreated it? Or was it one of the many acts of domination and control of Sennacherib, who was still considered present in his city? In case it might be perceived that I too focus upon power and control, let me stress that it is the fact that the Assyrians, and their Near Eastern contemporaries, believed the image or monument to be the person that I find fascinating. The "power of images" (Freedberg 1989), or in Mesopotamia more accurately the power of "the image/texts," was, and is, not only that they communicated the might of the ruler whose deeds are depicted and described. They are not mere signifiers of a signified that is all-important. It is as signifiers that the images and texts have their power. To the Assyrians they represented the survival of the ego, knowledge, and other concepts we still need to comprehend. Such other readings are possible, even necessary, in this post-modern age: the Assyrians were not just obsessed with war and propaganda; they believed in what we would call magic, they observed strange lands and peoples with amazement. Multiple readings of their texts, acknowledging these facts, may lead to a deeper understanding of Assyrians as human beings.

SARGON OF AGADE

Despite their wish for immortal fame, the large majority of Mesopotamian kings were merely remembered in lists of ancestors or king lists. A few of them became figures about whom tales were told that survived for many generations; of those only some became the heroes of detailed stories describing military feats, stories that seem to have caught the imagination of later audiences and remained popular regardless of the political vicissitudes of the region. These were the kings of the Akkad dynasty,[5] a short-lived group of highly successful military leaders from northern Babylonia, whose troops seem to have roamed over large parts of the Middle East in the twenty-fourth and twenty-third centuries. They represent to most modern scholars the earliest known example of empire builders, and under them Babylonia is thought to have ruled a territory from the Persian Gulf to the Mediterranean Sea. The awe these kings inspired in antiquity, as today, was enormous: they became the paradigm for all Mesopotamian imperial rulers to come, their shining example rarely, if ever, equalled.

The creator of this "empire" was Sargon, his greatest successor his grandson Naram-Sin, who did, however, see the beginning of its precipitous collapse. Scholars acknowledge that the histories of Sargon and Naram-Sin contain a mixture of data: some inscriptions left by these kings themselves, others legends told centuries, if not millennia, later. How to separate fact from fiction has been a primary concern, the degree of credence given to a first-millennium literary source, for instance, depending on the individual scholar. Confirmation of events related in them is sought elsewhere, but remains mostly inconclusive. For instance, Sargon's claim that he conquered Ebla (Frayne 1993: text 11)[6] was thought to be confirmed by the find of a burnt palace at the western Syrian site of Tell Mardikh. But Sargon did not leave any evidence there to stake his claim. Was the destruction really his work, or that of his grandson Naram-Sin who boasted of the same feat (Frayne 1993: 136), or a totally separate disaster? All three reconstructions of events are possible, and have their defenders (cf. Astour 1992), but none rests on more "proof" than another.

One can read the texts relating to the Akkad kings in another, more fruitful way, however, an approach urged by Liverani decades ago (1973), and only recently put into practice by a handful of scholars. We can look at them not as sources on Sargon and Naram-Sin, but as sources about themselves. Why did someone in the first millennium, almost 2,000 years after the death of Sargon, bother to describe his rise to power (Glassner 1993: 217–18), or at least copy out a composition that related this? And what does it tell us both about the fame of Sargon and the concerns of the people "remembering" him? The crucial difficulty for such an investigation lies in the fact that we cannot establish the date of composition of these traditions. We can date the manuscripts, but we do not know whether they were copies of older texts or new creations. Therefore the attempts at reconstructing why particular stories about Sargon had been composed remain highly tentative in themselves. Yet the history of an idea can be followed over time, through the manuscripts, revealing much about Mesopotamian ideology. This has been recently studied in an excellent way for Naram-Sin and the fall of Agade (Glassner 1986), and I will, in summary fashion, describe here the obsession with Sargon as it evolved through the centuries. All ancient sources regarding Sargon have been collected several times, based on a generic approach distinguishing between royal inscriptions, literary texts, omens, etc. (Hirsch 1963: 2–9; Lewis 1980: 125–47). Here I will study the tradition of Sargon as it developed over time, taking into account all genres of texts together, as these are often interrelated to such an extent that untangling the connections is impossible. Moreover, previous scholars have used evidence from omens to validate statements in chronicles, for instance, ignoring that these two genres are based on the same premises and sources (Liverani 1993: 43) Again, this leads to an attempt to evaluate the historicity of sources, something that is not my concern here. What I want to investigate is how the Mesopotamians themselves thought of Sargon, and why they looked at him in a particular way at each stage.

The remains of texts written in Sargon's reign itself (*ca.* 2334–2279) are sparse (Frayne 1993: texts 10, 16, 17, 2001–5): a handful of inscriptions with his name are preserved, primarily written for his daughter Enheduanna who was high priestess in the southern city of Ur. In the western Iranian site of Susa a very damaged stone stela was found, one side of which showed the representation of a man identified in the adjacent inscription as Sargon, another side contained the word "conquered" (ibid.: text 10). Although it is possible that Sargon himself set up the stela in Susa on a military expedition there, it is more likely that the stone was taken as booty by later Elamite raiders of Babylonia together with a number of other, more famous stelae and statues of the Akkad dynasty: the stela of Naram-Sin, the obelisk of Manishtushu, etc. A stone vase found at Ur was dedicated "for Sargon, king of the universe" (ibid.: text 2002). That title is found in several other inscriptions in which Sargon's family members refer to him.

In Sargon's reign the use of year names, started somewhat earlier by some Sumerian rulers, was continued, yet not applied throughout the regions he controlled. Some texts at Nippur use this dating system which commemorates at least two military events: a campaign in Elam, with the destruction of the city of Arawa on its border, and a campaign to Simurrum, the area east of the Upper Tigris (ibid.: 8). Since tablets found in other Babylonian cities were not dated with year names, we cannot state with certainty whether they were written under Sargon or under one of his successors. Certain stylistic elements, including the forms of certain cuneiform signs, of administrative documents from the early part of the dynasty are so distinct, however, that we can establish that a city such as Umma was controlled by Sargon or his sons. Based on these scanty remains we can state that Sargon called himself "king of the universe," claimed to have campaigned in the east, controlled Nippur in central Babylonia, and had a daughter who was high priestess at Ur. All in all it is not a very distinguished record, but the ravages of time and our failure to find Sargon's dynastic seat, Agade, may explain the scarcity of information.

Fortunately for his fame Sargon erected a number of statues of himself with inscriptions commemorating his military feats in detail. These statues were set up in the courtyard of Enlil's temple at Nippur, the Ekur, and stood there at least until the early second millennium (Buccellati 1993). He was not the only king who did so: his successors Rimush, Manishtushu, and Naram-Sin did like-wise, as did some kings of dynasties that replaced Akkad, Erridu-pizzir, the Gutian and Shu-Sin of Ur (e.g. Kutscher 1989: 49–101). Perhaps many other rulers followed suit. That these statues were preserved and respected is somewhat surprising. New dynasties controlled Nippur, and although we can perhaps say that the Old Akkadian rulers had already attained legendary status in Old Babylonian times, the appearance of statues of Erridu-pizzir, a member of a dynasty that was considered to have caused havoc in Babylonia, shows that a positive appreciation was not needed for survival of one's statue. The statues themselves have disappeared, but scribes went around copying the inscriptions down on clay tablets, as well as the epigraphs that identified people carved on the socles, most often defeated opponents of the campaigns described: "Lugalzagesi, king of Uruk," etc. Why these inscriptions were copied is unknown; their contents seem to have been what mattered, as the sign-forms used, although somewhat archaizing, do not imitate those to be expected on an Old Akkadian stone monument. Two manuscripts are preserved collecting such inscriptions from statues of Sargon, Rimush, and Manishtushu on the same tablet. In total, texts from sixteen statues of Sargon were collected, many of them poorly preserved because of damage to the Old Babylonian tablet rather than to the original Old Akkadian statues when they were copied.

The image we obtain here of Sargon is a lot more detailed than what is preserved in original inscriptions from his reign itself. His military feats described in the Old Babylonian copies fall into two categories: the unification of Babylonia, and conquests of wide-ranging peripheral areas. None of the campaigns is dated, nor can we establish a clear sequence of events based on other criteria. The conquest of Babylonian city-states was accomplished by defeating a coalition of fifty governors led by Lugalzagesi of Uruk, who had in previous decades united the very south of the region. The campaigns in the periphery dealt with Elam (south-western Iran) and Parahshum (central Iran), where Sargon seems to have imprisoned a large number of local governors and princes (Frayne 1993: texts 8 and 9, captions). The exploits in Syria are referred to in vaguer terms: he did honor to the god Dagan in Tuttul, a city on the Middle Euphrates. In return Sargon was granted control over the Upper Land: Mari, Iarmuti, and Ebla, Syrian territories from the Middle Euphrates to the west, which were given to him as far as the cedar and silver mountains, namely, the Amanus range in north-western Syria. He could thus claim not only the title "king of the universe," which we know to have been in use in his own time, but also that Enlil, the god of Nippur, gave to him the Upper and the Lower Seas (Frayne 1993: text 13), i.e. the Mediterranean and the Persian Gulf. The latter image clearly stuck in the minds of the Mesopotamians, as will be seen later.

There is no reason to doubt that these Old Babylonian tablets contain bona fide copies of inscriptions that had been carved in Sargon's days. No glorification of the king, beyond that produced by his own court, seems to be presented here. Whether it is fact or fiction is irrelevant for my purposes here. Neither can we say that Sargon and his Old Akkadian successors were singled out for this preservation of memory: though many statues had been erected by them and thus their inscriptions predominate in this record, they are hardly unique. Sargon had, however, attained a special status after his death – he was deified, and a cult existed for him. Although in the third millennium such a cult was not unusual, the survival of Sargon's (and Naram-Sin's) is impressive: we have evidence from the Ur III period (Hirsch 1963: 5) down to the Persian period (Kennedy 1969) of offerings made to Sargon as a god. The survival of this cult into the late first millennium obviously was related to the continuing fame of the man I will describe here.

Sargon's appearance in the Sumerian King List is a normal feature for kings of his era, although some extra information is given about him, which was unusual: "In Agade, Sargon – his father was a gardener – cupbearer of Ur-Zababa, the king of Agade, he who built Agade, was king. He ruled 56 years" (Glassner 1993: 140). This indicates that stories about him were in circulation, and indeed he figured prominently in literary and omen texts from the early second millennium. These are so varied and rich in nature that they clearly show a conscious acknowledgement that he was someone special, a great king who left a mark on history. While an appearance in omens and related chronicles (all of later date) is something a handful of early rulers could claim, only Sargon and his grandson Naram-Sin feature explicitly in long literary texts. To be sure, they share this fame with some epic protagonists such as Enmerkar, Lugalbanda, and Gilgamesh, but the latter may have been purely fictional characters, while Sargon and Naram-Sin certainly existed in reality. What do these stories tell us about Sargon? A number of them deal with his rise, a tale reflected in the Sumerian King List. He started out as a cupbearer of Ur-Zababa, ruler of Kish, and succeeded in overthrowing his master despite the latter's traps and even connivance with Lugalzagesi of Uruk (Cooper and Heimpel 1983). That he became king of Kish is not certain, as the Sumerian King List gives five native successors to Ur-Zababa, but Sargon did establish himself as king of Agade. His consolidation of power in Babylonia is not described, but obviously this could be a result of the loss of data as well as a lack of concern by the authors. People in the centuries after his reign were conscious of the image that he unified Babylonia and subdued the surrounding areas. For example, the "Curse of Agade," a Sumerian literary text that deals with the mistakes of Naram-Sin, possibly composed in the late third millennium and extremely popular in the early second millennium, starts with a summary descriptions of Sargon's rise to power:

> After Enlil's frown had slain Kish like the Bull of Heaven,
> had slaughtered the house of the lord of Uruk in the dust

like a mighty bull, and then Enlil had given sovereignty and
kingship from south to north to Sargon, king of Agade.

(Cooper 1983: 51 ll. 1–6)

Thus the defeats both of Ur-Zababa of Kish and of Lugalzagesi of
Uruk are alluded to here. Moreover, according to the same "Curse
of Agade" Sargon extracted tribute from Marhashi in Iran, while
when Naram-Sin became king, Sumer (southern Iraq), the Amorites
of the Syrian desert, Meluhha (India), Elam in the east, and Subir
in the north, all regularly supplied goods to Agade (ibid.: 53).

In the later texts dealing with Sargon himself, his far-flung
campaigns are of great interest, and special attention is given to
those in the northwest, to which only vague reference is made in
his own inscriptions. The campaigns in the east, however, which
figure prominently in his statue inscriptions, are mentioned only
obliquely in a fragmentary composition perhaps somewhat later
than Old Babylonian in date. There, in a monologue Sargon
states: "They will not block (my way) before Elam" (J. Westenholz
1997: text 8). Since, in a second manuscript of the same text,
Elam is replaced by the cedar forest, even this single reference to
the east may have to be disregarded.[7] His campaigns to the north,
the area from the Amanus mountains to the Upper Tigris,
i.e. southern Turkey just north of the Syrian border, appear to
have attracted more interest, however. Three Old Babylonian
compositions deal with them. In two, Sargon himself exhorts his
soldiers to be valiant. They are led into the Amanus mountains
where they reach the cedar forest and fight in the area of
Mardaman (i.e. Upper Tigris; ibid.: text 7), or campaign in the
land of one Uta-rapashtim (ibid.: text 6). The latter seems to me
to be an entirely artificial name, conspicuously similar to that of
the Flood's sole survivor in the Gilgamesh epic, Uta-napishtim,
"Seeker of life." The second element in the foreign king's name,
the adjective "broad," seems to refer to a geographical expanse.
The name either shows the germs of a later tradition that places
Sargon next to Uta-napishtim at the edge of the world, or had an
independent meaning and led to a later confusion (see below).
Sargon also boasts, in the Uta-rapashtim text, of a great number
of conquests: Amurru in the west, Subartu in the north, and
perhaps even Carchemish on the Turkish Euphrates (ibid.: text 6).
The final text dealing with this area is a fictive letter of Sargon
to eight men in which a request is made to Shamash for the

permission to capture Purushhanda, a city in central Anatolia (ibid.: text 11).

The military fame of Sargon may find some reflection in the omen literature of the time: several observations are said to indicate "the omen of Sargon," with some vague extra information. The statements "he ruled the entire world," "he had no rival," and "he went through darkness and saw the light" appear frequently (Lewis 1980: 136–7). Military valor is clearly intended, but the details thereof are not portrayed.

Sargon's image as a great conqueror is thus very strong in the Old Babylonian period. It was proclaimed by himself on statues still on exhibit in that period in Nippur, it dominated the literary tradition about him, and was reflected in the omens. "I am Sargon, beloved of Ishtar, who roamed the four quarters," states his auto-biography of Old Babylonian date (J. Westenholz 1997: text 1), and surely everyone who had read or heard the texts about him would have agreed. He was a man of lowly birth, a cupbearer, who had risen to power. His name Sharru-ken, "the king is legitimate," is probably a programmatic throne-name to convince people that he was legitimate. Why did he appeal so much to the elites of the early second millennium? Many royal houses were made up of new-comers, often Amorites who had perhaps entered Mesopotamia only in the late third millennium and grabbed power in various city-states when Ur's rule over Babylonia had disintegrated. A 200-year struggle for hegemony had culminated in the military successes of Larsa and then ultimately of Babylon, which in the eighteenth century had turned the entire area from the Persian Gulf to the Middle Euphrates into an ephemeral political union. All of the rulers involved were suspect in terms of royal descent. But Sargon did not appeal only to Babylonians: one of the literary compositions regarding him was found in the Diyala site of Tell Harmal (J. Westenholz 1997: text 7), and a king of Assur called himself Sargon. More importantly, perhaps, Shamshi-Adad, the great Amorite leader who for a short time in the early eighteenth century unified the entirety of northern Mesopotamia, saw the Akkadian kings as his models. He called himself "King of Akkad" (Grayson 1987: 58), he mused about Manishtushu when he rebuilt the Ishtar temple at Nineveh (Grayson 1987: 53), and he did stay in the city of Agade for a while (Dossin 1950: no. 36 l. 5). It is then not surprising to read that he had statues of Sargon and Naram-Sin set up in Mari and provided with sheep offerings (Birot 1980).

After the collapse of the Old Babylonian political system around 1600, textual information from the region becomes very scant. But literary production was not necessarily at a standstill. Babylonia may have been highly creative in this area and set trends for other cultural regions where we do find Babylonian literature in translation or in the Babylonian language. Texts regarding Sargon similarly find an audience abroad while in Mesopotamia his memory only vaguely lingers at this time, if our scarce sources are reflective of reality. Only two omens, one from Assyria, another from Babylonia, refer to him (Lewis 1980: 137). The contemporary Hittites in Anatolia and the Egyptians knew Sargon well, however. The material from the Hittite capital, Hattusas in central Anatolia, is the most extensive and shows the active participation of the local elite in developing his image. A new composition appears at this time, called "King of Battle," concentrating on Sargon's involvement in Anatolia (J. Westenholz 1997: text 9). We know of an Akkadian-language version of this text found at El Amarna in Egypt, possibly in two manuscripts (ibid.: text 9B–C), and a Hittite-language paraphrase, found in several, fragmentary, copies at Hattusas (Güterbock 1969). Since the story survives in Mesopotamia into the first millennium, it may be safe to assume that it was a second-millennium Babylonian composition that was exported to Hatti and Egypt together with a select group of other literary texts. The interest to the Hittites will become clear soon, but before we turn to the text itself, it should be pointed out that Sargon was not unknown to them even in their earlier history.

King Hattushilis I, the great conqueror of the Hittite Old Kingdom in the seventeenth century, refers to Sargon in his bilingual Hittite-Akkadian annals. There he states that Sargon had crossed the Euphrates and had destroyed a city called Hahha. Likewise, Hattushilis had crossed the river more than 600 years later – in the opposite direction, naturally (Güterbock 1964). The Old Hittite kings were very successful in long-distance campaigns, as their Old Akkadian counterparts had been in the past. They descended into northern Syria several times, defeated Aleppo and Urshum, not too far from where Sargon and Naram-Sin were supposed to have campaigned, and Mursilis I even succeeded in marching all the way down the Euphrates to Babylon, putting an end to Hammurabi's famous dynasty. Sargon was thus an example to them, if indeed they believed that he had penetrated into Anatolia.

The Anatolian campaign is the subject of the "King of Battle." The Akkadian version at El Amarna relates how Sargon wanted to go to war, but that his soldiers warned him of the dangers, a rather common literary motif where the ruler accomplishes glorious deeds against the advice of his men. Sargon was encouraged here by the spokesman of merchants from Purushhanda, a central Anatolian city, who complained of suffering extortion. The depiction of the wealth and abundance of Purushhanda seems to have convinced the Akkadians to set out. Their opponent is identified as one Nur-daggal, a name that contains the Akkadian element "light" (nur), and the Sumerian element, written syllabically here, "broad" (dagal). It is clearly a fanciful name, which may be a play on the name of Sargon's opponent in the Old Babylonian texts, Uta-rapashtim. The Sumerian term UD can also refer to the sun and light, while the Akkadian adjective rapashtum means "broad." In first-millennium traditions Nur-daggal is replaced by the good Akkadian name Nur-Dagan "light of the god Dagan," which may be what was to be understood originally.[8] It is, however, also possible that an outlandish name was invented here on purpose, similar to a good Akkadian one, but slightly skewed. The same would go for the Uta-rapashtim we met in the Old Babylonian material. Nur-daggal submitted to Sargon, who remained in Purushhanda for three years as its king. The Hittite version has some more detail about the march to Anatolia, including an offering made by Sargon at the source of the Euphrates, the identification of Nur-dahhi as king of Purushhanda, and the appearance of gods in dreams to Sargon and his opponent.

Liverani (1993: 52–6) has tentatively suggested that the story was composed in Shamshi-Adad's days, as a means to urge the king to re-establish trade contacts between Assur and central Anatolia. Purushhanda had housed a colony of Assyrian merchants before trade was interrupted by events in Mesopotamia, and, on Liverani's reading of the story, if Shamshi-Adad truly wanted to be like Sargon, he would have had to free the merchants there. Since Shamshi-Adad did try to emulate Old Akkadian rulers in his titulary that is a possibility, although difficult to prove considering the absence of manuscripts from Shamshi-Adad's days. The appeal of this story to the Hittite kings can be understood, however, but only if they saw the Old Akkadian rulers as their examples, and Nur-daggal not as one of themselves, but as a representative of the Anatolian rulers they themselves had subdued in the early centuries of the second millennium. Purushhanda could then be presented as a foreign city that had been captured by an illustrious ancestor. What stands out in the story is the description of the area of Purushhanda as rich and lush, something that must have appealed to a local audience. The appearance of this story in Egypt is less clear, but then we have a hard time understanding why any Babylonian literature found its way there. It is likely that the preserved manuscripts were written in Hattusas and then sent to Egypt (J. Westenholz 1997: 105).

In the second half of the second millennium Sargon's fame was thus maintained and spread over the entirety of the Middle East where the Akkadian language was understood. In the preserved textual material, very limited indeed, the Anatolian connection is emphasized, something Sargon's own inscriptions did not touch upon. This emphasis probably results from the fact that the later texts at hand derive from Anatolia itself, the locale of Sargon's feats.

In first-millennium Mesopotamia, Sargon's fame flourished, both in Assyria and in Babylonia. The textual material at hand is extensive and we know from a library catalogue from Nineveh that at least two additional compositions existed, entitled "Sargon, the glorious" and "Sargon, the strong" (Lewis 1980: 134). The stories about him became more detailed on certain aspects of his life, although a negative element in his career appears, a novelty in a tradition that previously had nothing but praise for him. The main aspect of Sargon's fame, his far-flung military conquests, still remains the focus of the literature about him. He is presented as having reached the limits of the earth in the endeavor. The most detailed and explicit depiction of Sargon as conqueror of the universe is a text now called "The Sargon Geography" (Grayson 1974–77).

Known to us in two manuscripts, a neo-Assyrian one from Assur and a neo-Babylonian one of unknown origin, it describes the various regions he controlled, either by identifying border points or by measuring their sizes in *bēru*, the Akkadian measure indicating a distance covered on foot in two hours (about six miles). The designations for the areas and cities are a mixed bag of terms in use in various periods of Mesopotamian history (Liverani 1993: 64): for instance, Marhashi (third millennium), Emutbalum (early second millennium), SURginiash (late second millennium), and Hanu (first millennium). Sometimes even contradictory uses of

terms are found: for instance, Magan is used to indicate both
Egypt and Oman (Heimpel 1981: 66–8). It is thus likely that the
author had available a number of older texts of various dates
relating to Sargon, and combined their information with his
own geographical knowledge. The designations of distant areas
with ancient and anachronistic toponyms was not unusual in neo-
Assyrian texts. It strengthened the propagandistic impression that
time stood still in these barbarian regions (Machinist 1986: 189).
Liverani has suggested that the author had the Old Babylonian
version of texts with Old Akkadian toponyms at hand, but I
see no evidence for that. The text seems to be a neo-Assyrian composition using anachronistic terms, perhaps thought to have been
correct in the days of Sargon himself. As Liverani points out, the
consistent use of the *bēru* in distance measures is something
only appearing in Late Assyrian royal inscriptions, and this text has
the same purpose as those accounts: the glorification of the king's
military actions which covered an enormous region.

"The Sargon Geography" has two summations of the king's
conquests:

> 120 double hours is the reach from the source of the
> Euphrates to the border of the land of Meluhha and Magan,
> which Sargon, king of the universe, measured and whose
> width he calculated when he conquered all lands covered by
> the sun.
>
> (Grayson 1974–77: 60 ll. 30–2)

Referred to here is the region from central Anatolia in the north
(the source of the Euphrates) to the very south of the earth,
Meluhha and Magan being the names for Nubia and Egypt in neo-
Assyrian times. A second passage states:

> Anaku (Cyprus) and Kaptara (Crete), the lands across the
> Upper Sea (Mediterranean), and Dilmun (Bahrain) and
> Magan (Oman), the lands across the Lower Sea (Persian
> Gulf), and the lands from sunset to sunrise which Sargon
> conquered three times. From Anzan (Iran) to Misri (Egypt),
> Surru (Tyre), Surshatak (?), Gablabi (Byblos?) to [ ], Kukun
> (upper Tigris?), Maganna (Egypt), Baza (Arabia), [ ], and
> the land of the Udaneans on the border of Sumer, as many
> as there were [ ], Teima (Arabia), . . .
>
> (Grayson 1974–77: 60 ll. 41–8)

The geographical references here are not always clear, but the general meaning is: Sargon had conquered the region from Crete to Oman, from where the sun rises in the east to where it sets in the west. Then a number of places are listed on the outer borders of that region. The message is blatantly clear: the whole known world was under Sargon's control.

The idea that Sargon reached the edge of the world is also expressed in the so-called "Babylonian map of the world" (Horowitz 1988). On a late Babylonian tablet a drawing was found of the universe, with its center in the city of Babylon and known regions. The land mass is surrounded by the ocean, outside of which are mysterious regions. The accompanying text talks about these regions as populated with exotic animals and monsters: it also makes reference to the god Marduk and creation, and states in one line: "Ut-napishtim, Sargon, and Nur-Dagan, king of Burshahanda" (Horowitz 1988: 148 l. 10). Here Sargon and his opponent of the "King of Battle" story are found together with the sole survivor of the Flood in the Epic of Gilgamesh, Ut-napishtim. In that text Ut-napishtim resides at the edge of the world across the ocean. The association of this man with Sargon is clearly due to a confusion in the names of the hero of the flood story and of Sargon's enemy, Uta-rapashtim, in the Old Babylonian Sargon story (J. Westenholz 1997: text 6). But there is here also an implicit acknowledgement that Sargon could, and did, reach the edge of the earth. And since the "King of Battle" text presents Nur-Dagan as his enemy in his furthest adventure, this man can be found at the edge of the world as well. That the "King of Battle" story is still known at this time is clear from two neo-Assyrian manuscripts of it (ibid.: texts 9 D–E). In them Nur-daggal's name is "corrected" to Nur-Dagan, as in the "map of the world" text. Sargon's conquests had thus reached the outer limits of the earth, a feat that could not be surpassed. Also the omen literature makes reference to this fact repeatedly: it mentions his campaigns in the east and the west and often just states "omen of Sargon, who ruled the world" (Lewis 1980: 138–9).

The first-millennium traditions also elaborate more on Sargon's humble beginnings. His birth, previously left unexplained except for the fact that his father was a gardener, is now the story of a Moses-style legend. Again several manuscripts of this text are known, from Assyria and Babylonia (J. Westenholz 1997: text 2). In them, Sargon is stated to have been born to an unknown father and a mother who was probably a priestess. She gave birth to him in secrecy and placed him in a reed basket in the river. He was picked up by a water-drawer, who adopted him as a son, and made him a gardener. The goddess Ishtar grew fond of him, and made him king. While ruler he embarked on difficult journeys in the mountains and over the sea. After these statements the majority of the text remains unclear to us. Such stories are common among usurpers to the throne (Lewis 1980). All references to people and places are deliberately vague or fictional: the father, mother, and uncle are unnamed, the city of birth, Azupiranu, is unknown, the water-drawer's name, Aqqi, means "I drew water." Only Ishtar and Sargon are "real" characters; no mention is made of his opponents Ur-Zababa and Lugalzagesi. The tradition that he grew up as a gardener can be based on the Sumerian King List's statement that his father was a gardener, but all other details, and perhaps more importantly the omissions, are new. They shift the focus from a man who fought his way from cupbearer to king of the universe, to one of mysterious birth who by the grace of Ishtar rose to rule all.

The tradition of his rise in the palace of Kish did not disappear, however, although the story becomes mysterious. In the Chronicles, the first-millennium compositions that deal with then-ancient history, Sargon figures prominently. In one this story is found:

> Ur-Zababa ordered Sargon, his cupbearer, to change the wine-libation cups of the Esagil: "Change them!" Sargon did not switch them; on the contrary, he was careful to deliver them to the Esagil. Marduk, son of the prince of the Apsu, looked with joy upon him and gave him kingship over the four quarters. He took care of the Esagil. [All who] dwelt in the palace [brought] their tribute to Babylon. But he himself [neglected] the word Bel (i.e. Marduk) had spoken to him. He dug up the earth of the clay pits and in front of Agade he built a new city and called it Babylon. Because of the transgression Sargon had committed, Enlil changed his word and from east to west his subjects rebelled against him, and he was afflicted with insomnia.
>
> (Glassner 1993: 217)

A new element enters the story here, one that is found in several other first-millennium sources: Sargon committed a sacrilege by building a new city, and therefore the gods caused his people to rebel against him. What city exactly is intended is confusing: the above chronicle states that he built Babylon next to Agade, yet Babylon is mentioned many times before in the same text, so this must be a mistake. Another first-millennium chronicle, "The Chronicle of Early Kings," has this version:

> He dug up earth from the clay pit of Babylon and made a counterpart of Babylon next to Agade. Because of this transgression the great lord Marduk became angry and wiped out his people with a famine. From east to west they rebelled against him, and he (Marduk) afflicted him with insomnia.
>
> (Glassner 1993: 219)

Also two omen collections of this period mention the building of a new city near Agade named Babylon and a general revolt against the old king (King 1907: 27–8; 34–5).

The glory of Sargon is still depicted in the "Chronicle of Early Kings," yet the end of his life, a subject never really addressed earlier on, is now one of disaster. Although the Sumerian King List mentioned that Sargon built Agade, this fact did not seem to have been of great interest prior to the first millennium. At that time it became a negative aspect of his career. How can we explain this? It was not unusual for Mesopotamian kings to build new cities, or totally to refurbish existing ones to act as their capitals. Several such kings are known throughout Mesopotamian history: the Babylonian Kurigalzu II in the fourteenth century; and the Assyrians Tukulti-Ninurta I (thirteenth century), Assurnasirpal II (ninth century), Sargon II (eighth century), and Sennacherib (seventh century). The remarkable aspect about these massive projects was that all but one of the rulers never boasted of this accomplishment. Although they commemorated the construction of new buildings or walls, the fact that an entire new city was founded was not mentioned in the royal inscriptions. The only exception to this rule was Sargon II of Assyria, an interesting character in his own right. He probably saw Sargon of Agade as his example, considering he adopted his throne name. He was a usurper to the throne, and may have wanted to distance himself from the existing powerful lobbies in his court by moving his capital to a new location. The building of that city, Dur-Sharruken which means "Fortress of Sargon," is commemorated in his inscriptions as a personal feat: he selected the site, made the plans, and supervised the work. The detailed description of his participation would not have been remarkable had other city-builders not been so silent about the urban character of their projects. Around the period that Sargon of Assyria built his city,[9] we find stories about Sargon of Agade having done the same, but the latter's act is described as a sacrilege, something for which he was punished in his old age. It seems thus possible that we have here a condemnation of Sargon of Assyria's project by his own contemporaries through analogy with the ancient king. I have argued elsewhere that the building of a new city by a mortal man was considered to be an act of *hubris*; only gods were allowed to found cities (Van De Mieroop 1997c: 52–61). Sargon's city was abandoned as capital upon his death, perhaps because it was considered doomed. We may find here then an ironic situation where a king consciously invoked the figure of an ancient ruler, who had died some 1,700 years earlier, to be his shining example. Yet in the eyes of some of his subjects, the Assyrian committed the sin of *hubris*: he built a new city. This was condemned by them in texts ostensibly dealing with the ancient ruler, whose character had been unblemished up to then.

The traditions of Sargon of Agade were thus manipulated in the first millennium to reflect contemporary events. On the one hand, he remained the epitome of the conquering hero, reaching the edges of the world. The neo-Assyrian kings who at the height of their empire controlled the Middle East from western Iran to Egypt came close to emulating him. On the other hand, he was portrayed as committing an act of *hubris* at home by building a new city. That was probably a reflection of the thoughts of some Assyrians under Sargon of Assyria, who planned a new capital. This use of the figure of Sargon of Agade for ideological purposes relevant to the people hearing or reading the tales was nothing new in the first millennium. It had started in the Old Babylonian period when he was made the paradigm for the up and coming new dynasties jockeying for power, many of them headed by usurpers. In the second half of the second millennium, the Hittites saw his exploits in Anatolia as an example for their own campaigns. In the first millennium neo-Assyrian rulers envied his world empire, but some of their subjects used his disastrous old age as a warning against *hubris* at home.

Can we disentangle from the mass of stories a historical truth about Sargon? It must remain doubtful, since there is so little known from the days of his reign itself, and because the later traditions are so firmly rooted in our minds that we cannot set them totally aside. As an example of the difficulty in establishing a single "fact" about his reign, we can look at the question of the city of Agade. Did he really build a new city to serve as his capital? That he built Agade is received wisdom in the discipline. Archaeologists have failed to locate the city so far, so it is impossible to test the hypothesis through excavation. But the technique of regional survey could reveal the sudden appearance of a new large center because of its effects on the distribution of sites in the region. The area of Akkad, northern Babylonia, was surveyed in the 1950s and the scholar analyzing the collected data could not come up with a site that would fit the picture we have of Agade (Gibson 1972: 7), a large site appearing in the twenty-fourth century. He suggested thus in a footnote that "Sargon did not found a totally new city" (ibid.: 14 n. 76). Textual references to Agade might help us out, but we cannot yet distinguish with certainty between pre-Sargonic and Sargonic texts, so when the name Agade appears we automatically call the text Sargonic. Yet there is a year name of a king of Uruk, Enshakushanna, found on a Nippur tablet where he claims to have defeated Agade (A. Westenholz 1975: 115). As king of Uruk, he would have preceded Sargon's opponent, Lugalzagesi, and Agade would thus have been in existence prior to Sargon. Since all information on chronology and dynastic succession for this period relies on the Sumerian King List, a document whose authors clearly manipulated facts for their own purposes, we could play around with the information contained in it to make Enshakushanna a contemporary of Sargon. This would amount to a lot of circular reasoning. Scholars who have acknowledged the fact that Agade was the name of a city that existed prior to Sargon have relegated it to the status of a small settlement, in order to safeguard Sargon as the founder of a new capital (Wall-Romana 1990: 207). So the vague references to this act of founding in texts with little historical value seem to need to be proven right at all costs.

Why is this the case? If we ignore all later traditions about Sargon, we would come up with a very meager record for a man whose fame lasted throughout Mesopotamian history. This fame intrigues us: it lasted 2,000 years, and we have revived it in the last century. When in 1931 the excavators of Nineveh found a stunningly beautiful copper head of a man, supposedly in seventh-century layers, it was decided on stylistic reasons that it had to be an Old Akkadian king. Despite the lack of an inscription, the possibility that it was a portrait of Sargon was very enticing, and, although now an exact identification is rarely made, the piece is still known as the "Sargon" head (Nylander 1980). Whether or not this identification is correct is entirely irrelevant to me; the fact that this piece of sculpture was immediately equated with Sargon of Agade is, however, of interest.

MESOPOTAMIAN HISTORY AND NARRATIVE

The long native tradition on Sargon of Agade presents a special problem to the historian attempting to write his history. Despite the awareness that the later tales about him may be purely fictional, can the information contained therein be ignored when writing about the ancient king? It is my contention that scholars have listened to these tales, not only because they seem like a source of factual information on an otherwise shadowy figure, but also because of their form. They are little stories, much more narrative in character than anything surviving from the reign of Sargon itself. This narrative form is what makes them truly "historical" in our minds, and thus more worthy of study, since we tend to equate history with a narrative form of writing.

An example of the practice of using later literary traditions in writing Sargon's history can be found, once more, in the standard reference work of ancient history, *The Cambridge Ancient History* in its latest edition:

A miraculous or a mysterious origin is essential to super-human characters, and Sargon was the first to show that the taste of the ancient eastern peoples was to be for the latter. Like several notable successors he had, and did not disguise, an obscure birth and a humble beginning. The account of this is not only explicit but conveyed in a form which purports to be his own words. Only the first few lines are preserved of Assyrian tablets which begin, "I (am) Sargon, the mighty king, king of Agade", and go on to relate birth and earliest years of the speaker, name in broken lines some of his subsequent conquests and then break off. It is not, indeed, likely that the words are an authentic utterance of the great king; the class of composition to which the text belongs was regularly cast in the form of personal record as though taken from an inscription, but there is much to suggest that they were the production of a later age, having a didactic bent and perhaps a certain philosophy of history. One such recorded inscription even purported to recount, in the god's own words, the life and beneficent achievements of "the god Marduk, the great lord". Despite this element of forgery, these accounts were certainly based upon authentic tradition, and there is nothing incredible in the statements attributed by this "legend" to Sargon. According to this, therefore, his mother was a priestess, his father an unknown wanderer. He was born in secret in an obscure village on the Euphrates called Azupiranu, perhaps "Safron Town", from a local product which kept its name almost unaltered. His mother, to rid herself of the child, enclosed him in a basket which she covered and made fast with pitch, and launched it upon the river. Miraculously preserved from drowning, he was carried downstream, and fished out by one Aqqi, a labourer in a palm-garden, who noticed the basket as his bucket dipped in the water. Aqqi took the child and reared him as his own, making him to follow the same profession.

(Gadd 1971: 417–18).

The modern historian goes through great lengths here to acknowledge that the source, which he then quotes almost verbatim, is a late composition of a genre of literature that is known to include purely fictional accounts. Yet he perceives in this text an authentic tradition, and finds nothing in it incredible. The tale allows him to describe in vivid terms the birth and upbringing of Sargon by paraphrasing the Mesopotamian narrative. The story on which his account is based is known only from manuscripts found in the first millennium. It reads:

I am Sargon, the mighty king, the king of Agade.
My mother was an *entum*-priestess, my father I do not know,
  my uncle loved the hills.
My city is Azupiranu, which is located on the banks of the
  Euphrates.
My mother, the priestess conceived me, she bore me,
she placed me in a reed basket and sealed its opening with
  pitch.
She threw me in the river, which did not rise over me.

The river carried me up and brought me to Aqqi, the
water-drawer.
Aqqi, the water-drawer, lifted me up when he dipped in his
bucket.
Aqqi, the water-drawer, took me as his son, and raised me.
Aqqi, the water-drawer, appointed me as his gardener,
and when I was a gardener, Ishtar took a liking to me.
For four and [ ] years I was king, the black-headed people I
ruled, I [governed].[10]

(cf. J. Westenholz 1997: text 2)

Why has the late date of this text, only known from manuscripts
written more than 1,500 years after Sargon's death, not prevented
it from becoming a historical source? It seems to me that its appeal
as a historical source lies partly in its narrative character.

The issues of narrative and of narrative in historiography have
been much debated in scholarship in the past decades: anthropologists, art historians, literary theorists, and philosophers have
all dealt with the universal human activity of narration. Narrative
in the writing of history has been of particular interest, since it
seems to be here that history finds its unique position between the
arts and sciences: while it purports to be a scientific discipline, it
presents most of its results in a narrative form, more akin to the
arts than to the "hard" sciences. Much of the scholarly discussion
has dealt with the narrative form of modern historical writing:
certain schools have portrayed the narrative as an "unscientific"
form of historiography (White 1987: 31–8), while critical
approaches to major nineteenth-century historians have revealed
the ways in which the literary form they employed informed the
contents of their work (White 1973). But the historical sources
themselves have also been analyzed for their narrative character,
since in the Western tradition, narrative history is considered to be
the "purest" form of historical writing. It is readily acknowledged
that non-narrative forms of historical representation, annals and
chronicles, exist, but these are considered to be "imperfect"
(White 1987: 4). For instance, the dominance of annals in the
early medieval period as compared to the glory of historical narrative in classical antiquity is seen as a sign of decline (Barnes
1963: 64).

Medieval European historians see three basic genres of historical
representation, annals, chronicles, and history proper, the first

two of which are inferior due to their lack of narrative strength. "Annals" are yearly records providing a date and a short statement regarding an event; "chronicles" are somewhat more narrative and comprehensive, and reach farther back in time. These two genres fail to achieve narrative closure, however; they merely end and do not conclude (White 1987: 5). In Western tradition "real" history requires narrative, i.e. a story with a beginning, a middle, and an end. To some, it needs a plot, a central theme whose origins are explained, that is developed, and drawn to a conclusion. Extraneous matters are cut out: there is a selection of information that is relevant to the plot, excluding unrelated things that happen to have occurred in the period of time covered by the historical text (Scholes and Kellogg 1966: 211).[11] Finally, a narrative in history contains a moral. By the mere fact that it organizes events, materials, and facts in such a way that there is a conclusion, it presents a world that is imaginary, and a story that is moralizing. "Could we ever narrativize without moralizing?" (White 1987: 25). The perceived superiority of narrative in historical discourse is thus due to the fact that it provides an image of life that has coherence, integrity, fullness, and closure (ibid.: 24). It gives a sense of Being that is complete, logical, and consistent; it gives an order to the events of the past that makes them present to us. The narrative character of the source also appeals to the historian, as narrative is so universal and translatable. As Barthes says, enjoyment of narrative is very often shared "by men of different, even opposing, culture" (1988: 95). It can thus be understood by people of distinct cultures, translated from the alien context to the familiar one of the scholar.

The narrative form of historical discourse also presents a fundamental paradox to the historian: its order, coherence, and completeness are appealing and intelligible, but are imaginary. Reality does not present itself in the form of ready-made stories that come to a logical conclusion. Events occur in a sequence that often has no beginning or end, that lacks coherence, and surely does not exclude extraneous facts. The realism of narrative historical representation is a dream (White 1987: 24–5). By using the narrative form, to some, "history" has abandoned its distinction from "fiction." Historical narrative is considered to be more realistic than the non-narrative source, because it employs a form that its borrows from and makes it akin to fiction. "So the circle of the paradox is complete. Narrative structure, which was originally developed within the cauldron of fiction (in myths and the first epics) becomes at once the sign and the proof of reality" (Barthes 1981: 18).

While narrative is universal, historical narrative is not. The Western tradition itself has its non-narrative historical forms, and in recent decades the concept of narrative history has been under siege (White 1987: 31–3). It was a form that took time to develop. The earliest and most prominent ancient Greek historians, usually thought to be at the roots of the Western historical tradition, failed to attain narrative closure in their works. These historians applied many of the required narrative elements, but still they ended their accounts abruptly, without a conclusion. Herodotus, "the father of history," wrote his 600-page long work in order to explain how the Greeks defeated the mighty Persian army of Xerxes in 480 BC. Although he adduced innumerable details regarding the earlier histories and customs of cities and states broadly involved in the conflict, the dominant theme of the work remained the Persian war and the superiority of the Greeks. But he did not end his account with the Greek victory at Salamis, and extended his narrative into the following year. There is a gnawing sense of a lack of conclusion of his work, the final passages merely relating a rebellion in Ionia and a story about the Persian king Cyrus. We feel that he could have continued to write in like manner indefinitely. The work ends abruptly, like a chronicle. With Thucydides a fuller and more coherent narrative is attained, as his story of the Peleponnesian war is more focused and stream-lined than Herodotus's. It is even molded in a tragic form where the early arrogance of the victorious Athenians stands in stark contrast to their miserable escape from Sicily at the end of Book 7. The work can be read like a Sophoclean tragedy in prose form (Damrosch 1987: 37). But still, Thucydides did not finish when he had depicted the tragic downfall of the Athenians. He continued to describe subsequent events, up to a point six years before the end of the war when he ended the work suddenly, in the middle of a sentence. In vain we look in Herodotus and Thucydides for something like Polybius's summing up: "now I have reached the end of my whole work" (Polybius 1927: 453). However narra-tive the main body of their works is, they end like chronicles, *in medias res.*

In some other cultures the historical narrative is not found at all, which has led to the opinion that history there is absent altogether. One often repeated example is India before the Moghul period. Hegel stated categorically: "It is because the Hindoos have no History in the form of annals (*historia*) that they have no History in the form of transactions (*res gestae*)" (Hegel 1956: 163). He acknowledged the existence of king lists, but these do not count as historiography in his opinion, because they lack a narrative form:

> The Hindoos do indeed possess lists and enumerations of their Kings, but these also are of the most capricious character; for we often find twenty Kings more in one list than in another; and should these lists even be correct, they could not constitute a history.
>
> (ibid.: 164)

Since all great Sanskrit narratives lack historical referents, and historical figures are only found in lists and chronicles, India has been declared a civilization without historical understanding, a condemnation that has only recently been challenged (Pollock 1989).

In the Western tradition we have arrived at an equation of narrative with history, which might be more intuitive than rational, but still governs our appreciation of the historical sources and their authors. Therefore, that "the writing of history . . . is a rare phenomenon: it has in fact developed independently only in three very different societies: Judaea, Greece, and China" (Murray 1991a: 214) can be stated in a reference work on the Greek world intended for a wide public without wondering what this means for the study of other civilizations. Where does that assertion leave the "historian" of ancient Mesopotamia?

The large majority of Mesopotamian historical writing corresponds to what scholars of European history would describe as "inferior" genres of historiography: annals and chronicles. These terms were adopted by the modern editors of Mesopotamian texts, although the documents designated as such do not exactly fit the European classification. What we call annals in Mesopotamia can be more elaborate than their medieval European counterparts. This "lowest" level of historiographical representation dominates the Mesopotamian material; annals are characteristically accounts of military campaigns in chronological order, often written in the first person (Grayson 1980: 150). Although they can provide substantial detail in their descriptions and can contain literary vignettes, they are not narratives. They organize material on a strictly yearly basis, list events without establishing connections between them, and begin and end abruptly. Most of them are integrated within building inscriptions, commemorating the foundation or restoration of a temple, palace, city wall or the like, on a particular date in the king's reign. The regnal years preceding the construction are identified by the military campaign that happened during that year. Thus the accounts begin with the king's first campaign and end with the one just completed when the building project is initiated. No causal links are established between the individual campaigns or between the conquests and the construction. These are merely enumerated as separate facts. Moreover, the royal annals are characterized by the fact that they cover solely the reign of one man, and references to the time before his accession are virtually absent (Renger 1996: 15–16, 19–20).

The chronicles from Mesopotamia may be somewhat more narrative than the annals in that they focus on a specific concern, such as the cult of a particular god. They remain, however, entirely attached to the idea of a sequence in time, moving from king to king in a strict chronological succession. They end suddenly and do not draw conclusions. If a didactic point existed in these texts, such as respect for a god, it was not explicitly spelled out. While annals and chronicles, as described here, are not the only Mesopotamian historiographic sources, they share with the large majority of the others the fact that they lack the basic requirements of the historical narrative: a story with a beginning, middle, and end.

Thus, when the scholar is confronted with sources regarding an ancient Mesopotamian individual, such as Sargon, ranging from the dry entry in a king list to a story about his birth, a difficult choice is to be made about what to do with the latter. On the one hand, something approaching our ideal of "true" history is available: a short story about a child whose birth had to remain a secret, who was abandoned by his parents, but survived and rose to greatness. Such a story is readily comprehensible and accessible.

On the other hand, we know that it is a story, something written perhaps more than 1,500 years after Sargon's death. All names, except those of Sargon and of the goddess Ishtar, are deliberately vague or fictional. The text's historical "truth" is highly suspect, and by all standards of historical methodology it should be discarded as a factual source on Sargon himself. It is an intriguing document because somehow first-millennium Assyrians and Babylonians found interest in its tale, but it tells us nothing reliable about Sargon himself. Yet it is difficult to discard this shred of history on Sargon's life, because it is a narrative and as such appeals to our historiographic sense.

So, what are we to do? To deny the existence of the tale is impossible, as it reads as one of the "best" bits of information on King Sargon. Thus the text needs to be interpreted, which can only be done in its own cultural context. That context derives from its date of composition and preservation, as I hope to have shown before, and makes the Sargon Birth Legend a source on first-millennium Assyrian history rather than a biography of Sargon of Agade. We cannot assume that the authors of the tale were more knowledgeable about Sargon than we are, nor can we make a judgement on the tale's historical value based on the fact that it sounds credible. Unfortunately, we cannot easily establish the date of composition of this type of text, but we can determine the date of its copy and preservation. It is within that time period that we have to study the importance of the tale. Although ignoring its contents as a historical source on Sargon is difficult, it is historically the only legitimate attitude.

By urging the disregard of this tale as a source on Sargon of Agade, I am also urging the discontinuation of the historical practice that dominates the study of ancient Mesopotamia. It is often the goal of the scholar to gather the greatest possible number of facts regarding a person, group, or event, which are then quoted with their sources. Data from varied periods and contexts are accumulated in order to establish a full list of references contained within the preserved ancient texts (Van De Mieroop 1997a: 303–5). The aim of the scholar is to be as comprehensive as possible, hoping not to have missed a single reference. The historical importance of the facts accumulated in this manner is not really considered, only the idea that the greatest number of facts will lead to the greatest understanding of the person, group, or event under investigation. This "philological history" has been attacked as methodologically and intellectually unsatisfactory for many decades now (Croce 1960: 294, 301 [originally published 1915]), but still flourishes in such disciplines as Mesopotamian history, where "facts" are relatively rare. It is a method that strives for the unattainable goal, set in the nineteenth century by Leopold von Ranke, to reconstruct the past "as it actually happened." This approach sees the narrative as coinciding with the event. All that can be known about the event is present within the source, and source criticism can replace historical criticism (Al-Azmeh 1981: 199–200). It aims at the creation of a modern narrative that paraphrases the ancient one, or tries to establish a logical sequence of various ancient sources. It privileges the narrative source, raising it to a level of history that it may never have had in its own cultural context, or ignores the way in which the source itself manipulated knowledge of events for its own, culturally defined, purposes.

Is narrative necessarily the superior form of historical recording? Perhaps in the Western tradition we may rank it above annals and chronicles as more pleasing to our minds, and even more accurate. But in many non-Western traditions, narrative may not have been the preferred form for recording history. I do not deny that narratives, stories, are crucial to the preservation of memory. All humans tell stories, but they do not necessarily write them down. We could also hypothesize that historical recording in texts was merely a tool, an *aide mémoire*, for narrators whose words formed the real historical text. Writing is not even required: scholars of pre-Columbian Meso-American cultures see purely pictorial representations and maps as historical documents that were used by narrators during ceremonial events (Boone 1994).

Besides the written records, the preservation of historical memory in Mesopotamia could have taken place in many ways and forms that are elusive to us. Oral and visual narration of the past with lessons for the present could have taken place in ceremonies and spectacles, for instance. We know virtually nothing about such events, but they certainly took place. The one festival that is somewhat known to us is the New Year's festival at Babylon, which did involve a procession along the major streets in the city, where the chief god's statue was carried from a temporary residence outside the city to his temple in the city center (Kuhrt 1987). The king's participation in this festival was one of his crucial duties, and while to us the event seems to have a purely mythological character, it may have had some historical connotations to the Mesopotamians. Other royal spectacles must have taken place, and probably involved large audiences. It is commonly acknowledged that visual and oral techniques played a role in the dissemination of royal propaganda in a highly non-literate society (Oppenheim 1979; Machinist 1993: 98–102), but were these merely limited to majestic buildings, stelae and reliefs, and readings of texts of the types that are preserved to us? Could more spectacular staged events have played a role? What ceremonies were held in places like Nineveh, Assur, and Babylon when the king returned from battle? Victory parades, so well-known in the West from Rome to Washington, may have dazzled the Mesopotamians as well. There might not have been a need to narrativize history in written form if story-tellers and visual displays conveyed the historical message to the people. Perhaps the Greek historians are testimony to a break-down of a system of communication rather than the inventors of a more sophisticated preservation of the past: Herodotus, fearful that Athenian imperialism might dictate the memories of the past; Thucydides, lecturing to his compatriots from exile. We simply cannot demand the same narrative sources in the very different political and cultural circumstances of Mesopotamia, nor can we deny ourselves the pleasure of narrating our own versions of the Mesopotamian past based on the "dry" written records they left us.

Chapter 3

History from Below

The bulk of the population of any pre-modern, and even modern, society is an elusive target for historical research. We know they existed and provided most of the labor that maintained the societies we study, but we do not know how to reach them. In societies with low levels of literacy, they cannot speak to the historian sifting through written evidence, and therefore they are often neglected. Some histories of the Assyrians, for instance, could leave one with the impression that the empire was created and maintained by a single man. How can we look for his subjects? Where can we find traces of their existence and learn something about them? We could look here at archaeology, the science that is not bound by writing to the people it studies. Excavations could reveal equally well the hovel of a day laborer as the palace of a king and show us what living conditions were. But, sadly, virtually no houses have been excavated, and none allow us to reconstruct how many people shared the same roof, how many pots and pans, and tools they had, where they slept, what they ate, and so on.

The term "history from below" has been applied in the last three decades to the study of the masses of people who are left undocumented by our official sources. The approach is interested in those people usually ignored by historians. As E. P. Thompson said it in his famous book *The Making of the English Working Class*:

> I am seeking to rescue the poor stockinger, the luddite cropper, the "obsolete" hand-loom weaver, the "utopian" artisan, and even the deluded followers of Joanna Southcott, from the enormous condescension of posterity. Their crafts and traditions may have been dying. Their hostility to the new industrialism may have been backward-looking. Their

communitarian ideals may have been fantasies. Their insurrectionary conspiracies may have been foolhardy. But they lived through these times of acute social disturbance, and we did not.

(1966: 12–13)

In this study of the working class organizing itself and demanding political representation, Thompson could rely on the writings of some of the participants: pamphlets, memoirs, periodicals, and so on. Few societies in history had ordinary people who could express themselves likewise, and the historian interested in them has to seek their words and thoughts in the documents of the elites and institutions with whom they interacted, often in situations of conflict. Thus the villagers of Montaillou in the early fourteenth century speak to us through the records of the inquisitional court (Le Roy Ladurie 1979). It is due only to the methodical mind of the Inquisitor, Jacques Fournier, that these records were well kept, and to his ambition to show how good he had been at the job, that they were preserved. Such bodies of evidence are rare in historical research.

Also in ancient Mesopotamia the mass of people did not write and are thus inaccessible to us directly through written sources. Since there is no "ethnographic" literature of elites musing about the conditions of the ordinary people either, we see the latter only in the records drawn up by institutions with which they interacted. They are often just names on lists; when they provided services these are accounted for, and payments to them are registered. Their own voices are thus not heard, but at least we may find some indications of what they were asked to do, how they were organized in their institutional labor, how they were rewarded, and sometimes how they suffered. Although the result may not be a vivid picture, at least we do not totally ignore their existence.

The concerns of history from below overlap to a great extent with those of social history, although the latter is more interested in general structures, the former more in how individuals and groups behave within these general structures. Moreover, social history can also deal with the well-documented elites. The social history of Mesopotamia is a rather chaotic discipline in that it is approached through a variety of techniques with numerous ideological backgrounds, rarely explicitly acknowledged. On the one hand, there are studies that seek to establish translations for ancient terms thought to refer to social classes. For instance, the hierarchy *wardum* – *mushkēnum* – *awīlum* found in the code of Hammurabi has led to endless debate. If *wardum* on philological grounds can be translated as "slave," and *awīlum* on contextual circumstances seems to refer to "a member of the elite," what do we do with the *mushkēnum*? A recent summary of the problem adopts the idea that it refers to "someone who is not a member of the palace organization," a "citizen" (Stol 1993–97: 492–3). Such translations remain somewhat meaningless if they are not placed within a general structural outline of society, however. What exactly does the term "slave" mean? Are we to see a Mesopotamian *wardum* as the equivalent of a Roman slave, whose body belonged to his owner, or as someone similar to the medieval European serf, tied to the land he or she worked?

A second group of scholars has thus been more involved with understanding the general structure of Mesopotamian society, mostly through models inspired by Marx and Weber, who were, at best, poorly informed about the ancient Mesopotamian material. This work is inseparable from considerations of the economic structure of Mesopotamian societies,[1] which makes sense if we define class structure along purely materialistic lines. I will thus relegate my remarks on the study of social structure to the chapter on economic history. Here I will discuss our capacity to study non-elite members of Mesopotamian societies. Admittedly, the term non-elite is vague in itself. I mean to indicate by it the non-ruling classes, those who were not part of the upper levels of temple and state hierarchies that directed the political life. Those non-elite people were not all unable to write, and certain, restricted groups did leave us written documentation, but that is almost entirely concerned with business. An analysis of their writings, especially their letters, can be very revealing, but unfortunately business concerns drown out personal matters. The large majority of people were non-literate, however, and can only be studied because they are included in the administrative records of the institutional households of temples or palaces, or because they were forced to interact with such households or literate businessmen for various reasons. In this chapter I will investigate two such cases as illustration of how we can work on this aspect of history. I will discuss the organization of voiceless workers in an institutional household and the effects of a military conflict upon the lives of common city residents and farmers. Moreover, I will look at one particular group of non-elite people who have left us with written remains, to show the opportunities and challenges we face in studying them.

PROSOPOGRAPHY

The silent subjects of history can be seen only when their lives intersected with those of writers. The Mesopotamian material is not of the type where we find descriptions of the lifestyles of the poor and the humble, but a great number of people did interact with the bureaucracies of palaces and temples. The latter would demand labor and services from certain sectors of society, and thus in times of economic centralization large groups of people become known to us. This is true to such an extent that we claim to know the names of tens, if not hundreds, of thousands of Mesopotamians, and approximately when and where they lived, but nothing else.

It would be futile to study these people as individuals with the evidence at hand, but we can investigate some aspects of their lives as members of groups. This technique is called prosopography in ancient history, "the investigation of the common background and characteristics of a group of actors in history by means of a collective study of their lives" (Stone 1987: 45). Prosopography has not been applied much in Mesopotamian history, but is very promising when we can identify groups of people, named or un-named, who appear in a set of records over a period of time.

One of the periods of Mesopotamian history where such an approach can be feasibly undertaken is under the so-called Ur III dynasty in twenty-first century Babylonia. This dynasty has been called "one of the worst totalitarian régimes known to history" (Diakonoff 1971: 20), because of its seemingly unstoppable urge to record. So far more than 30,000 texts from a 100-year period are published and many more are known to exist in museum collections, while excavations in the right places would unearth countless more. It is not so much the sheer number of known records that impresses, but their style. They are rigorous accounts of expenditures, receipts, and transfers, often of the same items day after day. In an organization that deals with some 77,000 animals in a year (Sigrist 1992: 34) the appearance of one fattened black sheep is recorded. Although this mass of material presents the researcher with an embarrassment of riches, and with difficulties in the manipulation of the data, the number of texts is really not that great considering we are dealing with a century-long period. In any case, the habit of the bureaucrats of the Ur III state to record on a periodical basis – daily, monthly, or yearly – a set of information regarding a particular aspect of economic life, presents us with a good data base for prosopographical studies.

In the province of Umma in south-eastern Babylonia the Ur III state controlled a number of thickets or copses of small trees and wild plants, which were taken care of by a group of men we may call "foresters" (Steinkeller 1987a). It was their duty to cut and trim trees, collect branches and twigs, and harvest wild plants and grasses in between the trees. The state demanded predetermined quantities of products. In good bureaucratic fashion the forests were divided into thirty units, each given a name. Groups of workers were responsible for one forest each, and a supervisory structure was established that made one man ultimately responsible for the whole operation. The organization of the labor units shows the importance of the family in such matters. This is visible both at the level of the workers and at that of the supervisors.

Each forest was taken care of by a group of workers, varying in size from one to five, most often two. These were almost always members of the same nuclear family, and their responsibilities and rewards were clearly determined by their status within that family. Several classes of workers existed: B-class headworkers in individual forests, responsible for a full-output and receiving a full ration; D-class half-output workers receiving half a ration; and E-class one-fourth-output workers receiving a quarter ration.[2] In several cases the father of the family was of class B, the eldest son class D, and the younger son class E. When the father died, the eldest son moved up to class B, the younger to class D, and an even younger one to class E. It thus seems to me that a family near a copse was given the duty of taking care of it. Purely for administrative purposes a system was invented where the head of the family was given the highest reward, the second-placed man half of that, the rest a quarter. Naturally, in reality the majority of the work may have been taken care of by younger children or the women, but bureaucratically that was irrelevant. A strict family hierarchy was maintained.

That was not only true on the level of the common worker, but also for the supervisory staff. Since the state did not want to deal with each forester individually, a pyramidal command structure was imposed on the workforce. The thirty forests were divided into three groups of ten, each under the control of one foreman, and the three foremen reported to an overseer. Family ties were important here as well. In the early period of our documentation, the overseer was one Ur-TAR.LUH; two of his sons, at least, were foremen of ten forests each: Ur-emash and E-urbidug. After the father died, the eldest son, Ur-emash, took over his position, while two brothers, E-urbidug and Sheshkalla, acted as foremen. The third foreman was seemingly not related by blood to them. All supervisors were listed as workers themselves, although they may have employed substitutes, which shows that, at least in theory, social advancement was possible. Family connections rather than expertise seem to have been the crucial factor for success, however. It may be that training for a supervisory position was given to the eldest son. Ur-emash, the last overseer, used the title scribe, which shows that he had graduated from school. An ability to read and write may have been a requirement for the job, as he kept the books demanded by the state bureaucracy.

The study of this small group of men shows that workers of this type lived with their families, probably near their place of employment. Family ties were strong and played a crucial role in promotion. Moreover, the dates on the records at hand show that only the supervisory staff was involved in this work year-round, and received payment in the form of rations and the usufruct of land full-time. The actual workers provided their services, and received rations, only for part of the year. In the last decade it has become clear that many of the workers in this seemingly highly centralized state-economy, worked part-time for the state, and consequently are only visible in the record part of the year. I determined that, shortly after the Ur III period, craftsmen in a centralized workshop of the state worked in alternating teams (Van De Mieroop 1987b). Independently this was concluded in studies on Ur III foresters (Steinkeller 1987a) and millers (Uchitel 1984), and other economic activities of the state were organized similarly (Steinkeller 1996). This shows that the Ur III state was not as centralized as we were led to believe, and, more importantly, the dangers of positivism in this type of research emerge. Indeed, virtually all the records at hand show people at work in the state sector of the economy in numerous tasks. But a simple listing of when each one of the men and women appears shows that they only worked periodically. When they were not working for the state, they were most likely occupied otherwise in a sphere that remains undocumented. It is too early to say that the entire Ur III economy recruited labor in this way – (the crucial agricultural sector has not yet been sufficiently analyzed) – but at least part of it was. The common worker in the state sector of the Ur III period, was thus only part-time employed by the state, worked with other family members, and spent a substantial amount of time engaged in a world unaccessible to us.

INNAJA, AN OLD ASSYRIAN MERCHANT

Another place and time where we can see the importance of family ties in society is the so-called Old Assyrian period, roughly the first three centuries of the second millennium BC. In the site of Kanesh in central Anatolia, some 20,000 tablets were found, the large majority dating to a period of at least eighty-five years, *ca.* 1910–1830 (Veenhof 1995: 862). The tablets were kept in the houses of merchants from the city of Assur in northern Mesopotamia, who had established a colony at the edge of the Anatolian town Kanesh. Their business was the import of tin and textiles into Anatolia, and the export of gold and silver to Assur in return. The archives contain a mixture of contracts, administrative documents, and letters, and seem to have been written by these merchants themselves, and by their associates in Assur and in other colonies. This corpus of texts is quite unique in Mesopotamian history: it is large, very coherent in contents, and it includes a large set of letters, which are very direct in their discussion of issues. We may then have here a means of access to the concerns and words of the people themselves, something lacking for most periods of Mesopotamian history.

The study of these men and women would be most fruitful if based on the reconstruction of their archives as they were found in their houses at Kanesh. Unfortunately the majority of texts published so far derive from illicit or early excavations when findspots were poorly recorded. The tablets found during the scientific excavations starting in 1947 can be located exactly in their archaeological context, and provide the opportunity to reconstruct archives as they were constituted in antiquity. Only very recently has the publication of these tablets been initiated, however, and we are still waiting for analyses of texts that belong together. Meanwhile scholars have relied on internal evidence, primarily the appearance of the same main characters, to reconstruct some merchants' archives. So far, at least seventy of them are known (Veenhof 1997), not all of them completely analyzed, however. In the future we can expect to be able to reconstruct the lives of these Assyrian men and women in great detail, a boon for Mesopotamian social history. I will discuss here some aspects of what we know about them, in order to demonstrate the opportunities and challenges these texts present.

One of the Assyrians who resided in Kanesh was a man named Innaja (Michel 1991). He lived in Anatolia in order to take care of his family's business, which like that of all other Old Assyrian merchants focused on the trade of tin, textiles, gold, and silver. The business was already in existence during the lifetime of his father, Elali, when Innaja had resided in Assur. There he had married Taram-Kubi, with whom he had several children. When Elali died, the eldest son Shu-Kubum took over control of the business in Assur, while he sent his brother Innaja to Kanesh. Several other siblings were active in less important colonies throughout Anatolia: Bur-Assur in the south-west and Enna-Sin in the west. Moreover, some of the sons of Innaja were also actively engaged representing the family firm: Assur-reşi was located somewhere on the route between Assur and Kanesh, Assur-taklaku was in Zalpa, possibly on the same route, Shu-Sin worked in the north, while Ikkupaja travelled to various regions. Moreover, a son of Shu-Kubum, Elali, supervised the caravans on their last stages from Assur to Kanesh. Although Innaja was thus involved in a larger family business, headed by his older brother, and may even have been its main representative in Anatolia, his archive from Kanesh focuses on what seem to be his personal commercial activity. We have no letters written to him by his brother, and only some where he addresses his brother. This may obviously be the result of the fact that we have to reconstruct Innaja's archive based on the appearance of his name in the texts, and perhaps his house in Kanesh contained a large number of directives where he is not explicitly mentioned.

Innaja worked very closely with his wife, Taram-Kubi, who had remained behind in Assur, where she gathered goods to be sent to Kanesh, and represented her husband to the authorities and other merchants. Eight letters from her to Innaja are known, as well as one from him to Taram-Kubi and other associates. Moreover, we have a number of letters written to Innaja by his sons. These people were thus closely related, but surprisingly the letters they wrote to one another were almost exclusively devoted to business matters: requests for silver, for textiles, complaints about lack of funds, and so on, dominated the exchanges. Very rarely a personal matter arose, and even then it always had commercial aspects to it. A typical example is this letter from Taram-Kubi, who is upset that her husband does not provide her with the resources she needs to acquire goods needed for export:

> Speak to Innaja; thus says Taram-Kubi. You have written me as follows: "Keep the bracelets and rings that are here, so that they can provide you with food." Indeed you have sent me half a pound of gold through Ili-bani, but where are the bracelets that you sent me? When you departed, you did not leave me a single shekel of silver. You cleaned out the house and have taken everything. Since you left a terrible famine has hit Assur, and you did not leave me any grain, not even a liter. I have to buy grain constantly to eat.
>
> Concerning the collection by the temple, I have given a standard in [ ], and I have paid my share. To city-hall I have paid the [ ] measures of grain which belong to Atata.
>
> What is then this extravagance about which you keep on writing to me? We don't even have anything to eat. Do you think we can do foolish things? I have gathered everything I have and have sent it to you. These days I live in an empty house! The (business) season has arrived. Send me the equivalent of my textiles in silver, whatever is my share, so that I can buy ten measures of grain.
>
> Regarding the tablet with the list of witnesses, which Assur-imitti, son of Kura has taken, he has caused much trouble to our house. He has hired servants. Your representatives have taken care of things. Finally, I have had to pay up until you come, yet he is not removing his claim. When you come you can discuss it. Why do you keep on listening to lies, and do you keep on sending me angry letters?
>
> (Michel 1991, vol. 2: 13–5, no. 3)

In another letter she seems to urge her husband to come to Assur: "I beg of you, when you see this tablet, come. Look at Assur, your god and the god of your household. May I see you while I still live!" (ibid., vol. 2: 15–18, no. 4, lines 22–6). But this outcry is contained in a long list of business requests, and seems to be more a cry for help than an expression of loneliness. Similarly, Innaja's son, Assur-reṣi, informs his father that his younger brother, Shu-Sin is ill, and that he left him behind in Zalpa (ibid., vol. 2: 64–5, no. 42). Again we see no display of concern or pity, only an explanation why he did not bring his younger brother. The lack of expressions of personal emotions in letters is not limited to this corpus. It is a common characteristic of Mesopotamian letters. As one scholar succinctly states it:

> Using the expertise of a scribe for writing a letter was worth the effort only if financial interests were at stake. In letters the only attested topics within the sphere of private life are complaints about insufficient allowances, outstanding marriage payments, and so on. No one wrote a love letter; illness was a rare subject.
>
> (Stol 1995a: 499)

Unless we assume that no such personal feelings existed among Mesopotamians, we have to explain why this is the case, especially since the Old Assyrian correspondents by all indications wrote their own letters and did not need to hire scribes. The Old Assyrian letters derive from business archives and it could be possible that parallel ones of a more personal nature were discarded. But then, we keep letters with a sentimental value, and why would this not have happened among these traders? One can thus wonder whether personal concerns were ever committed to writing. Letters were carried by intermediaries, associates, traders, caravan leaders, and perhaps were public record. Personal matters would not fit this context. They may have been confided to family members who, travelling to and from Assur, would relate the message in person. If so, they will always remain secret to us.

Innaja was assisted in his business affairs by his close family members, but the family ties attested in this trade were not limited to his nearest kin. We can observe that his relations to other merchant houses were very close, and that intermarriage between the various trading families was common. Thus Innaja's wife, Taram-Kubi was the sister of another famous trader, Imdi-ilum (Ichisar 1981; Larsen 1982). Since much of the commercial activity required the collective funding and gathering of goods by several merchant houses, this is perhaps not surprising. The men and women engaged in this trade must have been often in contact with one another for professional reasons, and personal relations between them might have developed easily. The general picture we obtain of these Assyrian traders, based on evidence available so far, is thus one of merchant families, headed by the elder member, closely collaborating. The various houses were joined through marriage and business ties, financing and organizing their ventures in a collaborative enterprise.

What was then the social status of these traders, both in Assur and in the colony of Kanesh? Since we have virtually no records from Assur itself, we have to rely on evidence from the Kanesh texts to investigate their position in the home-town, Assur. It has been estimated that some 2,000 inhabitants were simultaneously involved in the trade at its height, one-third of whom regularly travelled to Anatolia (Veenhof 1977). Of those remaining in Assur, a number were manual laborers engaged as producers of textiles or other goods needed for the trade. Yet, a large group was involved in the organization and management of the trade, some 1,500 individuals. The entire population of Assur at this time has been estimated to have been at most 15,000 (Larsen 1987: 52), so 10 percent of the residents of Assur were seemingly involved in this trade! This closely knit group seems to have had an enormous influence in all urban affairs.

Descriptions of society in Assur in this period (Larsen 1976) have portrayed it very much like a medieval European mercantile city-state, such as Venice, run by a body of elders. The heads of the great merchant houses seem to have gathered in an assembly that made decisions in the name of "the city." The executive was the "year-eponymy," a man chosen annually by lot, probably from among these elders. Although a king existed, his powers were limited: in the cult he was high priest of the city-god Assur, and he acted as head of the royal household as a pre-eminent family leader. Since the data for this analysis are found in letters and contracts of merchants, this may obviously be an extremely biased view. The king and the palace are barely mentioned; the world of these texts document rarely interacts with his. If this description is accurate, the balance between the two poles in Mesopotamian political life, the palace and the citizenry (Van De Mieroop 1997c: 118), was very much in favor of the latter, something that could be reversed by a strong king. The latter seems to have happened when a ruler from the west, Shamshi-Adad, seized the throne around 1810, and established himself as autocratic king (Kuhrt 1995: 88–9). Although he perhaps re-established the trade with

Kanesh, which had been abandoned earlier due to unknown circumstances (Veenhof 1995: 865), the power of the merchants was reduced, and the rule by elders was not revived.

In the Kanesh colony the structure of the mother city was duplicated to a certain extent only, as the political conditions were different. The traders ran their internal affairs without much interference of the local king, who resided in another part of town. But the latter was actively involved in the commercial activities of the traders: he collected taxes, imposed restrictions on the kinds of goods that could be traded, and he acted as supreme judge (Larsen 1976: 155–6). We find here either a different system of government, or a different bias of the documentation, which after all derives exclusively from the colony.

In both places the social status of the merchants seems to have been very high. In Assur we can perhaps talk of a merchant oligarchy, while in Kanesh the community was largely self-governed. How representative were they of Mesopotamian society in general? Was this a highly unusual group of people, or should we imagine that similar families were a constant feature in Mesopotamian history, at least when long-distance trade was conducted? All Old Assyrian texts derive from one colony only, and it is clear that Kanesh was merely one link in an extensive network of international trade. As the tin and textiles sent to Anatolia were imported into Assur, one can imagine that similar merchant colonies existed in the places were these goods were procured, Iran and Babylonia. Alternatively, it is possible that Iranian and Babylonian merchants had colonies in Assur. Moreover, similar networks must have existed for the trade of other goods, and in other cities (Larsen 1987). How many Assyrians, and inhabitants of other Mesopotamian cities had attained such high social status in the centuries of the early second millennium? In other periods of Mesopotamian history the geopolitical conditions certainly had a great deal of impact on long-distance trade. We can imagine that in a setting of large territorial states the organization of trade was very different, and that it was more controlled by the palaces. Still, in many, especially earlier, periods of Mesopotamian history the political conditions were similar to those in the Old Assyrian period, and merchant classes may have been equally powerful in society.

If so, why do we know so little about them? There is no lack of archaeological research on sites in the Mesopotamian periphery where colonies like the one at Kanesh could have been found. An interesting archaeological fact regarding the Kanesh colony is that the material remains excavated in the houses of the Assyrian merchants do not show evidence that these are foreigners. Their houses cannot be distinguished from those of local Anatolians save for the tablets found in them. It is thus conceivable that many of the sites in the Mesopotamian periphery housed natives of Assyria or Babylonia without this showing any trace in the archaeological record. This leads to perhaps the most remarkable characteristic of the Old Assyrian traders: they seem to have been highly literate people. That a large number of traders and their associates were able to write is suggested by the appearance of numerous hands and of levels of scribal ability. How unusual was this for such a community? The written form of Akkadian used by the Old Assyrian merchants is characterized by its simplicity in its choice of cuneiform signs. The writing is almost entirely syllabic, and only some 100 signs are commonly used (Larsen 1976: 305). In other periods and places we do not find the same level of simplicity, but why should we imagine that the Old Assyrian merchants were special? Once the initial threshold of learning how to record one's spoken language was passed, the number of signs used to do so remains only a secondary problem. Do we have to assume that other traders relied more heavily on professional scribes, or that our ability to recognize that they wrote their own letters is due to a relative scarcity of texts? The questions facing us, then, in the study of these very well-documented Old Assyrian traders remain thus very basic. Were they really politically as important as it seems?; were they unusually literate?; and most importantly, can they be used as a paradigm for the status and organization of Mesopotamian long-distance traders or are we to regard them as being exceptional?

THE EFFECTS OF WAR

Warfare, this horrible human activity that dominates our historical record, is often portrayed as the act of kings alone. But the lives of numerous people were critically affected by it, either because they were the soldiers, or because their fields, cities, and villages were in the path of the advancing armies. While today we are constantly confronted with images of civilians whose lives are ruined by war, in antiquity we often see only the glorious army commanders proclaiming victory. The other side of the coin, the destruction of common people's lives, is difficult to study as they are not described except in vague terms in some literary texts, but we have some windows of opportunity when war had repercussions on the interactions of these people with institutions and individuals who left a written record.

The effects of military activity on citizens can usually only be guessed at when we read, for instance, the Assyrian annals proclaim that thousands of people "great and small, male and female" were deported from one corner of the empire to another. Even the Hebrew Bible, the most narrative of the sources relating to Mesopotamian history known to us, does not describe the pain and suffering of the Israelites and Judeans whose lives were devastated by Assyrian and Babylonian armies. A glimpse of such suffering can be gleaned in a small archive from the seventh century, found in the Babylonian city of Nippur, belonging to one Ninurta-uballit (Oppenheim 1955). In the last decade of the neo-Assyrian empire, Babylonia gained its independence but certain old urban centers remained under Assyrian control. One of them was Nippur, which continued to acknowledge the Assyrian ruler, Sin-shar-ishkun, as its king, while the surrounding countryside was in the hands of the Babylonian Nabopolassar. The latter besieged the city in 620, preventing its inhabitants from leaving, and starving them into submission, something only accomplished three years later. The desperation of people is visible in Ninurta-uballit's dry legal records; they include nine contracts of parents selling a child, every time except once, to Ninurta-uballit so that he would keep them alive. One contracts states:

> [In the third year of] Sin-shar-ishkun, king of Assyria, [the town of Nippur] was under siege; exit through the gate [was]; the equivalent (of one shekel of silver) was one *sûtu* of barley; the town was [ ], the people [so]ld th[ei]r children [for money].
>
> (ibid.: 88; 2 NT 297 ll. 1–5)

Sometimes the parents received a small payment in silver for their own support, for instance:

> Nergal-ah-uṣur, son of Iqisha, said to Ninurta-uballit, son of Bel-usati, as follows: "Take my small (female) child Ṣullea-tashme and keep (her) alive, she shall be your small child!

Give me six shekels (of silver) so that I may give . . . and that
I may eat." Thereupon, Ninurta-uballit [accepted his offer]
and weighed and gave him in one [payment(?)] six shekels of
silver. Nergal-ah-uṣur guarantees against a vindicator or
a contestant on behalf of the small child. Nippur, month
of Dumuzi; 10th day; 3rd year of Sin-shar-ishkun, king of
Assyria.

(ibid.: 87; 2 NT 293)

Ninurta-uballit obtained thus a number of slave girls, more or
less for free, which he would have to raise at his own expense.
Oppenheim, the texts' editor, rightly suggests that he hid his
archive and fled the city when the Babylonians finally forced it to
surrender. His neighbors most likely did not appreciate his taking
advantage of the conditions of war.

Not only did civilians suffer in war, the soldiers who were forced
to do the fighting could also lose their lives and had to leave their
family and work behind to join their king on a campaign. The
recruitment of soldiers in Mesopotamia is difficult to discuss in
detail. The sources provide little specific information about how
the Assyrian peasantry and their provincial counterparts were
called up, equipped, and trained to accomplish the conquests for
which their kings took credit. We know from dispersed evidence
that, at the latest starting in the early second millennium, much of
the land owned by the crown was occupied by tenants who had to
provide services. The latter could be military in nature, but also,
for instance, the growing of provisions for the army. The core of
the army seems to have been made up by men subject to this obligation, however. Because the majority of the soldiers were thus also
farmers, they were only free to go to war after the harvest had been
gathered, i.e. late June. It is seemingly only in the Late Assyrian
empire that the existence of a core standing army made that
restriction obsolete (Manitius 1910). Even though the Assyrian
army included levies from the provinces, military duty must have
been a burden upon the peasantry of the heartland when the army
campaigned annually. Yet, the agricultural and military cycles did
not conflict when Assyria was the aggressor, and so the farmer was
able to fulfill both duties.

But in cases when the country was attacked by nomadic groups
or of civil war, the parties could not wait until the harvest was
collected to gather their forces, and the repercussions on the
farmers could be disastrous, even when they returned home safely.

A possible illustration of how civil war could destroy the livelihood of farmers is found in the late period of Mesopotamian history, when the region was part of the Persian empire. While the initial rise of that empire is quite well described in classical and Near Eastern sources, by the mid-fifth century documentation on it is extremely limited. Herodotus's account of Persian history ends with Xerxes, while Xenophon treats a later period. The only available classical source is the fragmentary *Persika* by Ctesias, a physician from Cnidos who resided for a while at the court of Artaxerxes II. He provides an account of Persian palace intrigues, which is usually considered of little historical value, but reveals that many successions to the throne were contested by armed factions. One of these struggles took place after the death of Artaxerxes I in 425 BC. According to Ctesias, he and his wife died on the same day, and their son ascended the throne as Xerxes II. Several of Artaxerxes's sons with other wives were unhappy, however, and after forty-five days Xerxes II was assassinated and replaced by his half-brother Sogdianos. The latter demanded allegiance from the rest of the family, but one of his half-brothers, Ochos, son of Artaxerxes and a Babylonian woman, rallied the support of a number of influential members of the court, was crowned king by them and, backed by an army, captured the Persian throne. Several of the potential other contenders were assassinated, and Ochos ruled as Darius II for nineteen years. It is clear that Darius II was considered in Babylon to have been the immediate successor of Artaxerxes, and his original power-base must have been situated there (Briant 1996: 605; Stolper 1985: 114–16).

The effects of these events on the lives of Babylonians would have been entirely obscure but for the existence of an archive of a firm involved in land management, the so-called Murashu family.[3] This archive consists of some 800 tablets, primarily from the period of Artaxerxes I year 10 (455–4) to Darius II year 7 (417–16). They were found in the city of Nippur and record the day-to-day economic transactions by this family of entrepreneurs. Their business was the management of land for absentee land-lords: they collected rents and taxes, leased unoccupied plots, provided tenants with water, seed, and plow oxen, privileges they acquired for a fee from the owners, Persian nobles or the state. Moreover, they turned the income they collected, agricultural produce, into silver which was wanted by the owners, uninterested in masses of perishable goods. When the tenant was unable to pay the dues, the firm could provide him with a loan against the land as guarantee, a transaction which resembles a modern mortgage. The records of this type are very standardized in phraseology, for example:

> 18,720 liters of dates are owed to Enlil-shum-iddin, son of Murashu, by Biruqa', son of Kullu-ki-il and the lords of his bow-fief of the corporation of Arabs. In month VII (Sept–Oct) of the first year (of Darius II) he will deliver these dates, 18,720 liters according to the measure of Enlil-shum-iddin, in the city Hambari. One will stand guarantee for the other, whoever is available will pay. The planted and cultivated fields of their bow-fief, bordering on the royal canal in the area of the city Hambari, bordering on the field of [PN], and bordering on the field of [PN] is at the disposal of Enlil-shum-iddin. Another creditor on this property has no right until Enlil-shum-iddin has been satisfied.
>
> In the presence of Umardatu, Belshunu, and Ishtabuzanu, judges of the canal of Sin. (names of witnesses and scribe) In Nippur. Month IV (June–July), day 25, year one of Darius, king of the lands. (Imprint of) their fingernails. (Seals of the judges). Their fingernails.
>
> (Donbaz and Stolper 1997: 138, no. 82)

This legal document indicates that Biruqa' received a payment from Enlil-shum-iddin equal to the value of 18,720 liters of dates. After the date harvest he would have to repay the loan with newly harvested produce. In the meanwhile his field became the possession of Enlil-shum-iddin, who could now charge a rent on its use until the loan was refunded. The Murashu firm thus gained title to a number of fields whose occupants were indebted to it, and who paid a rental fee. Combined with the cut in the profits of the real owners, the absentee Persian landlords or the crown, these activities enabled the firm to acquire substantial wealth. The Murashu firm was not unique in this period (Van Driel 1989), nor was this activity a Persian innovation; throughout Mesopotamian history landowners allowed private entrepreneurs to collect rents and taxes for them for a part of the profits (Van De Mieroop 1992: 208–10). Although it might impose some additional burden upon the tenants, the system must have worked well in normal times. But in unusual situations it might cause havoc.

Possibly as a result of the reforms by Darius I in 518, the majority of agricultural land in Babylonia was owned by the king, who issued its usufruct in two ways. Either large estates were assigned to nobles in his favor, who often did not reside on them. Thus the satrap of Egypt, Arsham, had estates in Babylonia. Or corporate groups organized by profession obtained land which they parcelled out to individual members. The land was given to them in return for military service to the crown, and the medieval European term "fief" is often used to describe its nature. We encounter "bow fiefs," "chariot fiefs," and "horse fiefs," which probably were granted in return for service as archer, charioteer, or cavalry-man, or for a financial contribution equal to the cost of a mercenary substitute (Renger 1995: 315–18). Fiefs were inherited through the male line, could be leased and subdivided, but not alienated (Stolper 1985: 25). The normal demands made on the fief-holders were probably not exorbitant, as we know that Babylonia flourished economically in the Persian period, but in exceptional circumstances, such as those described by Ctesias, the high politics of the Persian court might have had serious consequences for the lives of these tenants.

We see an enormous increase in the number of mortgages issued by the Murashu firm in the sixth and seventh months of the last year of Artaxerxes I's reign (September–November of 424 BC), and the first seven months of the full regnal year of Darius II (April–October of 423 BC): about thirty from the first period, about seventy-five from the second, while at the most ten contracts in any of the other years (Donbaz and Stolper 1997: 10–11). We know that loan documents of this type were destroyed when they were repaid, so what we have here is the evidence of a large number of unpaid debts to the Murashu firm. These surges in bad debts can be explained in various ways,[4] but the following explanation, inspired by Stolper (1985: 122–4), focuses upon a possible connection with the larger political picture.

We know that Artaxerxes died in the ninth month of the year, and that soon afterwards the various factions rallied their forces for a power struggle. In his power base, Babylonia, Ochos, the future Darius II, and nobles who supported him, such as Arsham, who held estates managed by the Murashu firm, increased the demands on their tenants. They needed men or money to hire mercenaries. The farmers still indebted to the Murashu firm from the last financial crunch before the harvest in month VII became unable to repay their loans. Their debt-notes remained in the Murashu archive, waiting to be repaid. Moreover, the increased demands led to even more loan requests early in the following year, in Babylonia Darius II's first full regnal year. The tenants were either forced to abandon their fields, which were ready for harvesting, to provide the required military service, or they had to find the money to hire a substitute at a time when their reserves were low, just before a new harvest would provide new income. Many of them thus turned to the Murashu firm for loans, which they were never able to repay. The Murashu firm got stuck with a lot of useless debt-notes which were held in the archive in the hope that they would be recovered later on. But seemingly this was futile and hence the records survived for us to read.

What happened to the hapless tenants is still not clear to us. Did they die in battle? Did they incur so much debt that they were never able to repay it? We do not know. But still we cannot ignore the fact that intrigues far away in the Persian court at Susa most likely had devastating effects on the lives of the Babylonian farmers.

These examples hopefully indicate that there are ways of studying the ordinary Mesopotamian in the written record, although the results may seem disappointing. They also demonstrate that "history from below," perhaps even more than other aspects of the discipline, requires a reliance on preconceived models. As Hobsbawn phrased it: "The grassroots historian cannot be an old fashioned positivist" (1988: 21). Instead of combing the evidence for what is indicated about the "ordinary citizen," the historian has to start from some assumptions, and know what to look for. For instance, in the case of the Murashu archive, one has to assume that warfare based on a system of military levies of tenant farmers would cause disruption of these people's lives when troops were raised. This presupposes a certain rationality behind the system of military levy combined with agricultural tenancy, a logic that cannot be documented. Similarly, the observation that workers in the late third millennium were only part-time on the books of their institutional employers, leads to the assumption that they worked for themselves for the rest of the time. The model employed assumes that people will try to gain as much income as possible, within reason, and use their time to that effect. But Sahlins has demonstrated that in many "Stone Age" societies this was not the case, and that most people took it easy (Sahlins 1972). Again, according to Hobsbawn (1988), model-building is necessary, but based on guesswork, and the models utilized need to be revised constantly to fit the new evidence. I would like to stress that we need to be explicit about the models we use, not only in the writing of "history from below," but in all aspects of history. One area where this especially a concern, and a problem in much current work, is economic history, to be considered next.

Chapter 4

Economic History

The cuneiform writing system was developed for the purpose of recording economic transactions, and throughout the three millennia of its use this remained one of its primary concerns. The number of cuneiform economic records available is unparalleled in the ancient world, except for Roman Egypt, and in many later pre-capitalist cultures. Tens, if not hundreds, of thousands of documents are known, many more remain unpublished in museum collections, and excavations constantly yield more archives. Considering the long time-span involved, the absolute numbers may seem small if averaged out per year, but the largest quantities are clustered in relatively short periods of time; for instance in Babylonia, in the twenty-first, eighteenth through sixteenth, and sixth centuries. For the study of the ancient economy these texts provide a unique data base. Unfortunately they remain insufficiently mined by scholars who are interested in broad economic structures rather than detailed analyses.

The study of economic history is closely tied to that of social history. Since we are unable to comprehend the native terminology that seems to refer to class, we have to base our social classification upon the materialistic criterion of access to the means of production. The moment these are controlled by a particular group, we have a "class society" (de Ste Croix 1981: 32). In any agricultural society, such as Mesopotamia, the means of production is land. Unfortunately, it is not always easy to determine exactly who could own land, and how extensive landownership by different groups in society was. A recent and detailed survey of the evidence (Renger 1995) shows that three types of landownership are attested in Mesopotamia: institutional, private, and communal, corresponding to three sectors of the society: the public institutions of temples and palaces; the private citizenry; and village communities. The relative importance of each type of landownership varied geographically, especially between the irrigation based systems in Babylonia and the rain-fed systems in Assyria, and temporally, with a movement over time towards increased private ownership. There is much disagreement among scholars about the extent of the three types of ownership: while some see the extent of communal land as negligible (Leemans 1983), others find private ownership a marginal phenomenon (Renger 1995). The fact that institutions owned a lot of land is acknowledged by all, but it remains hard to determine how dominant they were. A great danger lies in a positivistic approach to these matters. Indeed, the majority of records will refer to institutional land, but that is due to the fact that most large archives are institutional. The communal sector is hardly documented because its economic activities were not so complex as to require written records to keep track of them.

Every scholar thus works with a certain model of society in mind, consciously or subconsciously, and that model will crucially affect their views on social and economic history. In my own view Mesopotamian society was not a single hierarchical structure, but contained three interacting sectors, each with its own social hierarchy. The institutional sector had its elites, numerically small but extremely powerful and wealthy at certain moments in history, and its dependants, large in number and primarily in a "tributary" relationship with the institutions. The latter were granted tenancy of plots of land sufficient to feed their families after dues to the institutional owners were paid (Renger 1995: 318–19). In the communal sector social hierarchy was determined along family lines, but all members of the community owned the land which could not be alienated. This sector was under constant threat of absorption into institutional and private ones. Since it is the least documented, it is also the most difficult to study. Finally, within the private sector we see a distinction between the wealthy landowners, or owners of successful businesses, who accumulated substantial properties, and the poor individuals and families outside the institutional or communal sectors, who survived as hired laborers. These three sectors of society were not clearly distinct from one another, nor was their relative importance static. Throughout Mesopotamian history they existed in ever-changing relationships, determined by political, economic, even ideological circumstances. Their presence is not equally clear in the documentation, quite the opposite, which makes the study of these relationships so difficult.

The nature of the documentation has also determined what aspect of the economy has received the most attention in scholarship. The records we have focus upon exchange, since they were written only when two requirements were fulfilled: first, a transfer of property with a determined value had to be involved, be it silver, grain, commodities, luxury goods, real estate, or labor. Besides this, there had to be a perceived need for a record in order to counter future claims on the property or to justify the activity of an administrator to higher authorities (Van De Mieroop 1997b). Economic activity is not merely exchange; production and consumption are crucial aspects to keep in mind, but these will not be documented unless transfer was involved between various actors: individuals, institutions, or branches of institutions. The survey of existing theories regarding the Mesopotamian economy that I will provide presently will indicate that the focus of disagreement has been on exchange mechanisms. Most controversy has been around Polanyi's claim that the market played no role in Mesopotamian economic life. Yet many of his critics have not considered the roles of different exchange mechanisms which need to be evaluated within the context of the entire economic system. Moreover, there is a need to look at other aspects of economic life, beyond mere exchange. Production and consumption play a central role in economic life which cannot be ignored in this aspect of the study of history.

In this chapter I will provide first a description of theoretical approaches to the Mesopotamian economy, since many of them are rarely acknowledged in the discipline. Then I will provide one example of an economic activity to illustrate the opportunities we have and the difficulties we face.

THEORIES OF ANCIENT ECONOMICS

Any study of the social and economic history of the ancient Near East, however limited in its focus, is prejudiced by the author's conscious or subconscious views on ancient society and its economy. Few scholars explicitly express their views on these matters, however, and no models based upon ancient Mesopotamian material itself have been formulated. Most often the models used have been borrowed from "ancient historians," i.e. those who deal with Greece and Rome, who may or may not have had access to ancient Near Eastern material. As the most prominent approaches were developed in the late nineteenth–early twentieth centuries, when the study of the ancient Near East was in its infancy, they are based primarily on the classical material, taking only Hellenistic data into account when treating the Near East. Ironically, the classical material for economic history is quite limited in its extent. Although it has the benefit of some treatises, such as Aristotle's *Politics* or Pseudo-Aristotle's *Oeconomica*, the number of actual records of economic transactions is small. On the other hand, the Ancient Near East has no treatises at all, but there is an enormous abundance of actual records. As one scholar has stated it: "One should remember that classical sources are incomplete, peculiarly biased, and relatively impoverished compared to ancient Near Eastern cuneiform sources for direct and sustained accounts recording economic practices" (Kohl 1987: 8). In what follows I will provide a summary survey of the models that have influenced ancient Near Eastern scholars working with Mesopotamian material, with special reference to the literature explicitly dealing with that culture. A lack of acknowledgement of these background issues within the discipline has led to an absence of a proper economic history.

The primitivism–modernism debate

The most basic question concerning our study of ancient economies is whether we can approach them with concepts and models derived from the study of the modern economy, or have to consider them as being fundamentally different from our modern experience. The terms of this debate were framed a century ago, unfortunately with both sides using specious models presented in dogmatic terms. The primitivist position was presented by Karl Bücher in his *Die Entstehung der Volkswirtschaft* (1893) and stated a unilinear development from closed household economy to city economy to national economy, which more or less coincided with the ancient, medieval, and modern periodization of European history. This model was vigorously attacked by Eduard Meyer in an address to German historians in 1895 (Meyer 1924: 81–168; Schneider 1990: 430–43), where he stated that the Greek economy in the classical period had reached a stage of evolution paralleling that of modern Europe. Hence, he argued that the concepts and terminology of modern economics could be applied in the study of ancient Greece, and ancient society was driven by the same capitalist motives as modern society. These terms of the debate were not very useful as they oppose two fundamentally different, monolithic, systems, leaving little room for compromise: either the ancient economy was just like the modern one, only smaller, or it was so fundamentally different from ours that none of the modern economic behaviors and motives can be said to have existed in antiquity (Will 1954; Pearson 1957; Austin and Vidal-Naquet 1977: 3–8).

That debate is far from limited to the field of ancient history, but was and is paralleled by equally vitriolic ones among economists and anthropologists. At the time of the Bücher–Meyer controversy German and Austrian economists were involved in a polemic over whether or not there was a universal validity to economic analyses employed at the time. The Germans insisted on the uniqueness of all economic situations in order to be able to plead for protectionism of the developing German industry, against the laws of liberal economic theory. They found support for their idea in the historicism of Leopold von Ranke (1795–1886) and others who insisted that each historical period was unique and that models could not be used across chronological or cultural borders. Thus the free market, which had been absent in many historical situations, did not need to be the goal of the contemporary German economy either. On the opposite end of the spectrum there was the idea of the universal law of maximization of economic resources, which could be used in the analysis of any economy.

More recently economic anthropologists have been involved in the "formalist–substantivist" debate, sparked by the writings of Karl Polanyi, to be discussed later. Formalists see a use for classical economic models in the analysis of economies other than the modern European one. Substantivists do not; to them the absence of markets and "all purpose" money make such models entirely inapplicable.

What seems to be of importance in these debates' aftermath is the question whether or not we can apply such concepts as profit-motive, commercial enterprise, manufacturing industry, or market economy to the ancient world. When using such terms one does not necessarily have to adopt the entire modernist point of view, although that impression may inadvertently be given. It cannot be denied that many scholars perceive the ancient economy as if it was entirely modern in all its aspects, although these scholars do not state so explicitly. The primitivism–modernism debate is of great importance to the study of ancient Mesopotamia as well, yet explicit references to it in the literature are relatively rare (Van De Mieroop 1997c: 13–18). Many scholars investigating aspects of the Mesopotamian economy, such as prices, trade, craft production, etc., seem to adhere to a modernist point of view. It is remarkable, however, that all scholars who have formulated a coherent theoretical framework for the interpretation of the Mesopotamian economy have rejected that approach, and have insisted that the ancient Mesopotamian economy was fundamentally different from the modern European one. These "primitivist" views have been inspired by a variety of models derived from ancient history.

Although there is great variation in the "primitivist" opinions expressed, all are inspired by one of the two great sociopolitical thinkers of the late nineteenth–early twentieth centuries: Karl Marx and Max Weber. Before outlining the different systems, their basic area of agreement should be stressed: all believe in the importance of the *oikos*, the household unit, as the fundamental unit of production and consumption in antiquity. That household can vary enormously in size. In its smallest form it includes the patriarch and his sons and grandsons with their wives and children. Dependent labor was part of the household, which thus could expand enormously to a large palace or temple complex headed by a secular or religious leader with hundreds of dependent families. Such a household strove towards economic autonomy, both as a producer and as a consumer of its basic needs. How these households related to one another and to the outside world is interpreted in different ways.

Marxist interpretations

By the time Karl Marx died in 1883 only one of the ancient languages of Mesopotamia, Akkadian, had been recently deciphered, no economic records were published, and information on ancient Mesopotamia was still limited to confused accounts in classical sources and in the Hebrew Bible. Hence one cannot expect Marx or his collaborator Friedrich Engels to have had any knowledge of the Mesopotamian civilization or to have devoted special attention to it. Yet their basic ideas on economy and society in antiquity have been extremely important for the subsequent study of Mesopotamia, and they still provide a useful frame of reference. Marx and Engels' ideas evolved during their lifetimes, and their abundant writings can be interpreted in various ways. Thus they have provided the foundations for different influential schools of thought.

Their most fundamental contribution lies in the emphasis on the "relations of production": "the social relations into which men enter in the process of production, which find legal expression to a large degree either as property relations or as labour relations" (de Ste Croix 1975: 16; 1981: 32). These relations are thought to determine every other aspect of a person's social consciousness, and a historian needs to study the economic conditions of the period under investigation to understand it. The ownership of the means of production, which in antiquity was basically land, is of crucial importance in our consideration of ancient societies. Here Marx and Engels seem to have changed their minds over the years, from considering the "Orient" as having known a separate development, to one that considers the entire world to have gone through the same evolutionary stages, although not all at the same time.

The idea of a separate development in the East, which may be taken to include the entire non-Western world, finds expression in the concept of the "Asiatic Mode of Production." Marx and Engels never explicitly stated what they meant by the term, and it is hard to develop a coherent picture of it. But the following elements seem fundamental to it: the absence of private property of land, the presence of large-scale irrigation systems in agriculture, the existence of autarkic village communities combining crafts with tillage and communal ownership of the soil, the stagnation of passively rentier or bureaucratic cities, the domination by a despotic state machine, which hoarded the bulk of the surplus and functioned not merely as the central apparatus of repression, but also as the principal instrument of economic exploitation. Also characteristic are the lack of an intermediary between the villages and the state, the fact that the interaction between villages and the state was purely external and tributary, and the fact that the state's fortunes did not affect the villages (Anderson 1974: 462–549). The concept of the Asiatic Mode of Production has been vigorously attacked, especially in the so-called former Eastern bloc countries, for its lack of an empirical basis and its Orientalist ideology of Asiatic stagnation.[1] It is still sometimes appealed to by classical historians who seek a way to exclude the Near East from their field of inquiry (e.g. Finley 1985: 27–9, n. 39). A recent attempt by the Italian scholar Carlo Zaccagnini to revive the Asiatic Mode of Production as a useful model for the study of the ancient Near East (1981b; 1989: 1–126), focuses so much on the idea of the communal ownership of land, that the resulting picture is hardly distinguishable from other Marxist schools of thought, to be discussed presently.

The Asiatic Mode of Production formed the basis of a theory that did gain much more acceptance among Western scholars, a theory that was put forth in great length in Karl Wittfogel's book entitled *Oriental Despotism* (1957). The author was more interested in the authoritarian regimes of his days than in antiquity, but he sought to relate the growth of absolute power in areas outside Europe to the management of hydraulic resources. In his theory the rise of the state in Mesopotamia, among many other regions, can be explained as resulting from the need to coordinate large irrigation projects indispensable for survival in areas with insufficient rainfall for dry-farming. After an initial popularity, the theory has lost its appeal due to its uncritical mixture of evidence from widely varying cultures, and its lack of an empirical basis in many of the areas discussed by Wittfogel. For instance, the large irrigation projects imagined by him did not appear until late in Mesopotamian history, long after the rise of the state, and the need for a supra-regional authority for successful agriculture is not demonstrated. Moreover, we can say that Wittfogel takes the Orientalist view of the otherness of Asia to an extreme: Oriental despotism becomes the main characteristic of any civilization attested there in history and is portrayed as the defining attribute of Asia.

Marxist scholars who have dropped the concept of the Asiatic Mode of Production still employ many different models for the study of ancient Mesopotamian society and economy. The most important school of thought among them is centered on I. M. Diakonoff, a most prolific writer in the Academy of Sciences of the former Soviet Union. His ideas and those of his students are not universally accepted among former Soviet scholars, but have gained prominence world-wide. The "Leningrad School" bases itself upon the model of universal evolution developed by Marx and Engels when the latter abandoned the Asiatic Mode of Production. Pre-capitalist evolution knew three stages: primitive, slave-owning, and feudal. The idea of the primitive Mode of Production was borrowed by Engels from the American anthropologist L. H. Morgan, who in his book *Ancient Society* (1877) described a pre-class society where the means of production were owned by the community. According to the "Leningrad School," and others, the survival of the community remains a crucial characteristic of ancient Near Eastern society, at least until the end of the second millennium BC. In that sense it does not seem to differ much from what scholars such as Zaccagnini emphasize in their defense of the Asiatic Mode of Production. Parallel to the community, however, a class society developed with the growth of the state. Kinship ties were abandoned for a territorial community, an economic surplus encouraged a division of labor, which in turn enabled the intensification of production, and a hierarchy of non-productive state functionaries grew over a majority of exploited productive laborers. Although there is a great amount of evolution afterwards, and the relative importance of the community and state sectors shifts to the advantage of the latter, the basic mode of production henceforth remained the same in Mesopotamian antiquity. The majority of labor was provided by a slave-like class, not chattel slaves in the classical sense who were the property of their owners, but dependents who owned no property and were deprived of the products of their labor through physical or ideological coercion (Diakonoff 1991: 1–66).

The parallel existence of a state and a communal sector is also basic to the view of ancient Near Eastern society held by the leading Western Marxist historian in the field, Mario Liverani (1976). He juxtaposes the domestic mode of production in the village communities to the palace mode of production in the cities. The latter extracts its resources from the villages for such non-productive purposes as ostentatious display and infringes upon the rights of the community through the commercialization of the land. The distinction between free and dependent in Mesopotamian society was not paralleled by a separation between wealthy and poor, but rather the opposite. The free community members lived at a level of subsistence, while the palace dependants could become very wealthy but were never economically or politically free. In later history these dependants became so powerful that they were able to demand exemptions from taxes and services, hence acquiring freedoms of real importance. But the latter remained essentially promotions within a chain of dependency.

Max Weber

By the time Max Weber published his "Agrarverhältnisse im Altertum" in 1909, better known in the English-speaking world by its inclusion in *The Agrarian Sociology of Ancient Civilizations* (1976), in his own words "about 200,000 cuneiform texts ha[d] been brought to light," and such important sources as the code of Hammurabi of Babylon were known to him in translation. Although most of the material was inaccessible to the non-specialist, Weber did discuss Mesopotamia as one of the ancient societies on which he based his economic theory of antiquity. Despite his statement that Mesopotamia and Egypt profoundly differed from Greece and Rome due to their irrigation-based agricultures, Weber regarded the Near Eastern economies as having many of the same basic features as the classical European ones. Unfortunately, his work is virtually unknown among ancient Near Eastern scholars, or if known, is ignored by them.[2] It has been extremely influential in the study of the social and economic history of classical antiquity, however, especially after it had been provided with a solid empirical basis for Greece by J. Hasebroek in 1928. Weber insisted that the ancient economy could not be regarded as separate from its political institutions. While in the Middle Ages a mercantile class strived for economic gain through commerce based on intensive manufacture, in antiquity the citizenry, who held all political powers, lived off the rents of the fields worked by unfree laborers and from the spoils of war. Those revenues were divided among the citizens, not to be used for further profit-making, but for the enhancement of their social status. Commerce and manufacture were left to outsiders.

Despite these social restrictions on profit-making enterprise, Weber acknowledged that a great deal of seemingly capitalist enterprise did take place, and that Babylonia in this respect set an example for the entire Near East. Mesopotamian partnerships in trade were not much different from those found in medieval Islam and Genoa (Weber 1976: 101). Most useful for the study of ancient Mesopotamia, in my opinion, is this statement: "What has been sketched above indicates that somewhat complex economic institutions existed, but it is not now possible for us to judge the relative importance of these phenomena for the economic structure of Mesopotamia" (Weber 1976: 103). This statement, made in 1909, still holds true today.

Weber's influence in the field of ancient Near Eastern studies has been important, however, in that he inspired Karl Polanyi, whose work has had an enormous impact on anthropology and history in general. In the 1950s Polanyi brought together at Columbia University a number of scholars whose meetings resulted in a volume entitled *Trade and Market in Early Empires* published in 1957. Among the contributors was the leading Assyriologist A. Leo Oppenheim, who remained influenced by Polanyi's ideas, although he somewhat distanced himself from them later on. Oppenheim's own masterpiece, *Ancient Mesopotamia* (1977), shows that influence, although Polanyi is not mentioned in the book, which remains a basic reading for any student in the field. Yet several articles by Mesopotamian scholars critical of Polanyi have appeared more recently, and one can say that his views have been rejected by all but a few Assyriologists. His critics have focused on one aspect of Polanyi's theories, the idea of market-less trading. Unfortunately, this focus has led to a refusal to acknowledge the broader concepts he introduced, which do merit consideration.

Polanyi's most fundamental concept is that the economy of any ancient or non-Western society was or is embedded within social relations. He thus adopted Weber's idea of embeddedness, but shifted the emphasis from political circumstances to the social realm. Social relations determine the exchange of goods in a society, and according to Polanyi, three modes of exchange exist:

1 reciprocity among symmetrically arranged groups;
2 redistribution within a society with a powerful center;
3 exchange through price-making markets, which only appeared in nineteenth-century Europe and enabled the separation of the economy from its social context.

Since neo-classical economic theory is only aware of this last form of exchange, Polanyi argues, its theories and models cannot be applied to the study of societies where markets did not exist. Markets belong to what Polanyi calls formal economics, a set of rational actions that dictate choice in a situation of insufficient means. They enable the acquisition of all goods and services for a price, expressed in amounts of money. Non-market situations fall within substantive economics, which concentrate on the fact that man interacts with his natural and social environment for a supply of material needs. These interactions are not dictated by rational actions but by social interactions.

To substantiate his claim on the absence of markets in Mesopotamia, Polanyi wrote a very poor paper on "Marketless trading in Hammurabi's time" (1957), which has since provided an easy target for criticism. In it he argued that there were no markets in early second-millennium Babylonia, basically because Herodotus stated that the Persians did not know markets; because there was no evidence for a drastic economic change between the Old Babylonian and Persian periods; and because there is no evidence in the archaeological and textual evidence for markets. However, none of these arguments is really valid: Herodotus probably had a Greek *agora* in mind when he talked about Persia; markets need not to be held in open spaces recognizable in the archaeological record, as modern Middle Eastern cities clearly show, and terms for a market place exist in the Akkadian language (Röllig 1976).

The second part of Polanyi's article dealt with the Old Assyrian traders of the early second millennium whose records found in the Anatolian site of Kultepe-Kanesh seem to demonstrate the existence of a capitalistically minded business community. He portrayed these traders as state agents who transported textiles to Anatolia on commission for the city of Assur in order to obtain copper there. They ran no financial risks as they worked with advances from the treasury, and price differentials were set by the authorities. Again, it has been easy to destroy his arguments with empirical data: Old Assyrian traders were not state agents, financial losses were common and a worry to them, and Assur did not import copper from Kanesh, needed for manufacture, but only silver and gold, purely for the accumulation of wealth (Gledhill and Larsen 1982).

In a posthumously published book, *The Livelihood of Man* (1977), Polanyi came to acknowledge the existence of some market-style exchange in the ancient Near East, yet not of price-setting markets, and this point has been studied at great length by one of his staunch supporters in the field, Johannes Renger (1984). One cannot ignore the empirical data within the Near Eastern record for the existence of some market mechanisms with the concepts of profit and loss, with price fluctuations, and with situations of scarcity. But the fundamental difficulty lies in determining the relative importance of the exchange through a market within the totality of the ancient Mesopotamian economy. Polanyi's most lasting contribution lies in his demonstration of alternative means of exchange, reciprocity, and redistribution. The existence of the latter in the Mesopotamian economy is obvious: the third-millennium public institutions of temples and palaces supported numerous families through a system of rations of barley, oil, and wool, or with prepared bread and beer. Adult men and women, children, babies, and old people were accorded certain amounts of these goods (Gelb 1965). During the second millennium the ration system was replaced by a wage system, but the support of numerous people by the central institutions continued to exist. The role of reciprocity has been less explored. It assumes the existence of groups of equal status exchanging goods not necessarily because of material needs, but in order to enhance social relations. We know that the exchange of gifts played an important role in the international diplomatic contacts between Egypt, Hatti, Babylonia, Mitanni, and so on in the second half of the second millennium, but its role in the local economy is less clear. Polanyi has been accused of romanticism by having "an utopian model of primitive society which minimizes the role of conflict, coupled with a model of man which emphasizes innate altruistic and cooperative propensities while playing down self-interest, aggressiveness, and competitiveness" (Cook 1968: 213). In such an idyllic society, reciprocity would lie at the root of most of the exchange of goods. Was Mesopotamia such a society, was it one dominated by institutions redistributing goods, or did it have a flourishing market to which people could routinely turn for their provisions? Again, I think that we cannot determine the relative value of these three modes of exchange at any time within Mesopotamian history, nor can we say that any one of them was absent at a particular moment in time.

Both Weber and Polanyi had a great influence on the work of the historian Moses I. Finley, who expressed his ideas on the ancient economy in many articles and most explicitly in his book *The Ancient Economy* (1985). Although the contents of that work have been heavily criticized by ancient historians, the book cannot be ignored, as it presents a major milestone in the study of ancient economic history by its introduction of a systematic approach to many questions. Finley did not include the Near East among the ancient societies he discussed. In fact, throughout his writings we can perceive a dislike for anything Near Eastern. He seems to have believed firmly in the "Greek miracle" and could not see any similarities between the Graeco-Roman world and the Near Eastern.

> What matters is the way in which the two civilizations (or complexes of cultures) diverge fundamentally at every point, in their social structures, in their power structures (both internally and externally), in the relationship between the power structure and religion, in the presence or absence of the scribe as a pivotal figure.
>
> (Finley 1985: 28)

He envisioned a Near Eastern world that reeks of Oriental despotism. Its economies he described in these terms:

> The Near Eastern economies were dominated by large palace- or temple-complexes, who owned the greater part of the arable, virtually monopolized anything that can be called "industrial production" as well as foreign trade (which includes inter-city trade, not merely trade with foreign parts), and organized the economic, military, political and religious life of the society through a single complicated, bureaucratic, record-keeping operation for which the word "rationing", taken very broadly, is as good a one-word description as I can think of.
>
> (ibid.: 28)

Politics before Greece was non-existent, only kings who might have been influenced in their decision by courtiers (Finley 1981). It seems that even freedom was impossible in the Near East in his opinion: "It is impossible to translate the word 'freedom', *eleutheria* in Greek, *libertas* in Latin, or 'free man', into any ancient Near Eastern language, including Hebrew, or into any Far Eastern language either, for that matter" (Finley 1985: 28).

If we take a less Orientalist point of view and allow the ancient Near Eastern cultures to be part of antiquity, as Weber did, we need to consider Finley's contributions to economic history. His work is important in that it provides a well-developed system of ideas on the ancient economy from a "primitivist" point of view, which, ironically, can well be applied to the ancient Near East. The topics discussed in his book were obviously not considered on the basis of Near Eastern material, but his statements about Graeco-Roman antiquity can be used as guidelines for the study of the Mesopotamian economy. Of particular interest are his observations on the role of commerce and credit, his ideas on ancient slavery, and his development of Weber's characterization of the ancient city as a "consumer city."

Trade supposedly was a low occupation in the ancients' minds, and in any case not of great financial importance to the cities. It did not act as an impetus to increase manufacture, as most products were intended mainly for local consumption. Credit was also issued primarily by people of low esteem or by friends of the debtor, and loans were never taken out for productive purposes, except in the case of maritime ventures. The loans we have documented were used by the debtors in order to survive, usually to the next harvest, not to improve their agricultural property or craft workshop.

The issue of slavery is extremely complex in that there were many nuances between the extremes of free and slave, and that both slaves and freemen can be found in almost all kinds of civilian employment. Important is the idea that the development of a labor market was very hard in antiquity, because two difficult conceptual steps were needed: first, one had to be able to separate a man's labor both from his person and from the product of his work. Second, such a market required the development of a method of measuring labor, usually by introducing a second abstraction, labor time.

The designation of the ancient city as a consumer city is closely associated with the idea that commerce played a minor role in its economy. In the medieval European city, manufacture was intensive and intended for export, and both created wealth for the city. The ancient city, however, lived as a parasite on its hinterland, never returning anything more in goods or services than what it extracted in rents and taxes from it. These ideas resound in the work of those historians of Mesopotamia who have provided systematic reconstructions of its ancient economy, seemingly because they were inspired by the same influences that we see in Finley's work. A challenge for the future would be to write an equivalent to Finley's book regarding the ancient Mesopotamian economy.

Modernist approaches

The "modernist" view, which finds the same economic motives and behavior in the ancient and in the modern worlds, seems to be commonly accepted among scholars of ancient Mesopotamia, although it is rarely explicitly acknowledged. Many studies seem to assume that such concepts as maximization of profits, financial gain, or investment, are universal, or at least important, in the thoughts of the Mesopotamians. Hence, capitalist-style behavior is considered to be the norm. For instance, studies on loan contracts use terms such as "commercial loans" or "partnerships" (Skaist 1994), or long-distance traders are accused of being motivated by "filthy lucre" (Larsen 1982: 42). Since most studies analyze records of transactions that seem capitalist in nature, that is not a surprise. If documents of interest-bearing loans to various individuals form the archive of an individual under study, it is easy to conclude that he was a creditor who made a living as a usurer. If real estate acquisitions are dominant in the records of one man, we can imagine that we are dealing with a speculator in land. Again, it is important to keep in mind that such records are the only ones that were written, as they registered a transfer of property and guaranteed protection against future claims.When a man bought a piece of urban property he kept the sale documents in order to be able to demonstrate the legitimacy of his ownership. If he granted a loan, he kept the record until the loan was repaid to justify his claim on the debtor (Van De Mieroop 1997b).

Our main problem is to evaluate how important these transactions were to him: was the moneylender a landowner whose estates provided him with all his needs and who would help out his friends and neighbors with amounts of silver to tide them over in difficult times? Or was he an entrepreneur with access to silver who tried to increase his funds with well-planned investments in short-term loans? What percentage of the economy did money-lending occupy, when the mass of the remaining economy is unknown? Such questions cannot be answered with empirical data: the landowner's agricultural business will not be documented if all production and consumption took place within his household. Certainly the absence of records concerning any other economic activity cannot lead to a conclusion that this did not take place. Arguments from silence are especially weak in the ancient Mesopotamian context where the use of writing was very restricted. We can only evaluate the importance of attested economic transactions if we have a view on the economy in general, much of which remains undocumented. If we take the transactions attested in the sources as the only, or even dominant, economic activities, we will privilege those activities that seem capitalist in nature. Our documents focus on the transfer of property as a record of the goods involved was needed, but that does not mean that transfer was the most important economic activity in Mesopotamia. A positivistic attitude leads to a skewed view of economic life.

Some scholars have tried to argue explicitly that such capitalist-style activity characterizes the Mesopotamian economy (e.g. Silver 1985). Unfortunately, most of this has been done by attacking Polanyi's ideas on exchange, especially his assertion that the market did not exist. That is indeed an easy target for criticism, as evidence exists for buying and selling, fluctuating prices, and even native terms for "market." But the existence of market exchange, the extent of which remains unclear, is insufficient reason to depict the Mesopotamian economy as a capitalist one. More nuanced views are needed. The recent proposal by D. Snell (1997: 154–6) to see an opposition between "the household and the market," one a social unit with non-economic interaction, the other "a system of information about what is available for purchasing at what price, in what place, under what conditions," uses incompatible terminologies and, misleadingly, presents an image of static versus innovative. But is does indicate that we have to imagine a co-existence of various economic actors and structures whose relative importance varies over time (cf. Powell 1978).

In my opinion, the behavior of the ancient Mesopotamians cannot be understood using contemporary economic theories, imagining a free-market capitalist economy. The embeddedness of the economy in the society led to a Mesopotamian attitude that was quite different from our own. Our contemporary aversion to state control of the economy, and the ideology that free enterprise is the panacea of all social and economic ills, should not lead to the perception that non-capitalist behavior in antiquity would have led to economic stagnation. The wish to promote the free entrepreneurs of Mesopotamia as the driving force of that economy is, I believe, driven by a desire to see in the past a fulfillment of present dreams. On the other hand, within the social setting of Mesopotamia, economic actors could, and did, behave in ways we see as similar to contemporary capitalist behavior. Individuals needed to survive outside institutional or communal contexts, desired profits, and took advantage of business opportunities. Neither should we see ancient Mesopotamia as a society in which state-organized redistribution or community exchange could satisfy everyone's needs. A recognition of the modern basis of the free-market system, with its own cruelties, should not lead to an utopian view of a better, more communal, society in distant days.

The challenge to the economic historian of Mesopotamia remains, in my opinion, the proper evaluation of the available textual data within a larger structure that does justice to the importance of the individual transaction records, without a loss of proportion. I would argue thus for the use of an inductive method, studying the empirical data at hand in the light of a broader view of the nature of the Mesopotamian economy. If we allow the texts to dictate our views, we will focus upon a limited set of economic actions, especially exchange. Just as the accident of recovery once determined our views on the predominance of temple, state, and private sectors in various period of history, we should understand that what was recorded presents only a fraction of economic life at any time. If we focus solely on that recorded aspect, we present an unbalanced view of the total.

AGRICULTURE IN UR III LAGASH

The potential – and the frustrating shortcomings – of cuneiform texts for the study of ancient economic history, can be demonstrated by an example taken from one of the best-documented periods of Mesopotamian history, the twenty-first century when the kingdom of Ur ruled southern Babylonia. One of the characteristics of this period is the existence of a bureaucratic apparatus that recorded aspects of the state economy in great detail. Various state archives have been found, unfortunately most often by illicit diggers, including one at Puzrish-Dagan that deals with animal herds, an agricultural archive at Umma, and several of manufacturing workshops at Ur. I will focus here on information from the city of Girsu in the province of Lagash, where numerous texts relating to the agriculture of cereals have been found in a large governmental archive. Since cereal cultivation was the basis of the Mesopotamian economy, its study should be at the center of economic research, but this example will demonstrate some of the difficulties we face.

The province of Lagash under the kingdom of Ur was located at the south-eastern edge of the core of the state, bordered on the south by the sea, and on the east by the river Tigris. To its north was the province of Umma, to its west those of Uruk and Ur. The southern, eastern, and western borders were probably not well fixed, as marshlands and steppe areas were located there, while to the north lay an agricultural area that had been a bone of contention between Umma and Lagash for centuries while they were independent city-states (Pettinato 1970–71).

The province, and earlier city-state, was somewhat unusual in that it contained three important urban centers along the major canal running through the area: Girsu, Lagash, and Nina, all within 25 kilometers of each other. Girsu was an important administrative center for several centuries from the mid- to late third millennium. Perhaps as many as 30,000 cuneiform documents were found there; it seems that local diggers knew of the location of a massive store of them, which they looted before they informed the French archaeological team of its whereabouts in the late nineteenth century (Jones 1975: 41). The limited archaeological information available suggests these tablets were found in a governmental building of the royal administration (Zettler 1996: 84). Any study using these texts is faced with two problems: there is a mass of material including many long and complicated texts, and the material is dispersed over numerous museum collections, which are not always fully catalogued, as much of it was sold on the antiquities market. Since a full publication of these 30,000 tablets is not likely to be accomplished in the near future, nor perhaps a desideratum, studies on the economic activities they record need to be undertaken knowing that they are provisional.

No comprehensive study of cereal agriculture in Ur III Lagash has ever been attempted and the following remarks are thus to be seen as mere pointers to what could be accomplished. For this study I will utilize a number of texts that are summary accounts covering one or several years, but those are not the most common in the archive. They were created by the ancient bureaucrats on the basis of sets of smaller accounts, providing information either on a limited geographical area or for a shorter period of time. I do not believe that any of the texts quoted here were based on actual observation in the field, measurements of acreage, of yields, etc., but that they were compiled in the office using a string of reports. Therefore their accuracy seems sometimes pedantic: for instance, an account including entries of 318,293,000 liters of barley, will bother to record an expenditure with an accuracy of half a liter (Maekawa 1981: 50, text 1, see below). We have no idea how many records lay at the basis of these summary accounts. The calculations involved were not always correct. For instance, the individual entries of "optimum" fields in a text I will use here (BM 14615) add up to 1,825.75 iku[3] while the text itself gives a total of 1,700.50 iku in its summation. Corrections were made on the tablet after it was written, as the scribe erased certain numbers (Pettinato 1977: 80–1, pl. IV). Although any scholar who has added and subtracted numbers in such accounts, even with the help of a calculator, may sympathize with the Sumerian scribe's mistakes, these discrepancies create a sense of exasperation, as we do not know what exactly to believe.

In the early years of Ur's control over Lagash, several surveys of agricultural land were undertaken. One of the resulting records dates to the thirtieth year of King Shulgi, and covers to my knowledge the largest region (Maekawa 1987: 111–12, text 52).[4] The text is laconic, and reads:

A: 222,374 iku (= 799.90 sq. km.) land (to be cultivated by) oxen, 600 old units

B: 630 iku (= 2.27 sq. km.) issued by the king

C: 5,220 iku (= 18.78 sq. km.) individual plots at hand/as tenant land[5]

D: 4,428 iku (= 15.93 sq. km.) in the fields named E.SU.DAR, eden, and Lugal-gaba

total: 232,652 iku (= 836.88 sq. km.)

Out of which:

1) 22,155.5 iku (= 79.70 sq. km.) issued by the king, under the responsibility of Ur-Lama and of the sukkal-mah-official

2) 4,428 iku (= 15.93 sq. km.) to be taken care of for the god Enki

3) 17,292 iku (= 62.20 sq. km.) to be divided into long fields, next to the field of Gu'abba

4) 7,038 iku (= 25.32 sq. km.) drained from stagnant water

To be inspected at the order of the shabra-official:

50,913.5 iku (= 183.15 sq. km.) individual issues and with stagnant water

5) One plow team (is used) for each 348 iku (= 1.25 sq. km.); the [total area] is 167,040 iku (= 600.86 sq. km.), (thus)

480 units of land (to be cultivated by) oxen and as allotments for personnel.

6) 14,698.5 iku (= 52.87 sq. km.) at hand/as tenant land.

To be plowed by 600 (teams of) oxen. Account of the governor of Girsu. Via Urnigar the royal field assessor.

[Year:] the king's daughter [was married to the governor of An]sh[an]

The account begins with an assessment of land that is available, a total area of 836.88 sq. km., within which is 799.90 sq. km., divided into 600 units, that is plowed by oxen belonging to the palace (entry A). The second part of the text explains how the total area is used: the first four entries are added separately, as 183.15 sq. km. Together with entries 5 and 6 they add up to the grand total of 836.88 sq. km. Entry 5 is of special importance as it indicates the land that is directly managed by the royal administration, 600.86 sq. km., which is divided into 480 units. On the basis of this, and similar, texts it can be concluded that the total area of Girsu was divided into 600 units, 480 of which were directly managed by the public institutions (Maekawa 1987: 98–9). The size of these units corresponds to the area that can be plowed by one plow team: one cultivator, three oxdrivers, and the necessary animals to pull the plow. Each year an alternating half of the area was left fallow (Heimpel 1995: 74). The units are about 1.3 sq. km. in size, but there seems to be slight variation: in the text translated above the 600 units of entry A measure on average 1.33 sq. km, those of entry 5 only 1.25 sq. km. These divisions are thus not entirely mathematical, but must reflect observations in the field. It is not clear that all the land documented here was owned by the palace, only that the palace had it surveyed.

The total area recorded in this text, 837.5 sq. km., is enormous. How much of the province of Lagash it includes is hard to determine with certainty. In a homogeneous ecological zone, one could draw a circle with a 16.3 km. radius around the city of Girsu to cover the recorded area. But it is more likely that the agricultural area was concentrated along the irrigation canal, named "Canal going to Nina," and that it would form a long rectangular zone, which could incorporate the whole length of the province of Lagash.[6] Gelb has claimed that close to the entire province was accounted for in documents of this type (1986: 159–60), but he may have been misled by the sheer size of the areas involved. A text from the preceding Sargonic period lists fields that may all have been located in the Lagash province, whose areas add up to 444,505 iku, i.e., 1,600 sq. km. (Gelb *et al.* 1991: 88–90, text 24). If the latter text indeed only lists fields in the province of Lagash, and if that province had remained similar in size in the Ur III period, the area surveyed in the Ur III text studied here makes up only 52 percent of the entire province.

The text translated above makes only limited remarks about the quality of land involved, such as that it was drained from stagnant water. Other, more detailed surveys are more specific in this respect. We have two records dated to the thirty-sixth year of King Shulgi[7] that provide information on the quality of plots of land for two large adjacent regions: Truro 1 (Walker 1973: pls. XVII–XVIII) and BM 14615 (Pettinato 1977: 70–81).[8] Both tablets contain eight columns of text, recording details of individual fields in the first five columns, and totals and summaries in the succeeding three. In both texts there are discrepancies between our additions of the single entries and the totals provided, and I will here only discuss the totals given by the ancient scribes. Both surveyed areas are located in the district called Gu'edena, situated between Girsu and Umma (Pettinato 1970–71), and they may actually cover parts of the Umma province (Civil 1994: 200). That the surveyed areas are adjacent to one another is implied by the appearance of the "field of Alla, the wagoner" in BM 14615 (col IV: 10–12) and of "the field next to the field of Alla, the wagoner" in Truro 1 (col I: 21). The totals in the two texts list similar types of land, but not altogether the same. In tabular form their contents can be represented as shown in Table 4.

Their concluding sections read:

> at hand for the governor of Girsu. Distributions made by the king. Duga and Urmes measured. Measured fields of Girsu. Via Inim-Shara the royal field assessor. Year: Shulgi, the strong man, the king of Ur, the king of the four quarters, made Nanna of Karzida enter his temple.
>
> (Truro 1)

and

> measured fields at hand in Girsu. Lu-Ninilduma and Ur-Lama measured. Via Inim-Shara the field assessor. Year: Shulgi, the strong man, the king of Ur, the king of the four quarters, made Nanna of Karzida enter his temple.
>
> (BM 14615)

Table 4 Comparison of Truro 1 and BM 14615

Type of land[9]	Truro 1		BM 14615	
	iku	sq. km.	iku	sq. km.
Optimum	11,299	40.64	1,700.5	6.12
Good, steppe land	2,792.75	10.05		
Good			175	0.63
Good, pasture	835	3.01	3.5	0.01
Good, uncultivated	370	1.33	504.75	1.82
Mediocre	8,107.25	29.16	2,066.5	7.43
Drained	11,839	42.59		
Optimum, drained			49.25	0.18
Path	616	2.22	1,447.75	5.21
With stagnant water	[	]		
Basin and channel	3,267	11.75		
Basin			76	0.27
Channel			82.5	0.30
Very bad	2,797	10.06	953.5	3.43
Cultivated, not with barley	73.25	0.26	835.5	3.00
[ ], steppe land	360	1.30		
Hill	16	0.06	72	0.26
Forest	79	0.28		
Orchard			16	0.06
Habitation and orchards	396	1.42		
River	562.25	2.02	412	1.48
Closed off from irrigation			69.5	0.25
Well			3.75	0.01
Habitation			39	0.14
Totals	at least 43,409.5	at least 156.15	8,507	30.60

In addition to rating the quality of fields, these texts are much more detailed about features in the landscape that occupy space and do not produce cereal yields: wells, paths, habitations, orchards, and forests. This information was probably needed in order to calculate the potential yield the entire area could produce. One could not well demand income of barley from an area covered by a forest after all. It is likely that many such records were produced for the province of Lagash, and other Ur III manuscripts of this type are found, unfortunately all but one[10] without a date (Civil 1994: 200–1). Again, one can ask whether or not they covered the entire province, and whether more marginal zones were surveyed in this manner as well. The texts indicate that the fields were at the disposal of the governor of Girsu; in

Truro 1 it is even stated that they were issued to him by the king. These are thus royal lands, belonging to the state economy. How much land existed outside that sector remains unclear.

None of the texts quoted so far dealt with the cultivation of the land. They all record areas, most of which are available for cultivation, but not necessarily farmed at the time. Only part of the region was indeed cultivated, and of that not more than one-half each year, as the farmer had to respect the fallow system in order not to exhaust the soil. The land that was owned by the palace was exploited under three systems of management, which had been in use for centuries before the Ur III period: domain land, allotment land, and tenant land. Unfortunately, there is only one text that gives a detailed account of all three systems simultaneously, for an estate in Lagash named after an earlier city-ruler, Namhani (Maekawa 1986a). The account dates probably to the second year of Amar-Sin, and the survey may have been made due to the fact that it was to be converted into the "estate of Amar-Sin." The text identifies seventeen fields belonging to the estate, covering a total area of 7,773.5 iku (= 27.96 sq. km.), and indicates then in great detail how its exploitation was managed under three arrangements: 5,250 iku (= 18.88 sq. km.) was domain land, 1,876.5 iku (= 6.75 sq. km.) was issued as allotments, and 586.25 iku (= 2.11 sq. km.) was rented out. A small area was not included in these calculations. This is all land under cultivation that year, so the total estate must have been approximately double in size. This text indicates thus that institutional land was divided up into three types, domain land, allotment land, and tenant land, at a rate of approximately 68 percent, 24 percent, and 8 percent each (cf. Postgate 1992: 186). Some scholars have taken the information contained in it as representative of how all institutional land was managed (Renger 1995: 285), but this is impossible to assess as the text remains unique (de Maaijer 1997: 47).

The domain land was cultivated by institutional laborers and equipment, organized in plow teams under a supervisor. Each team was responsible for one of the units of about 1.3 sq. km. in size, as mentioned above. This type of exploitation was very expensive for the institution as it had to support the staff year round, including times when there were no agricultural tasks (Maekawa 1986a: 101–5). Allotments were issued to various officials as a reward for services they rendered to the institution. This provided them with an income, but probably also with the responsibility to find personnel to work the fields, as their occupations suggest that they were unable to do so themselves (ibid.: 105–16). Finally, a part of the land was rented out to individuals, both officials and people not attached to an institution, who probably did so in order to sublease the lots to farmers (ibid.: 116–29).

Difficulties arise when we try to recognize this tripartite division of land in other accounts of surveys, especially the large-scale surveys discussed before. The first text I discussed, the survey of the Girsu region (Maekawa 1987: 111–12, text 52), uses the Sumerian terms found in the Namhani-estate survey, but perhaps with different meanings. The Namhani-estate survey distinguishes between gán-gu$_4$, "domain land," gán-ŠUKU, "allotment land," and gán níg-gál-la, "tenant land." These three Sumerian terms are found in various sections of the Girsu survey: the first half of the account includes gán-gu$_4$ (entry A) and gán níg-gál-la (entry C), but does not mention the third type of land, gán-ŠUKU. The second half has again these two types of land (entries 5 and 6), and indicates allotments, ŠUKU, but as part of the domain land, and seemingly for lower personnel only. The parts of estates set aside as rewards for higher officers are not explicitly mentioned, unless they are referred to here as issued by the king. Moreover, the term níg-gál-la does not always mean "tenant land," but more often is used for "available," and the standard Sumerian term for "tenancy" is apin-lá (Maekawa 1986a: 92). That term appears at the end of the Girsu account, but most likely is to be translated there in a more generic way as "to be plowed." These examples should suffice to demonstrate that one cannot easily take the translation of a term from one text, and uncritically transpose it to another.

All institutional land was owned by the palace in the Ur III province of Lagash, but was managed by administrative units that were called estates or households, most often named after a god, but sometimes after a person or a city. There were probably twelve of these households in Lagash, all listed in a summary account dated to the forty-seventh year of King Shulgi (Maekawa 1984: 90–1). Each one of them contained a grouping of smaller temples or households, spread over the province. For instance, the household of the god Nanshe had fourteen shrines that acted as administrative offices in the Nina district (Heimpel 1995: 74–6). These larger households were probably the survival in name of an original system in which temples indeed had been the primary landowners, but whose assets had been usurped by the secular authorities, probably already by the twenty-fourth century. When the city-state of Lagash was incorporated into the Ur III state, the ultimate authority over them was passed on from an independent city-ruler to a governor, subject to the king in Ur. Probably very roughly between 200 and 300 sq. km. of land were cultivated by these institutions themselves every year. Two texts covering the periods Shulgi year 28 to 32, and Shulgi year 42 to Amar-Sin year 3 attest to this:[11]

74,426 iku (= 267.72 sq. km.) of field, its grain is 124,035 royal gur (= 37,210,500 liters)

from which 129,000 gur 5 sìla (= 38,700,005 liters) were deli[vered]

[excess of 4,965 gur 5 sìla (= 1,489,505 liters)]

[Year: (Shulgi year 28?)]

[. . . iku of field, its grain is . . .]

from which 118,200 gur (= 35,460,000 liters) were delivered

deficit of 7,502 [+] gur (= 2,250,600 + liters)

Year: the royal daughter married the king of A[nshan] (Shulgi year 30)

76,698 iku (= 275.89 sq. km.) of field, its grain is 127,830 gur (= 38,349,000 liters)

from which 78,462 gur 100 sìla (= 23,538,700 liters) were delivered

deficit of 49,407 gur 200 sìla (= 14,822,300 liters)

Year: Simurrum was destroyed for the third time (Shulgi year 32)

[Fields?] divided among five shabra-officials
(Thureau-Dangin 1903: no. 407)

636,586 iku (= 2,289.88 sq. km.) of field

The grain used for seed and as fodder for the plow oxen is 52,724 gur 1 2/3 sìla (= 15,817,201 2/3 liters)

The yield of grain is 1,060,976 gur 200 sìla (= 318,293,000 liters)

from which 779,293 gur 205 sìla (= 233,788,105 liters) were delivered

60,000 gur (= 18,000,000 liters) were from KUD.DU fields

Total of 839,293 gur 205 sìla (= 251,788,105 liters) were issued.

221,682 gur 295 sìla (= 66,504,895 liters) is the deficit of the yield.

3,805 gur 80 sìla (= 1,141,580 liters) for grain xx

29,536 gur 71 1/2 sìla (= 8,860,871 1/2 liters) grain at hand (?)

5,890 gur 140 sìla (= 1,767,140 liters) for stipends for the governor('s household)

2,730 gur 60 sìla (= 819,060 liters) for stipends for (the households of) the governor's children

2,428 gur 100 sìla (= 728,500 liters) for stipends for the shabras' (households)

2,524 gur 110 sìla (= 757,310 liters) for the e-kinga and the harbor??

Total: 46,914 gur 261 1/2 sìla (= 14,074,461 1/2 liters) delivered in individual years.

From the year Shashrum (Shulgi 42) to the year Throne of Enlil (Amar-Sin 3). Ten years.

(Maekawa 1981: 50, text 1)

The first text indicates exactly how much land was cultivated in each one of three years (268 and 276 sq. km., and a broken number), while the second text provides the information that over a ten-year period a total of 2,292 sq. km. was cultivated, thus an average of 229.2 sq. km. per year. These figures correspond to the information found in the summary account dated to the forty-seventh year of King Shulgi (Maekawa 1984: 90–1), in which a total of 242.66 sq. km. is cultivated under the management of the twelve administrative households of Lagash (ibid.: 74–5). These texts also record the amounts of cereals, mostly barley (but probably also emmer), that were harvested, without taking into account the various yields for different soil qualities, the productivity of individual areas, the amounts of seed, and so on. The texts are thus not a good basis for the study of yields in this period, a problem that has been extensively investigated (see Halstead 1990), and which I will not address here. The accountants were solely concerned with the total amounts of cereals that were available. The quantities produced on these institutional domains were immense: the 37,210,500 liters recorded for Shulgi year 28 in the above text would be sufficient to provide the basic ration of 1.5 liters of barley a day to 68,900 persons for an entire Babylonian year of 360 days (cf. Renger 1994: 178–9).

Obviously the whole harvest was not redistributed in equal rations to the general population of the province. A record dated Amar-Sin year 2 provides a detailed record of the expenditures for the entire province of Girsu in one year (cf. Grégoire 1970: 233):

84,666 gur 47 sìla (= 25,399,847 liters) grain, measured according to the standard of King Shulgi, grain from domain lands

1,902 gur 20 sìla (= 570,620 liters) grain from xxx, grain derived from fees[12]

13,026 gur 285 sìla (= 3,908,085 liters) old grain

Total: 99,595 gur 52 sìla (= 29,878,552 liters), total available assets

From which:

49,790 gur 161 1/2 sìla (= 14,937,161 1/2 liters), expended for the central tax-contributions

12,270 gur 195 1/3 sìla (= 3,681,195 1/3 liters), in the Girsu district

6,442 gur 185 sìla (= 1,932,785 liters), in the district at the banks of the canal to Nina

11,326 gur 140 sìla (= 3,397,940 liters), in the Gu'abba district, for offerings and grain rations;

5,073 gur 251 1/4 sìla (= 1,522,151 1/4 liters) grain for fields to be plowed

117 gur 180 sìla (= 35,280 liters) grain for fields to be "turned over"

86 gur 120 sìla (= 25,920 liters) grain for young plow oxen

2220 [+] gur (= 666,000+ liters) [   ]

[   ] 40 sìla [   ], grain for [   ]

(Total:) 89,461 gur 143 2/3 sìla (= 26,838,443 2/3 liters), deductions in one year

14,400 gur (= 4,320,000 liters) grain for Enlil

A grand total of 103,861 gur 143 2/3 sìla (= 31,158,443 2/3 liters) was expended;

an excess of 4,266 gur 91 2/3 sìla (= 1,279,891 2/3 liters).

Account of the grain in the totality of the Girsu province.

Year: Amar-Sin, the king, destroyed Urbilum

(King 1899: pl. 8, BM 12926)

The account is extremely accurate in its calculations, including amounts as small as a quarter liter. At the beginning of the year a total of 29,878,522 liters of grain was available from three sources: the income from domain lands,[13] grain brought in by palace dependants as fees, and grain left over from the year before. The figures provided allow us to calculate the approximate size of the domain land cultivated that year. For calculations of harvest yields a figure of 30 gur (= 9,000 liters) per bur of area (= 18 iku, i.e. about 0.064 sq. km.) was expected in Girsu accounts of the Ur III period (Maekawa 1984: 83). According to this standard the 25,399,847 liters from domain land would have been produced on an area of some 180 sq. km. Taking into account that only one half of the agricultural area was cultivated in a single year, the total area of domain lands would thus only have been 360 sq. km., much less than the 799.90 sq. km. mentioned in the first text discussed above (Maekawa 1987: 111–12, text 52). So the entire income of the province's domain land recorded here derived from only a small part of the area accounted for by the palace. This income, together with the grain from the two other sources, formed the assets at hand. From that enormous amount, deductions were made over the year, which added up to 26,838,443⅔ liters: these included taxes to the Ur III state, offerings and grain rations in each of the three districts of the province, and expenditures for current agricultural work. On top of these deductions, a round amount of 4,320,000 liters of grain was given to the god Enlil. Thus the grand total of expenditure exceeded the income by 1,279,891⅔ liters. These great amounts of barley harvested in the Lagash province were thus not entirely used for the support of the inhabitants. The quantities that were to be given to the Ur III state amount to almost half the entire reserve available at the beginning of the year. Moreover, Enlil, the chief god of the state pantheon, received a substantial amount as well. After expenses, what remained for the local cults and for payment of personnel rations amounted only to 9,011,920⅓ liters. We are not informed how that amount was divided up between the two types of recipients, but the entire stock was sufficient only to provide daily basic grain rations to some 16,690 people over a whole year.

The ration system, in which set amounts of barley, oil, and wool were issued to dependants, was a hallmark of early Mesopotamian history, and is especially well documented in the Ur III period. The amounts issued varied according to status, age, and gender, and they were paid out only while the recipient was in the employ of the state (Postgate 1992: 237–40). It is thus hard to calculate how many people in the Lagash province received rations from the amount of barley mentioned in the account of the year Amar-Sin 2. Not all personnel worked full-time for the state, as I mentioned in the last chapter. Agricultural workers may have been engaged for the entire year, but craft workers were not. Moreover, the size of the rations varied: the majority of male laborers received two liters of barley a day, female laborers only one liter a day. But some specialists could easily collect ten liters a day (Waetzoldt 1987: 121–3). We can at least conclude that not more than 16,690 men and women[14] could be provided year-round with the amounts for rations attested. But the actual number was certainly smaller, as several individuals received substantially more than the basic ration. Although the maximum number of 16,690 individuals fed through rations is still substantial, it is highly unlikely that it includes the entire population of the Lagash province, which contained three urban centers. So how were other people able to eat?

Three additional sources of food supply were available within the state sector. First, probably not all of the central tax-contribution to be made to the state, almost exactly 50 percent of the total amount of grain available in the text cited above (King 1899: pl. 8, BM 12926), was sent outside the region. Most likely a substantial part was used to support the state bureaucracy within the province. If the entire amount recorded for tax was consumed as minimum year-round rations for men and women, it could feed another 27,660 people. A second source of grain was provided by the allotment fields issued as compensation to certain personnel, usually high-ranking officials (Waetzoldt 1987: 128–32). The recipients could cultivate the plots, or, more likely, have them cultivated by their own staff. Such allotments seem to have been in lieu of rations, but unfortunately we are unable to estimate how much grain they produced, as we do not know the size of the land apportioned in this way. A third way in which land, owned by the state, was cultivated, was by renting it out to individuals for a fee. This arrangement is well attested at Girsu (Maekawa 1977), and it is clear that primarily high officials were the lessees. They must have sub-leased those plots to farmers for cultivation, just as they did with their allotment fields. Again we cannot estimate the income from such land, as we do not know how much of it existed.

A limited number of field rental agreements are known from the Ur III state (Kraus 1975). With many of them, a major problem of interpretation faces the scholar: was the land leased owned privately by the lessor, or was it assigned or leased to him by the state? Some scholars have suggested that rental contracts do attest to the existence of privately owned fields that were rented out by their owners (Gelb 1971: 152; Neumann 1993). Others are not convinced of that at all, and point out that it is a false assumption that a lessor not explicitly associated with a central institution in the texts is a private owner of the field leased. To these scholars the private ownership of land was virtually non-existent in the Ur III period (Renger 1995: 286–8). Both opinions can be supported by shreds of information that either suggests the existence of privately owned land, or makes it a rare occurrence at best. On balance, I believe that there is sufficient evidence (Neumann 1992: 164–6) to suggest that privately owned land existed. But when we have to determine how important that land was in the general agricultural economy of the Ur III state, we are at a loss. It seems probable that the survey of Girsu discussed above (Maekawa 1987: 111–12, text 52) does not cover the entire province, yet we cannot determine how much larger it was than the area of 837.5 sq. km. recorded, and whether or not only marginal land was unaccounted. How significant scholars rate the existence of private landownership is determined by their basic ideas about the structure of the Ur III economy, and those ideas are biased by their intellectual background as I discussed before. A purely positivistic approach is meaningless as the evidence needs to be placed within a general structure that cannot be developed on the basis of our sources alone.

I hope that this survey of some of the information available on agriculture in Lagash has demonstrated that we have a great deal of evidence at hand, of a type and detail that is rare in the rest of the ancient world. An incredible amount can be learned from this evidence about usages of land, yields, income, and expenditures. But, in the final analysis, some fundamental questions will remain unanswered. For instance, what part of the population was fed by the state, were there fields outside this state organization that provided food to many people, or did taxes remain in the area or were they transported elsewhere? Those questions were not addressed in the documentation, not because they were unknown to the accountants of antiquity, but because they were so obvious to them that they did not require mention (Civil 1980: 225–6). This leaves us to fill in the gaps in order to comprehend the system we are studying, and by doing so we impose our views on the ancient economy upon the evidence. The least we can do, then, is acknowledge whence these views derive.

Chapter 5

Gender and Mesopotamian History

No historical discipline can take itself seriously today without paying attention to the issue of gender. Ancient Mesopotamian history is no exception, and even though it has not taken a lead in any theoretical considerations in this research, it has to a certain extent, and with some delay, followed the general trends in gender scholarship. This scholarship has moved from a primary concern with the place of women in history to a study of the construction of gender, so I will use this broader term here, although much of Mesopotamian scholarship has been concerned with the identification of women in the record. As Mesopotamia is a civilization of the distant past and located in the Middle East, the study of gender is often colored by preconceptions and *a priori* assumptions based on ideas on women in classical antiquity and in the Islamic Middle East. This is especially visible in the use of such terms as harem and veil, or the assumption that women were necessarily economically dependent on men. Such preconceptions need to be resisted, as the position of women needs to be studied within the particular cultural context of Mesopotamian society.

After a survey of the developments in gender scholarship since the 1960s and the ways in which they have influenced the study of ancient Mesopotamia, I will provide an example of how the position of women in Mesopotamian society was particular to that culture. The bibliography on "women in ancient Mesopotamia" is quite substantial, so my survey will be far from exhaustive and will focus on how the various "waves" in feminist scholarship have had their repercussions on Mesopotamian studies.

The developments in scholarship regarding gender have been fast and momentous, driven by social and political changes in the Western world. Certain academic disciplines, such as

Mesopotamian studies, have lagged somewhat behind, often due to the distinct career paths of men and women, the latter typically being tolerated only in the earlier stages of scholarly training and the lower levels of academic employment. But still, the attention paid to women in today's scholarship is infinitely greater than was the case before the 1970s. Three waves of feminist scholarship can be distinguished in the general academy, not clearly delineated in time but often overlapping chronologically and focusing on somewhat different questions (Kandiyoti 1996: 2–7).

The first wave of feminist studies arose from the awareness that traditional history, and scholarship in general, had neglected half of the world's population by studying only the accomplishments of men. A goal of research was to identify women's contributions to history, which by itself presented a fundamental break with previous practices. These investigations required a change in attitude, since even clear references to women in the historical record earlier on had often been neglected due to the fact that research had dealt primarily with questions of male activities. This attitude was exacerbated by the fact that the historical documentation on women is often lacking, or does not yield the desired information on a superficial reading. Women's history does then require an approach where the scholar meticulously sifts through the record to identify references to the activities of women. In Mesopotamian studies this search started seriously only in the mid-1970s when a number of scholars began writing on "women in" a particular period of time. The clearest sign that the discipline had finally accepted the presence of women in Mesopotamian society as a valid concern, came in 1986 when its annual international conference, the Rencontre Assyriologique Internationale devoted a meeting to "La femme dans le Proche-Orient antique" (Durand 1987b). The collection of data on women continues today. It fits well within the philological approach to Mesopotamian history, in that it encourages the search through the extensive sources for references to women. These references can then be chronologically and typologically organized to arrive at a catalogue that is as complete as possible.

Due to the nature of the sources, the focus of attention has been on particular aspects of the woman's role in society. Prominent women, queens, and high priestesses, have received substantial coverage as they appear in such sources as royal inscriptions, court correspondence, and public administrative documents. Women at various levels in the cult are readily studied, as many contracts and the like indicate the professions of individuals mentioned, and for women these were often of a cultic nature. Moreover, archives of temples are often preserved as well as the large archive of what has been called a "cloister" in Old Babylonian Sippar (Jeyes 1983). The less privileged women are known especially from private contracts related to marriage, divorce, and widowhood, while female dependent laborers appear in large institutional households as menial workers, who primarily weave and mill.

The second wave of feminist scholarship shifted the focus from establishing the presence of women in history to an attempt at explaining why women were found in subordinate positions. Such an approach was intended to inspire women to throw off their secondary roles in society, and to establish relations between academia and feminist movements in the real world. Although many explanations of women's subordinate roles in society were presented, a majority of scholars saw an age-old system of patriarchy as the culprit, and historical foundations for this situation were sought. And here ancient Mesopotamia played a crucial role in the writings of some feminist scholars, who stated that patriarchy was not like "human nature" but that it had developed culturally in the late-prehistoric and early historic periods of "mankind." The development could be studied in the ancient Near East, as that was after all the region where history began. These scholars believed that a primeval system of matriarchy, where women had equal or greater authority than men, had evolved over time into the historical situation where men were, and still are, in charge. This theory picked up on ideas developed in the nineteenth century by such scholars as Bachofen, Morgan, and Engels, but which had lost popularity in the early twentieth century (Merrill 1979). They were now revived, as the demonstration of an earlier existence of a matriarchal society was thought to be able to inspire women to work for a return to such a situation in the future.

The most elaborate statement of this idea was published in 1986 in an extremely popular and acclaimed book by Gerda Lerner, *The Creation of Patriarchy*. It presented a teleological narrative describing an evolution from a matriarchical society as evidenced in the seventh-millennium Anatolian town at Çatal Hüyük to a purely androcentric Hebrew society where women were considered to be essentially different from men, their sexuality only important when beneficial to the latter. The biblical tradition, combined with the misogynous classical Greek one, led then to the Western patriarchal system that has survived till today. Mesopotamian history played a crucial role in this narrative. One could study there the gradual deterioration of women's status, in that states increasingly intervened by codifying their subordinate position in the legal systems. While in the third millennium women were only privately subjected to men, in the late second millennium the Middle Assyrian state had proclaimed laws that made it illegal for any woman who was not a prostitute to appear in public. Many other social changes resulted from the change in women's status: private property developed after women's reproductive capacity had been appropriated by men, the idea of enslaving foreigners was inspired by the oppression of women within the household, the sexual control of women was fundamental for the establishment and maintenance of social classes, and a religious shift from a supreme mother-goddess to an all-powerful male god justified and coincided with the rise of male dominance. Thus the creation of patriarchy was seen as being at the nexus of the growth of a whole set of inequalities based on gender, race, ethnicity, and class. Lerner's book was not the only account of such an evolution, nor the first one. It belonged to a series of statements that asked *why* patriarchy had developed, and had looked at the problem in evolutionary terms. Reasons for this evolution were found in the formation of the state and militarism (Rohrlich 1980), the appearance of private property and the division of labor (Engels 1884), or the development of agriculture and the commodification of women's sexuality (Lerner 1986).

The idea that patriarchy was a cultural development in history required proof that a matriarchal system had existed at some point in time. Evidence for matriarchy was sought in prehistory, and relied heavily on the concept of the cult of the Mother-Goddess in neolithic societies. Much has been written on this subject, especially inspired by the work of the prehistorian Marija Gimbutas, and the idea of the Mother-Goddess has become integrated in such contemporary Western ideologies, or fads, as New Age spiritualism and ecofeminism. Its scholarly merits are heavily criticized (e.g. Meskell 1995), and the search for a matriarchal past derives to a great extent from a desire to find a golden age in history – no war, no private property, no gender inequality, no pollution – which could inspire the struggle for a better future.

The study of prehistoric religions is certainly very complex, as it is based on extremely fragmentary evidence, statuettes, rock paintings, later myths, that can inspire varied, even contradictory, interpretations. The mixture of this study with contemporary trends makes any conclusion even more equivocal. Subsequently the acceptance of a matriarchal system in the distant past seems to be based more on contemporary beliefs than on scholarly argumentation.

The controversial character of the entire theory perhaps explains why the community of Mesopotamian specialists has refused to engage with the issue of the development of patriarchy. It is notable that Gerda Lerner's book, which devotes most of its pages to ancient Mesopotamia, has been totally ignored within the scholarly literature on Mesopotamia. I have been unable to locate a single review of the book within its journals or a single reference to it in one of the many subsequent studies on women in Mesopotamia. Meanwhile, the book was praised in the historical community in general, and became a standard feature on syllabi on women's history in American universities. Obviously a work of this nature, written by an outsider, is vulnerable to criticism as its use of empirical data is often faulty and undiscriminating. Moreover, its chronological and cultural boundaries cross the disciplinary limitations we impose upon ourselves, so it may have been hard to find a Near East scholar willing to address the work in its entirety, and possibly the popular appeal of the book may have immediately earned it the label of unscientific among specialists. Although it is not my intent to defend the thesis of the book, or its use of Mesopotamian (and other) data, it remains startling that the basic idea of a matriarchal society developing into a patriarchal one in early Mesopotamian history has neither been cogently addressed nor refuted.

It is, however, commonly insinuated in the Assyriological literature that the living conditions of women deteriorated over time in Mesopotamian history. In the third millennium upper-class women at least are seen to be very active in political and economic life, and there may even be evidence that polyandry existed at some time before the mid-third millennium, which to some scholars seems a sign of women's superiority within the household. Uru'inimgina, ruler of Lagash in the early twenty-fourth century, stated in his so-called reforms: "Women of former times each married two men, but women of today have been made to give up that crime." Scholars have been quick to point out that the interpretation of this passage is far from clear, however, and that it may actually refer to women "having to perform marital obligations" to two men because of their husband's debts (Cooper 1986: 77–8). The same passage states that a woman who speaks disrespectfully to a man will have her mouth crushed with a baked brick, hardly a sign of superior social status. The somewhat rosy picture of women's position in early Sumerian society depicted by some (e.g. Kramer 1976: 12–17) is thus categorically denied by others (Harris 1992: 948). The perceived deterioration of women's status in Mesopotamian society remains an unexplained evolution (Frymer-Kensky 1992: 79–80). In any case, the basic idea that women had a secondary status in Mesopotamian society seems to be generally accepted by scholars in the discipline, and the reasons for this situation are not investigated. It seems to be regarded as "human nature."

Feminist scholarship abandoned the totalizing views on women in the late 1980s under the influence of postmodernism, and focused instead on gender as a social construction. Teleological and essentialist histories such as *The Creation of Patriarchy* find no place in such scholarship. The world is not divided into two monolithic blocs of men and women, because there are multiple categories where gender intersects with race, class, wealth, ethnicity, sexual orientation, age, etc. Gender has thus been redefined as "an expression of difference within a field of power relations" (Kandiyoti 1996: 6), and of interest is how gender roles are socially devised. Again there are many different approaches to this issue, and reactions against this movement away from a politically active feminism, which I cannot detail here. One of the consequences in historical research has been an increased interest in the body and how it is perceived in various societies. Numerous studies have appeared on this topic (cf. Meskell 1996), but in ancient Mesopotamian studies the effects of this shift in scholarship have been minimal. The male has come to be included in studies on the body and sexuality (Winter 1996), and criticism of seeing a purely male/female dichotomy in the Mesopotamian conception of gender has been initiated (Asher-Greve 1997a). But in general the discipline is still committed to searching for attestations of women within the record, a continuation of the first wave of feminist studies.

The collection of attestations of women from a variety of sources faces several difficulties, however. First of all, it is ironic that we now have several accounts of "women in Mesopotamia," when no one would think of a similar study of "men in Mesopotamia." This very fact reduces women to a secondary status, as it assumes that by default men are the primary agents in Mesopotamian history. Second, on the very basic level of data gathering, it is not always easy to recognize women in the sources at hand, textual, archaeological, or iconographic. In texts we identify the gender of individuals through various means: their names, their titles, or their familial affiliation. Mesopotamian personal names, in both the Sumerian and Akkadian languages, are often gender-specific, due to grammatical elements or what we understand to be the contents of the name. The Akkadian name, Shu-Ishtar, "He of the goddess Ishtar" seems without a doubt to refer to a man, while Shat-Ishtar, "She of Ishtar," must refer to a woman. But the gender of the person named is not always clear, especially with names in the Sumerian language which does not distinguish grammatically between the masculine and the feminine. A Sumerian name such as Bau-zimu "(the goddess) Bau is my life" contains no indication about the gender of its bearer. Moreover, we know that some names could be given to both men and women in the same coherent group of texts (Harris 1977: 50). The enormous problems this poses to a researcher interested in questions such as the participation of women in the economic life have never been addressed. If an individual, only defined by a name that is not clearly gender-specific, appears in a text, it is customary among scholars to identify that person as a man, unless the activity described seems one that women would regularly undertake. The preconceptions regarding gender roles will then be reinforced by this attestation. The identification of individuals in literary texts is often similarly based on the assumption that men are the main characters, without a clear indication that such is the case. Thus it is stated that women only appear in secondary roles in such texts, while that may be due to our own automatic identification of the leading figures as males (Pollock 1991: 368–9). We often find our preconceptions reflected in the search for women in texts; for activities where we imagine male dominance we identify the individuals involved as male, and similarly we find women only in contexts that we consider to belong to the female realm.

In many Mesopotamian administrative and economic texts, individuals are not only identified by their names but also by a professional title or a familial affiliation. This was simply necessary in societies where several names were very popular, and confusion could easily arise about the identity of the individual. When such designations are found with women, this has ironically led to a confirmation of the *a priori* ideas about their status in society. When they are identified as the wife or daughter of someone, they are considered to be subservient to their male relatives. It is often perceived that otherwise they could only be active in the legal and economic sphere if they belonged to a certain professional group, usually some type of priesthood that can be clearly identified as reserved for women. Thus a woman who appears in a witness list as daughter or wife of someone, is thought to act under the authority of her father or husband, while for a man the designation as son or, indeed, sometimes husband is merely seen as a help in identifying the individual. Although I am not arguing that this is an entirely false perception, it has never been clearly demonstrated that women appear in the legal and economic record only as subservient to a male relative, as belonging to a particular professional group, or in a capacity different from males.

Gender studies in archaeology have often dealt with buried people, whose sex ideally can be determined through a physical examination of the skeleton. The accompanying burial goods could give us an idea about the wealth, social status, and appearance of the buried person during his or her lifetime, and might indicate the social position of women in the society under investigation. But again circular reasoning is often used to identify occupants of burials when the skeletons have not been sexed, which is usually the case with earlier excavations. What we think to be female gravegoods, such as certain types of jewelry, is interpreted as evidence leading to the identification of the buried as women. Careful study of this problem has indicated that especially lower-class females are difficult to distinguish from their male companions through burial remains (Pollock 1991: 376). In other aspects of the archaeological record, such as domestic architecture (Tringham 1991) or technology (Wright 1996), the distinction between male and female usage is very difficult to establish and often relies on ethnographic parallels that are impossible to verify. Even in the iconographic record the identification of women is not always clear; several Sumerian statues, for instance, have no clear gender in our eyes, as is exemplified by the varied identifications of temple-singer Ur-Nanshe as male, female, or castrato (Asher-Greve 1997: 438 and n. 37).

In the interpretation of these three groups of sources there is thus always the possibility that the identification of the sex or gender of the individuals studied is ambiguous, and it is up to the scholar to determine whether a man or a woman is involved. It is easy to let *a priori* assumptions about gender roles prejudice that identification: women are found only when what we think to be the female domain is involved. Otherwise they are excluded. This attitude is indicative of a larger and more fundamental problem in the collection of data about women. The search for such data and their categorization and classification are often guided by the preconceptions we have about women's roles in Mesopotamian society. Therefore, the search for women will concentrate on particular aspects of life: the domestic world, marriage and sexual behavior, the cult. It will see ownership of property as unusual, and as originating from a male relative, most often the father or husband. It will thus impose the views we have of the role of women in Mesopotamian society on the data we have, without questioning these views. Since so many of the data are isolated tidbits of information, individual attestations, scholars are faced with the task of organizing them into categories, which are dictated by the conceptual framework in which they work. That framework is very much an unquestioned androcentric view of the Mesopotamian world, the basis of which needs to be questioned and argued before it is used.

A first step in gender scholarship is thus to investigate the conceptual background we use in studying women in ancient Mesopotamia (J. Westenholz 1990). This background has never been openly argued and is not a conscious one, but it strongly influences how we interpret the individual data on woman and place them within a larger context. Since it is for the most part subconscious, it is far from monolithic, yet it shows overall assumptions that see women in Mesopotamian society in a particular light. In my opinion, this framework has been informed by Mesopotamia's position on the crossroad of two cultural areas for which strong views about gender roles exist: antiquity and the Middle East.

Although few scholars see Islam as inspired by ancient Mesopotamia, indeed most scholars see no connection between ancient and medieval cultures of the Middle East, the description of the status of women in Mesopotamia is often inspired by Western views on the Muslim world. The Orientalist stereotypes regarding Islamic women, found in scholarship and popular culture alike, are so strong and complex that they have inspired an enormous body of critical literature. Since these ideas influence the scholarship on Mesopotamia at the subconscious level only, recent post-colonial critiques of gender-stereotyping of the Islamic world have remained unnoticed and have not changed the general attitude of regarding Mesopotamian women in an Orientalist light. Those views present an intriguing paradox: the Middle Eastern woman is oppressed yet lascivious. She is kept out of the public eye, hidden in the harem or behind the veil, while being simultaneously sexually alluring (Alloula 1986). The complexity of this paradox needs to be studied in the context of the portrayal of the Other as radically different from us, a rich field of inquiry in post-colonial criticism that has been barely acknowledged in Mesopotamian studies. It cannot be reviewed here, but I will try to point out how some of the paradoxical Orientalist stereotypes emerge in Mesopotamian scholarship.

The harem and the veil are two tropes that dominate any discussion of Middle Eastern women: countless books and articles use the terms as buzzwords alerting the reader to the essential confinement of these women and their oppressed status in society. Although the pre-Islamic and Islamic periods in Middle Eastern history are strictly separated in the minds of most scholars, the terms harem and veil ironically are standard in studies on Mesopotamia as well. The idea of the harem calls up the image of a secluded area in a private house or palace where one or more women are kept, sometimes guarded by eunuchs. The term is also used as a collective noun to refer to the women in that area, the wives and concubines of the male head of the house. More broadly the harem has been taken to include all women in a household, married or unmarried, young and old, mistresses and servants. Any large household would thus have a harem. Yet by using this term scholars call to mind the stereotypical image of several women at the sexual disposal as the wives and concubines of one man. Since the term harem is an Arabic word, it is particularly associated with the Middle East, and would not be found in a description of a medieval European household, for instance.

In Mesopotamian studies royal "harems" have received the most attention, as any palace having a list of female personnel can be said to have contained such an establishment. Scholars using texts usually find "harems" first in Ebla in the mid-third millennium and in Mari in the eighteenth century, both cities in Syria, and then see them firmly established in Assyria from the fourteenth century on. But we know that earlier Babylonian kings had several wives as well; the Ur III kings, for instance, are known to have married many wives designated by various titles we cannot fully understand (Van De Mieroop 1989), so by these definitions they would have had harems as well. Moreover, archaeologists have designated many areas in palaces from the entirety of Mesopotamian history as "harems," when they are considered to have restricted access (e.g. Heinrich 1984). These designations are often contested as the uses of areas in buildings are never clearly established, but descriptions of Mesopotamian palaces with "harems" are routine beginning with the earliest explorers.

What life in these "harems" would have been like is not described in the textual material at our disposal, but has not prevented scholars from imagining it. Once the term "harem" has been chosen, a whole set of images arises in our minds, confirmation for which can then be sought in the available textual data. One group of texts especially has been interpreted as substantiating the idea of the Mesopotamian "harem." From eleventh-century Assur we have a set of fragmentary tablets that were published under the title "Palace and harem edicts of Assyrian kings of the second millennium BC" (Weidner 1954–56). These texts enumerate twenty-three decrees by Assyrian kings going back to the fourteenth century, regulating the behavior of palace personnel. By using the term "harem decree" the original editor immediately placed them within the conceptual framework of the stereotypical Middle Eastern harem, and this has continued to bias their interpretation until today.[1] His own description of the context of these texts clearly demonstrates this:

> Most of the edicts contain rules for the king's harem. There numerous women live together surely in a confined area, and it is understandable that friction often arises and that it is not easy to keep peace and tolerable concord.

Or:

> In general the palace-women are restricted to the area of the harem and thus they try by all means to deal with the deadly boredom, whereby gossip, quarrels, and fights occur all too often, and the smallest occasions have to serve to satisfy female curiosity.

(ibid.: 261)

It is remarkable that Weidner's rather peculiar views on the group behavior of women, which demonstrate the fact that he had some stereotypical "harem" in mind when he published these texts, have never been challenged by feminist scholars of Mesopotamia, who continue to take these texts as clear evidence of the oppressed status of women in Middle Assyrian society (e.g. Cifarelli 1998: 226–7, note 25). It is clear that the views about the cultural background of these texts also influence their translation, even by those scholars more restrained in their Mesopotamian harem fantasies. As the "edicts" are unique in character the translation of individual terms and of sentences is determined solely by the context within these texts themselves. For example, a recent translation reads:

> Royal court attendants or dedicatees of the palace personnel who have access to the palace shall not enter the palace without an inspection; if he is not (properly) castrated, they shall turn him into a (castrated) court attendant for a second time.
>
> (Roth 1995: 205)

From this translation it seems that only fully castrated men could enter the palace. First of all, we have to adjust the latter in our minds to indicate the harem, as it seems unlikely that the entire court was made up of women and castrated men. Second, the translator has allowed for a great deal of interpretation as the Akkadian term she translates as "castrated," in all other contexts seems simply to mean "checked."[2] I do not deny that castrates existed in the Assyrian court and that they could rise to high office, but nothing in these texts demonstrates that they are referred to here.[3] A less fanciful, although less exciting, reading would just deny access to the palace in general to male personnel who were not "checked" for whatever purpose. Similarly, another passage in these edicts seems to state that a court attendant would get 100 lashes if seen talking to a palace woman with bare shoulders (Roth 1995: 206 ¶ 21), but both the interpretations of the terms for "shoulder" and "to bare" are highly conjectural.[4]

Although we do get a general sense that these decrees strictly regulate access to, and behavior in, the palace, the suggestion that they deal with the harem sheds a particular light on their interpretation that derives more from our imagination than from the texts themselves. It is far from certain that the women involved were all royal concubines; an unfortunately broken passage refers to women married to men from outside the palace and living with their husbands (ibid.: 198 ¶ 3). This suggests strongly that we are dealing here with female palace personnel in general, and that they are far from women locked up in a harem. The terms "women of the palace" or "women of the king," which are found throughout Mesopotamian texts, are often translated as "harem women," thereby suggesting that they were available for the sexual pleasure of the king, but quite likely they were just general personnel. The 232 women that King Zimri-Lim of Mari had in his "harem," included singers, teachers, chamber-maids, and scribes (Durand 1987a: 85–6). By the common use of the term harem to refer to these women, scholars have invoked the stereotypical idea of the Middle Eastern palace harem, where women were supposedly locked up, guarded by eunuchs, and at the mercy of the insatiable despot. At the same time it perpetuates the assumption that anytime a female name or a group of women is found in connection with the palace, they must have been there for sexual purposes rather than for their technical skills.

A similar message of oppression is given through the idea of the veil, a piece of cloth worn by women to cover at least the hair, and often part of the face. The evidence for the veiling of Mesopotamian women in iconographic sources is almost totally absent, and in texts we can only surmise it in one document, again from the Middle Assyrian period. The Middle Assyrian laws contain a collection of statements regarding legal practices, often the punishment of certain social transgressions. The first tablet (A) deals primarily with laws where women appear as perpetrators or victims, and two paragraphs extensively treat what has commonly been interpreted as veiling (Roth 1995: 167–9 ¶¶ 40–1). They state that two groups of women should be veiled when outside the house during the daytime; married women and "concubines" who were veiled by their husbands in the presence of witnesses. Unmarried women could not be veiled, however. Prostitutes and slave-women who veiled themselves were subject to severe punishment: the former's clothes were given to the informant, they were given fifty lashes and had hot pitch poured over their heads, the latter had their ears cut off and their clothes were given to the informant. Moreover, men who did not report them were harshly punished as well, with whipping, piercing of the ears, loss of clothes, and a month of compulsory labor for the king. The exact intent of these rules is difficult to grasp. They group unmarried women with prostitutes and slaves as opposed to married women and publicly acknowledged concubines. The Akkadian term translated as "to veil" again appears in this text only,[5] and even though some type of head dress is most likely involved here, the choice of the term "veil" in the translation immediately calls up a set of associations with the covering of women in the modern Middle East. Some scholars have taken this then as a basis for designating any cloth cover as a veil (cf. J. Westenholz 1990: 515). If women were veiled in any period of Mesopotamian history, it is unlikely that this practice had anything to do with what we today consider to be the purpose of veiling in the Middle East, the protection of their face from the male gaze.

Thus the idea that the Mesopotamian woman was sequestered from the outside world runs as an undercurrent in much of what we say about them. That idea has a great deal to do with our perception of the Middle Eastern woman today, which, ironically, is an attitude in total opposition to the commonly accepted discontinuity between pre-Islamic and Islamic periods. We can thus find this statement by a prominent scholar: "And one must wonder whether this general invisibility of women in Mesopotamia does not reflect deeper cultural mores regarding distinctions of public and private along gender lines – a practise entirely consonant with parts of the Middle East today" (Winter 1987: 201). The restriction of women to a private world becomes thus a fact of life in the Middle East, frozen in time from antiquity till today.

But paradoxically the descriptions of Middle Eastern women's seclusion in Islamic times have a highly tantalizing sexual flavor to them. While nineteenth- and early twentieth-century Western travellers to the Middle East wrote extensively on how the movements of women were extremely restricted, they also described these women as lascivious and sexually engaged in acts that Victorian society could hardly imagine (Kabbani 1986; Mabro 1991). The harem in nineteenth-century imagination was not only a place of repression, but also one of erotic pleasure and Oriental luxury. What took place in the ancient Mesopotamian harem has not been explicitly discussed by scholars as no ancient document describes it, although some scholars have intimated that there was some sort of illicit sexual intercourse (Steiner 1987: 150) and of singing and dancing (Kinnier Wilson 1972: 46). The Mesopotamian woman as an active sexual partner is situated by scholars in the public sphere, as the prostitute. Much of the image of prostitution in ancient Mesopotamia derives from the following enigmatic statement of Herodotus in his description of Babylon:

> There is one custom amongst these people which is wholly shameful: every woman who is a native of the country must once in her life go and sit in the temple of Aphrodite and there give herself to a strange man. Many of the rich women, who are too proud to mix with the rest, drive to the temple in covered carriages with a whole host of servants following behind, and there wait; most, however, sit in the precinct of the temple with a band of plaited string round their heads – a great crowd they are, what with some sitting there, others arriving, others going away – and through them all gangways are marked off running in every direction for the men to pass along and make their choice. Once a woman has taken her seat she is not allowed to go home until a man has thrown a silver coin in her lap and taken her outside to lie with her. As he throws the coin, the man has to say, "In the name of the goddess Mylitta" – that being the Assyrian name for Aphrodite. The value of the coin is of no consequence; once thrown it becomes sacred, and the law forbids that it should ever be refused. The woman has no privilege of choice – she must go with the first man who throws her the money. When she has lain with him, her duty to the goddess is discharged and she may go home, after which it will be impossible to seduce her by any offer, however large. Tall, handsome women soon manage to get home again, but the ugly ones stay for a long time before they can fulfil the condition which the law demands, some of them, indeed, as much as three or four years.
>
> (Herodotus 1954: 121–2)

This passage, long known in the West before any Babylonian texts were understood, not only inspired Orientalist views of a decadent Babylon, but also confounded and continues to confound scholars with the task of how to explain it. If Herodotus really visited Babylon, as many believe, which misunderstood, but actual, practice inspired his depiction? Most often cultic prostitution is considered to be the answer.[6]

Throughout Mesopotamian history the cult personnel especially of the goddess of love, Sumerian Inanna or Akkadian Ishtar, included a number of women who acted as "prostitutes," priestesses who had sexual intercourse with men to whom they were not married. These women might early on have been involved primarily in sacred marriage rites, where the ruler had sexual intercourse with a woman representing the goddess in order to promote general fertility, but from the early second millennium on included a great variety of priestesses whose exact roles remain unclear to us. An assortment of titles is used to designate these women (Lambert 1992), so their number seems to have been substantial as well. But we are extremely poorly informed about their duties and activities, including their sexual acts which are only described in a couple of literary texts (Bottéro 1992: 190), such as the Epic of Gilgamesh where a prostitute introduces the wild man Enkidu to civilization by having intercourse for six days and seven nights. So scholars keep on referring back to Herodotus's account to conceptualize what the cultic prostitutes could have done in earlier Mesopotamian society (Beard and Henderson 1997: 489–90).

What these scholars have been unwilling to accept is that Herodotus and other classical historians talked about the sexual practices of the East with similar Orientalist attitudes to those we find in nineteenth- and twentieth-century travel literature. To the ancient Greeks sacred prostitution was a sign of the Orient: they saw it in Corinth as an eastern import, in Cyprus, Syria and Phoenicia, Armenia and Babylon. The classical accounts cannot serve as providing information on sexual practices in these places, as they were written in order to underscore the alterity of the East as a place of lust and desire (Beard and Henderson 1997). That such accounts were accepted as containing a kernel of truth and became pivotal in the nineteenth- and twentieth-century imagination of sexual life in ancient Mesopotamia, can hardly be seen as unrelated to the images of women in the Islamic Middle East provided in Orientalist literature and art. In order to properly understand the functions of the "cultic prostitutes," and sexual practices in general we will need to shed these stereotypical views, and look at Mesopotamia on its own account. Whether that would lead to a comprehensive picture is unclear, but it seems to be the only valid historical practice.

Mesopotamia is also an ancient society and many of our views on the position of women in it are influenced by views on antiquity in general. Research on gender in classical antiquity has flourished in the last three decades and, especially for the Greek world, the lot of women has been considered pitiful. They were accorded few, if any, political, legal, and economic rights; they were seen as subject to the man in the household; and even their procreative role was robbed from them. Authors like Aeschylus portrayed them as mere incubators for the male seed, which by itself developed into a child without a mother's contribution. In classical Athens in particular the legal and economic rights of women are considered to have been very limited. Even if they had their own wealth they were not allowed to manage it themselves, and if they worked outside the house they were reduced to tasks that were extensions of their domestic duties (Pomeroy 1975: 73). Although the great restrictions on women's activities may have been more the ideal found in the official rhetoric than in day-to-day practice (Schaps 1979), our contemporary views on Greek society tend to state that the woman's world was the private one, the man's the public one. When scholars look then at the legal and economic roles of Mesopotamian women, they repeat this view, and seek to explain the numerous exceptions as special cases: queens, widows, prostitutes, priestesses, and cloistered upper-class girls (Harris 1989). The "normal" woman could act in the economy only with the authorization of her male superior, the father or husband (Diakonoff 1986: 225). The abundance of material where this was not true, however, indicates that we may have to look at these matters not under the influence of scholarship on classical Athens, but in a context that fits Mesopotamia proper.

My suggestion that the status of Mesopotamian women is seen as a mixture of classical Greek and Islamic customs may seem far-fetched as it combines two such different traditions. But somehow, when women's history is involved, a very atemporal attitude emerges in scholarship, as if a woman's lot is a natural condition. This quote from a recent discussion of the poor treatment of women in Athenian society exemplifies this attitude perfectly:

> It is not easy to come to terms with such attitudes, however common they may be in peasant societies, if only because we idealize the Greeks as the originators of western civilization. But we should remember that (polygamy apart) the position of Athenian women was in most important respects the same as that of the 200,000,000 women who today live under Islam.
>
> (Murray 1991b: 255)

Plus ça change, plus c'est la même chose!

It is thus our task to study gender roles in Mesopotamia within its own cultural context, a task that requires the shedding of pre-conceptions based on the study, or assumptions, made for other societies. This is not easy as the data are fragmentary and need to be made coherent by the scholar. In what follows I will attempt to elucidate the context of some of the economic activity of upper-class women that we can observe in early Mesopotamian history. It is not my intent to demonstrate that their position in society was exalted and evidence of an ideal past where women *did* have power equal to that of men, but to show that the information avail-able can be interpreted outside the frameworks we usually impose upon them. Throughout early Mesopotamian history we observe the existence of households of rulers' wives, which were self-contained and self-sufficient. They demonstrate the participation of women in the economic sphere separate from their husbands and on the same terms, although on a smaller scale. They show that there was no economic division between public and private along male/female gender lines in this period, and that the observed inequality of women is one of scale, not of area of activity. I will illustrate the presence of such households with two well-documented examples from the period of *ca.* 2400 to *ca.* 2000. Traces of others are visible elsewhere and it does seem that these women's households were a standard concept throughout the period, but I will not attempt to describe all the evidence we have for them.

The earliest and best-documented "women's household" is actually the source of the first comprehensive administrative archive we have from Mesopotamia, the so-called Bau-temple archive from Girsu in the early twenty-fourth century. The enormous tablet find at Girsu in the late nineteenth and early twentieth centuries AD, partly through excavation, partly through looting, includes some 1,600 tablets from the end of the early-Dynastic period, when southern Babylonia was politically divided in city-states. The dates of the tablets span a period of about eighteen to twenty years from the reigns of the last three independent city-rulers of the state of Lagash: Enentarzi, Lugalanda, and Uru'inimgina. They belong, however, to an administrative unit called in Sumerian, é-MÍ, the "women's household," referring to the wives of these rulers who were in succession Dimtur, Baranamtara, and Shasha. Due to political changes by the usurper Uru'inimgina the household was renamed "household of (the goddess) Bau," but in practice this did not have an effect on its functioning, and it remained in the charge of the ruler's wife. This renaming has been the focus of scholarly attention as it led to the mistaken concept that early Mesopotamian society was one of temple-cities, and has perhaps diverted attention from the interest of this institution as a major force in the economy under the control of a woman.

The archive documents the existence of a fully functioning and autarkic economic organization, a real household in the context of the *oikos* economy discussed before.[7] It controlled an agricultural area of some 45.83 sq. km., which does not include orchards and reed-beds. The focus of the archive, as preserved, is agricultural activity: fieldwork, canal maintenance, animal husbandry, and fishing. The household took care of all steps involved from sowing to the final milling of the grain to produce bread and beer. It also had a weaving mill where women produced the cloth needed for its dependants, and it had access to traders for external relations and the acquisition of goods it did not produce itself. The documents state explicitly that the wife of the city-ruler was the ultimate authority. Ration lists, for instance, often state that the food was given by her, texts regarding income end with the assertion that the goods were given to her. Moreover, when there was a peaceful change of city-ruler, the incumbent head of the woman's household did not change: when Dimtur's husband Enentarzi died, she remained in charge for a while when her son Lugalanda ruled the city-state. Only later, presumably upon Dimtur's death, Lugalanda's wife, Baranamtara, became the head of the é-MÍ. That this system was not limited to the state of Lagash is demonstrated by the fact that Baranamtara conducted a gift exchange with the wife of the ruler of the city Adab, probably indicating diplomatic relations between these two women.

The perceived autonomy obviously may have been an administrative fiction. When Uru'inimgina usurped the throne of Lagash, he put his wife Shasha in control of the "woman's household," but did not interfere substantially with its functioning. After two years he radically reformed several aspects of his government, including changing his own title from "governor" to "king" and renaming his wife's household as the "temple of the goddess Bau." He terminated the existence of the households of several other royal family members, and transferred their personnel to his wife's household. The Bau-temple became thus very substantial in size as a result of the ruler's actions, who probably also increased his role in its daily functioning (Maekawa 1973–4).

Although we cannot say thus that the household of the ruler's wife was fully independent and in control of its own affairs, the ideal of an autarkic estate for the wife existed. It seems that each family member of the ruling house had such an estate at his or her disposal for their support, the size depending on the importance of the owner. The power relations within the family probably determined the relations between the estates. The ruler himself had the largest organization for his needs, his wife something smaller, and the children probably even smaller estates. When Uru'inimgina restructured this system by naming the estates after gods, he did not need to make any fundamental changes: family relations in the divine sphere paralleled those of the earthly ruling house. The gods Ningirsu, Bau, and Igalima, stood in for the royal family: king, queen, and prince, who remained supported by their estates now considered to be divine. Even if in practice the male head of the family may have had the ultimate say over what happened in these organizations, we see that, ideally at least, the wife had her own support system that encompassed a substantial part of the economic resources of the state.

During the Ur III period, when most of Babylonia was politically unified under a dynasty from Ur, the royal family was very extensive due to the practice of multiple marriages, probably to cement the king's relations with the elites of the leading cities whose daughters he married (Van De Mieroop 1989: 58–62). At this time royal involvement in the economy was very substantial, and the enormous number of documents preserved from this period almost all derive from the palace bureaucracy, which was dependent upon the king. The numerous officials attested often had seals where they declared their loyalty to his person, and the ideology of the state focused upon the, now divine, ruler at its head. Within this highly centralized structure royal wives were able to maintain a position of economic responsibility on their own. There is no longer any evidence of a self-contained estate for their support, but this may be due to the origin of the available texts. The most encompassing economic organization of the state documented in this period deals with the collection and distribution of livestock, provided by all subject regions for the support of the palace and its cults. Tens of thousands of animals went through the system which was created by Shulgi, the king responsible for organizing the Ur III state (Steinkeller 1987b), as the keystone of his centralization policies. It was one of several distribution centers through which the products of the various provinces and subject peripheral regions were exchanged. The livestock center was located by him near Nippur in a place renamed Puzrish-Dagan, but it was not created *ex nihilo*. Previously there had existed a smaller organization under the auspices of a queen, Shulgi-simti, which continued to function when Shulgi's large structure was in place (Sigrist 1992: 222–46; Sallaberger 1993: 18–25). Shulgi-simti's organization collected sheep and goats, cattle, fowl, and pigs from various contributors, who included numerous women: princesses, high courtiers, and the wives of state officials. The latter were identified only as "the wife of so-and-so" (Sigrist 1992: 231–2), which shows their status to be dependent upon their husbands' status, but still they had access to resources on their own to contribute to the queen's organization. The beneficiaries of the institution were the queen herself and a number of cults. Among the latter stands out a cult devoted to two otherwise rarely attested goddesses, Belat-Deraban and Belat-Shuhnir, which seems to have been brought by Shulgi-simti to Ur from her home region, probably in the Diyala area (Sallaberger 1993: 19–20). A succession of officials were in charge of the organization (Sigrist 1992: 226) and while only one of them has certainly a female name, it is possible that several more of them were women (Van De Mieroop 1989: 57). Shulgi-simti died very soon after her husband and this particular archive ceased to function, but later royal wives continued to be committed to certain cults, especially one on the day of the new moon, which was seen as the day the moon disappeared by the Sumerians (Sallaberger 1993: 60–3). This practice shows that women were involved in public economic activity in the Ur III state, even if their role was integrated within the larger system under the control of the king. Their functions were to a certain extent autonomous, and interestingly involved primarily the participation of other women as contributors and perhaps as officials. It seems that the involvement of women in the economy was usually interacting with other women, as if in a world parallel to the one where men worked.

The position of queens as we see it in these two places was thus one where they had access to substantial economic resources. They were not at the mercy of the husbands for their livelihood, but were supported by a system that they themselves, at least nominally, controlled. The households that they headed were public households in that they functioned on the same basis as the king's household. Royal women were involved in public life, parallel to their husbands, perhaps primarily in contact with other women. For several decades it was popular in scholarship to see an opposition of public/private along male/female gender lines. This approach asserted that women were reduced to the domestic, private, sphere in their activities, while men acted in the public sphere and therefore were more visibly engaged in cultural, political, scientific and other developments that define cultures. Only recently has this stark opposition in gender roles come under attack. First, it is too essentialist and simplistic, as it ignores race, ethnicity, class, and wealth, as important elements that determine the women's role in a given society. Second, it has become clear that the public/private dichotomy is a modern Western notion, that reflects historically developed ideas about the interrelations between gender and politics (Peirce 1993: 6–7). Moreover, when the activities of women are studied in more refined ways, it can be determined that they were more active in the public sphere than traditionally thought. (see Helly and Reverby 1992). Also for ancient Mesopotamia, and for the ancient Near East in general, the opposition has been too readily applied in my opinion. It has been customary to see the woman's role as entirely domestic, and to portray exceptions as aberrations. Queens who were prominent figures in their time are discussed with a sense of amazement. In Mari we see the wife of King Zimri-Lim taking care of state matters, including receiving correspondence from vassals, which scholars usually explain as her taking care of business in her husband's absence (Batto 1974: 16). In Assyria queens Sammuramat and Zakutu were able to erect their own inscriptions, so they are thought to have been unusually influential (Seux 1980–83: 161–2). In the Hittite state Queen Puduhepa received correspondence from kings of equal states, such as the Egyptian Ramses II, and from vassals, which is explained as a result of her earlier training as a priestess (Bryce 1998: 315–20). These women were active as public figures and therefore draw our special attention. But by being so amazed we may be like the ancient Greeks and Romans, who were surprised that women could rise to great prominence in the East, and so developed the myth of Semiramis to express their unease with these cultures (Capomacchia 1986). This shows once more that we should be careful not to impose ancient Greek and Roman views of the East onto our study of ancient Mesopotamian gender roles.

Conclusions

> Historians tell of true events in which man is the actor; history is a true novel.
>
> (Veyne 1984: x)

In order to make the past present, historians today looking back at societies of the past attempt to tell a story that their audiences will find interesting and believable. Their work is a creative act, taking observable data and placing them in a context that seems logical to the writer and the reader. Historians are thus at the mercy of two elements they cannot control: the presence of data and the logic of the present. Both critically inform the work that can be done: without data there is no history to write, without a logical context any data, however plentiful, cannot be understood. In both areas historical research constantly develops: the search for data has become ever more wide-ranging, refined, and integrating evidence that was previously ignored. On the one hand, there is no real limit to what could be uncovered as historical data on any period of time. New archives or historical writings might always be found, even for the best-documented moments in history. On the other hand, historians are using new types of information that can yield new insights, such as weather patterns or oral traditions. The contextual frameworks used by historians enable different analyses of primary sources, making their interpretation comprehensible to the contemporary audience. They are often inspired by developments in other intellectual disciplines, such as anthropology, economics, literary criticism, and philosophy, and reflect the concerns and intellectual trends of the period in which the historian works.

The writing of Mesopotamian history in these fundamental respects is no different from writing histories of other periods or places. When compared to the study of other historical periods, especially those of the Western tradition, it is a discipline in the early stages of development. Only since the 1850s have we been able to consult the written documents of its civilization directly, and one of the major tasks of the Near Eastern historian remains the uncovering and primary edition of the sources. This time-consuming task is never-ending. Older excavations and looting of sites in the Middle East have already led to the presence of numerous barely catalogued texts in museum collections around the world. If all excavations ceased today, there would still be enough work of primary study for generations of scholars on the basis of what is currently available. Meanwhile legitimate excavations continue, unfortunately mostly in peripheral areas of Mesopotamia, especially Syria and Turkey, while the Iraqis are able to undertake some in the heartland of Mesopotamia itself. Once the international political situation for Iraq improves, we can expect a return of archaeologists there. Every excavation in Mesopotamia has the potential to yield innumerable new texts. Even if Iraq is off-limits today to foreign archaeologists, the looting of sites is encouraged by the economic conditions there, and Western scholars will continue to examine the information produced by texts thus uncovered. Obviously, when 3,000 years of history are involved, the aggregate amount of material that was produced and potentially survived is immense. The textual material is written in languages that are still difficult to understand, and ancillary sciences such as paleography and lexicography are still relatively underdeveloped. Thus the basic work of making the material known in a format comprehensible to the scholarly community is a major project, whose end is not in sight. Some scholars have concluded that this is the only task presented to the student of Mesopotamia at this point in time, and that any interpretative work on history, literary criticism, and the like, needs to be postponed until more data are known. That is a fallacy, however, as even primary editions provide an interpretation of the texts influenced by the scholar's ideas on the Mesopotamian past. The collection of data already contains an element of classification that needs to conform to logic of the present time, and that fits the scholar's conceptual framework. If anything has been learned from the recent criticisms of scholarly practices in the humanities and social sciences, it is that no aspect of our work is free from bias.

The techniques of analysis available are also constantly becoming more refined. Texts that were taken at face value when first discovered, are now submitted to criticism that potentially yields new insights about their function and increases their value as historical sources. New theoretical approaches such as those inspired by gender or post-colonial studies enable the scholar to utilize long-known sources in new ways, to pry from them information previously ignored. Throughout this book I have excluded evidence other than textual data, except in very peripheral ways, but it is important to point out that numerous other historical sources exist in the archaeological, iconographic, and geographical records of Mesopotamia. Each of these areas entails specific problems of research, some overlapping with interpreting textual remains, others particular to the discipline. The historian needs to remain aware of the developments and interpretations in these areas, often relying on the expertise of the specialists. The disciplines dealing with these other records are becoming ever more developed. For instance, research on geographical features in the rural environment can provide information on agricultural techniques, settlement patterns, roadways, and so on. Such research is undertaken now with the help of satellite photographs, for instance, and involves computer and other technology unheard of ten years ago. All these data somehow can find their way into the historian's work.

Despite this embarrassment of riches, we have to be careful, however. There are indeed many periods of Mesopotamian history where the source material is more abundant than for some periods of European history. For instance, the economy of twenty-first century BC Babylonia is better known than that of tenth-century AD Flanders, and we may know more about Sennacherib of Assyria than about Charlemagne. But in general the record is slim for the long history that is being studied, especially since it fails to talk about so many areas of interest to us. The texts derive from a particular urban background of large institutions and wealthy entrepreneurs. They most often require the reader to be familiar with their context or background, which remains unstated as it was so obvious at their time of composition. They are the result of the accidents of production, preservation, and recovery. As I stated before, innumerable new texts will be uncovered in the future, and the potential that they will document sectors of the society now poorly known is great, yet writing was always an exclusive affair in Mesopotamia, and therefore limited in what it will reveal to us. The sources available to us have been compared to "incidental points of light in a vast, dark room" (Adams 1984: 82), the outline of which is hard to fathom. Thus we have to be aware that as historians the data we rely on for our reconstruction of the past is quite scant. We write history as it has already been written for us by the unequal preservation of traces of the past (Veyne 1984: 17). When data are lacking we cannot make them up to complete a picture that is readily available for another period or place. This does not prevent us from writing history, however.

The second requirement for our writing of history is that we present what we think we know about the past to our audiences in ways that are logical. Most often we weave a narrative that simply seems to make sense of what we have observed about the subject of our inquiry. The historian is thus like a novelist who addresses the reader in terms comprehensible to both. Here lies the greatest danger, however. What seems logical to us is informed by our own vision of the world, a vision that derives from our historical condition. Much of that vision is unconscious, and we often become aware of its limitations only due to external influences. Thus the interest in gender in the historical profession in general was encouraged by socio-political changes in the Western world that forced scholars to acknowledge the androcentric bias of their work. Discourse analysis, the investigation of contemporary political and intellectual influences on scholarship, is now an integral part of many historical disciplines. The writings of the scholars of the past are scrutinized as products of their time and social background. For Mesopotamian scholarship this work has barely begun: the construction of the discipline in the nineteenth century as a by-product of European imperial expansion in the Middle East is still not readily accepted, and most scholars see the early explorers as heroes rather than colonial agents (cf. Bahrani 1998b). Only German scholars of the early twentieth century have been criticized for their political usage of Mesopotamian material, and especially their anti-Semitism. Since that distasteful and regrettable episode in the scholarly history did almost cause the disappearance of Assyriology, it is indeed of value to look at its sources and developments, but it does not excuse us from investigating other influences on the discipline.

It is crucial that we recognize our own biases in the research we undertake. In this book I have tried to point out how the historian of Mesopotamia is influenced by views on the structure of this ancient society which are often derived from those we hold on antiquity or on the Middle East: for instance, views on the classical economy inform Mesopotamian economic history; views on women in Islam bias studies of Mesopotamian women, and so on. These ideas directly influence the analyses of specific problems and questions. But also in broader terms we need to become aware of our general attitude towards our object of study. The position of Mesopotamia in our historical consciousness is complex. On the one hand, many of us see there the roots of the Western civilization to which most scholars of Mesopotamia belong. In a teleological view of world history Mesopotamia lies at the beginning of an evolution that continues till today. Numerous are the books and articles that state that the history of the West starts in the Near East, the "birthplace of civilization" (e.g. Bottéro 1992). While classical Greece is still considered the high point of the ancient world and the place where our political, intellectual, and cultural ideals were born, it is now generally accepted that it did not originate *ex nihilo*, that it was influenced in such areas as science and technology by the earlier cultures of the Near East. This view often presents a justification for the work we do: we are not just looking at a civilization that is interesting for its antiquity, but at one that has contributed to the formation of our own. This teleology of history, while providing a rationale for much of the scholarship on Mesopotamia, is highly problematic: it is ethnocentric, privileging histories that have a presumed connection with the Western tradition (van der Toorn 1995); it employs evolutionary models that are intellectually suspect; and it denies the Middle East its own antiquity (see provisionally Van De Mieroop, forthcoming). Despite its intellectual flaws this attitude is important as it provides a *positive* attitude towards the field of study.

The "birth of the West" idea contrasts then with the second major influence on our perception of Mesopotamia. Mesopotamia is the East, the hostile Other as seen by the two cultures that form the cornerstones of the Western tradition: ancient Greece and Judah. That alterity and hostility were firmly ingrained in the Western mind before Mesopotamian studies originated in the mid-nineteenth century, and although our knowledge has developed to an infinite extent since then, it lingers in our scholarship. We are heirs to the Enlightenment tradition which structured its views of the world with Western man at its center in a period of European control over most of the globe. The otherness of the East in antiquity, which provided the Greeks with a means of self-identification, became part of the Enlightenment image of the structure of the modern world. It became a crucial part of the intellectual and philosophical traditions in which we still work, paradoxically opposed to the idea that the ancient Near East is part of our Western civilization. But such ambivalence is not uncommon in the way people deal with the Other, as post-colonial criticism has pointed out (Bhabha 1994: 66–84). This complex attitude towards our object of study in the end informs all the work we do, even if it is not readily recognized or acknowledged. A more detailed investigation of it remains another book to write.

Notes

INTRODUCTION

1 Among the recent works in the English language, I recommend Kuhrt (1995) or Hallo and Simpson (1998) for detail, Nissen (1995) and Charpin (1995) for handy reference.

1 THE FIRST HALF OF HISTORY

1 I owe this title to Hallo (1990).

2 Powell (1981). For a different opinion, see Walker (1987: 7–9).

3 For a concise description, see Walker (1987: 7–21).

4 The earliest preserved text, a treaty between two cities in the Diyala region, Nerebtum and Shadlash, dating to the nineteenth century is still not fully understood (Greengus 1979: no. 326).

5 See Renger (1996: 15–16) for references in Sumerian and early Babylonian texts, pp. 19–20 for references in Assyrian and neo-Babylonian texts.

6 For instance, the humorous tale "Why do you curse me?", see Foster (1993: 835–6).

7 For a translation, see Katz (1993).

2 HISTORY FROM ABOVE

1 Quoted here is the 1929 edition, slightly revised from the original 1926 text.

2 Unfortunately she uses the term "national image" which has all sorts of anachronistic connotations of nationhood and nationality, which are modern terms rather than ancient concepts (cf. Liverani 1992: 1031).

3 He is not entirely convinced by Parpola's argument.

4 The Medes must have felt a bond with the Elamites who had ruled the south-western corner of Iran.

5 A number of terms to indicate this dynasty are in use: Akkad, Old Akkadian, or Sargonic. Their capital city is called Agade, Akkade, or Akkad, the region around it also Akkad.

6 For Sargon's inscriptions in this work, and for all texts in J. Westenholz (1997), I will refer to the text number in the edition rather than to the exact page numbers.

7 I doubt that J. Westenholz's statement about a possible cedar forest in the east (1997: 94) is correct.

8 The Hittite version Nur-dahhi could be explained as a misreading of Da-gan as Da-hé.

9 The date of composition of both chronicles is unfortunately hard to establish. Only one neo-Assyrian manuscript is known of the so-called Weidner Chronicle (Grayson 1975b: 145, manuscript A), and its exact date is unclear. All other manuscripts are of neo-Babylonian origin or even later date. The connection between Sargon II's building activities and the composition of the chronicles is thus uncertain, but I believe it to present a likely explanation for the appearance of a negative element in the stories on Sargon of Agade. That such negative image did not exist prior to the first millennium is indeed based on an argument from silence, but the second-millennium literature on Sargon is extensive enough to make this a likely assumption.

10 The rest of the text is very fragmentary.

11 That story and plot are not the same in historical narrative, has been convincingly argued by Hayden White (1972).

3 HISTORY FROM BELOW

1 See Snell (1997: 145–58) who seems to lament this situation, but then continues to focus almost entirely upon economic exchange.

2 I follow here Steinkeller's classification (1987a: 78–9).

3 The following discussion is based on Stolper (1985), with additions in Donbaz and Stolper (1997).

4 Van Driel (1987, 1989) in particular has objected to Stolper's interpretation of events, adopted here.

4 ECONOMIC HISTORY

1 For a critique based on Mesopotamian material, see Komoroczy (1978).

2 The references to his work known to me are few. *Agrarian Sociology* appears in the bibliography of Butz (1980–83: 471), but has not influenced the contents of that article. Snell (1997: 148) refers to the same work, without going into detail. Weber's work *The City* (1958) was misunderstood and thus rejected by Gelb (1979: 4). Proper use of his work, without actual reference to his own writings, however, seems to have been made only in very recent years. Renger (1989, 1994) mentions Weber primarily as an inspiration to Polanyi. Michalowski (1987) uses his models when discussing bureaucracy.

3 One iku measures approximately 3,600 sq. m.

4 Note that the editor dates the text to the year Ibbi-Sin 5, but the damaged year name can also be read as Shulgi 30, which would place the text in the same period as the other surveys, and among the

bulk of illicitly excavated tablets to which it belongs. This redating was communicated to me by K. Maekawa during a lecture in March 1996.

5 For the problems of translation here, see below.

6 I base my information here on the maps in Zarins (1992: 58–9), and de Maaijer (1997: 54). The latter has a very detailed map of the Lagash area, which unfortunately lacks a scale.

7 Their date is Shulgi year 9, according to Civil (1994: 200). This is impossible as it would extend the career of the surveyor, Inim-Shara, over more than thirty-five years, at which point he became governor of Girsu (communication K. Maekawa).

8 Both texts seem to have duplicates, which indicates that these records were produced in several copies: for Truro an unpublished duplicate was reported in the British Museum (BM 23583; Maekawa 1986a: 114), while the remains of a fragmentary text published by Maekawa (1986b: 346–7) correspond almost exactly to entries found in BM 14615 (Civil 1994: 200).

9 The translations used here are those suggested by Pettinato (1977: 82–90), except for his idea that sù means "fallow." If this were correct we would have to conclude that all other areas were under cultivation, which would be entirely too large a percentage of the available land. Therefore, I use his earlier translation of "uncultivated."

10 Another of such texts from the year Shulgi 36, unfortunately very fragmentary, is Gomi (1982: no. 883) (reference courtesy of K. Maekawa).

11 Again we are confronted here with mistakes in the calculations that we cannot explain.

12 I translate še dusu here as "grain from *ilkum*," i.e. delivery of part of the yield of land held from a higher authority (Oppenheim *et al.* 1956– : I/J, 73).

13 That this grain was the income of all temple households of the Lagash province, is demonstrated by a summary account of the same year (King 1900: pls. 18–19; reference courtesy of K. Maekawa).

14 Each receiving an average ration of 1.5 liters a day.

5 GENDER AND MESOPOTAMIAN HISTORY

1 See Roth (1995: 195–209) for the latest translation of these texts. Note that she is careful to place the term "harem" in parentheses, and to refer to the texts as palace decrees.

2 As is acknowledged by the translator in the parallel passage in these edicts on p. 200. The Akkadian verb used, *murruru*, means "to check," and is only translated as "to castrate" in these edicts, cf. Oppenheim *et al.* 1956– : 223. The editor of the *Chicago Assyrian Dictionary* at the time that volume was published asserted elsewhere in a footnote that the Akkadian term "to check" was a euphemism for "to castrate" (Oppenheim 1973: 330, n. 17). He assumed thus that our discomfort with this practice was shared by the Mesopotamians.

3 Again it has to be assumed that the Akkadian term for "attendant" used here, *mazziz pani* (cf. Oppenheim *et al.* 1956– : 440–41), is a substitute for the term *ša rēši* which at times, but not always, means "eunuch" (Oppenheim 1973: 330–1).

4 Akkadian *naglabu* is translated as "shoulder blade, scapula" in Oppenheim *et al.* 1956– : 119–20) based on a sequence of anatomical terms found in a lexical list. Von Soden (1965– : 711) translates "hip" instead. "To bare" is an interpretation of the common verb "to open" (*petû*, ibid.: 861); the translation "to bare" is only used here and in editions of the Middle Assyrian laws.

5 The verb *puṣṣunu* and the derived adjective *puṣṣunu* (ibid.: 840) appear outside these laws in two unclear Middle Assyrian passages, where the translation "to veil" would be highly problematic.

6 For a detailed survey of the scholarship on this question, see Wilhelm (1990).

7 Unfortunately we still have to rely on the earliest descriptions, Deimel (1931) and Schneider (1920), for a comprehensive overview of this organization despite substantial progress in the understanding of individual texts and problems.

Annotated Bibliography

1 THE FIRST HALF OF HISTORY

Surveys of the available cuneiform materials are outdated, but Chiera (1938) is still of value. A nice introduction to the cuneiform writing system, the various languages recorded in it, and document formats, is provided in Walker (1987).

2 HISTORY FROM ABOVE

The number of books and articles dealing with royal inscriptions in general is enormous. Publications and translations of these texts dominated the field of Mesopotamian studies in its early decades. For Assyria, the two-volume collection of translations by Daniel David Luckenbill, *Ancient Records of Assyria and Babylonia*, University of Chicago Press, volume I, 1926, volume II, 1927, presents a capping stone of that work. Babylonian and Sumerian inscriptions never were presented in a similar fashion in translation only. A series entitled *Vorderasiatische Bibliothek* initiated in Leipzig in 1907 intended to make every text of relevance to the history of the (Asiatic) ancient Near East available in transliteration and German translation, and had an ambitious schedule including all Sumerian, Babylonian and Assyrian royal inscriptions. The project seems to have been terminated due to the First World War, and only the contributions on Sumerian–Akkadian (Thureau-Dangin 1907), Achaemenid (Weissbach 1911), and Neo-Babylonian (Langdon 1912) royal inscriptions, as well as an edition of all Assurbanipal texts (Streck 1916) were completed.

After this initial period only individual texts or isolated volumes of royal inscriptions were published. This changed in the 1970s when several projects of edition and/or translation were initiated, probably due to the abundance of research funding at that time. Most elaborate is a project at the University of Toronto, *The Royal Inscriptions of Mesopotamia*, that intends to re-edit all inscriptions from the earliest Sumerian to the late Babylonian ones. The volumes published so far cover Sumerian and Akkadian texts from *ca.* 2350 to 1595 (Edzard 1997; Frayne 1990, 1993, 1997), Assyrian texts from the early second millennium to 745 (Grayson 1987, 1991b, 1996), and Babylonian texts from 1157 to 612 (Frame 1995). The large corpora of texts of the late Assyrian kings remain thus to be edited. Recent individual monographs have dealt with some or all inscriptions of most of these kings, however: Tiglath-Pileser III (Tadmor 1994), Sargon (Fuchs 1993), Sennacherib (Frahm 1997), and Assurbanipal (Borger 1996). A project at the University of Freiburg has re-edited all Sumerian and Akkadian inscriptions of the third millennium (Gelb and Kienast 1990; Steible 1982, 1991).

For the study of these inscriptions the work of A. T. Olmstead, *Assyrian Historiography: A Source Study*, Columbia, Missouri, 1916 presents a milestone. In the 1970s–1980s they became a concern again, with important conferences in Toronto (cf. Grayson 1980), Jerusalem (cf. Tadmor and Weinfeld (eds) 1983), and Cetona, Italy (cf. Fales (ed.) 1981), and a string of articles by various scholars.

A recent review of the political history of the Old Akkadian period can be found in Kuhrt (1995: 44–55). The traditions regarding the rulers of this period were first studied by Hans G. Güterbock, "Die historische Tradition und ihre literarische Gestaltung bei Babyloniern und Hethitern," *Zeitschrift für Assyriologie* 42 (1934): 1–91; 44 (1938): 45–149. The recent studies by Glassner (1986) and in Mario Liverani (ed.), *Akkad: The First World Empire*, Padua: Sargon srl, 1993, contain theoretically informed re-evaluations of those traditions. Easily accessible is Sabina Franke, "Kings of Akkad: Sargon and Naram-Sin," in Sasson (ed.) (1995: 831–41).

For the communication of political messages to Mesopotamian audiences, see Mario Liverani, "The Deeds of Ancient Mesopotamian Kings," in Sasson (ed.) (1995: 2353–66).

3   HISTORY FROM BELOW

Evidence for the lives of Mesopotamian commoners can be found primarily in economic documents of the large institutions, which will be discussed in the bibliography of Chapter 4. The numerous letters from Mesopotamia are often published in editions that concentrate on their philological aspects, which even if presented with a translation, are often opaque. A nice selection of letters from all periods in a fluent English translation is provided by A. Leo Oppenheim, *Letters from Mesopotamia*, Chicago and London: University of Chicago Press, 1967.

The large collections of letters from Kanesh are available in dispersed publications only, e.g. Emin Bilgic, *Ankaraner Kultepe-Texte* III, *Texte der Grabungskampagne 1970*, Stuttgart: F. Steiner Verlag, 1995. A major research project in Leiden has edited and translated into German or English a large number of Old Babylonian letters, published in the series *Altbabylonische Briefe in Umschrift und Übersetzung* (13 volumes). In the Old Babylonian palace at Mari in Syria a very large number of letters have been found, primarily published, with a French translation, in the series *Archives royales de Mari* (27 volumes). A selection is provided in a recent French re-translation by Jean-Marie Durand, *Les Documents épistolaires du palais de Mari*, Paris: Éditions du Cerf, 1997. Neo-Assyrian palace correspondence from Nineveh is being republished in the series *State Archives of Assyria*, edited in Helsinki. Three volumes of letters have appeared so far. Letters from other periods are available in smaller quantities only or in older publications.

4   ECONOMIC HISTORY

Although no economic history of ancient Mesopotamia has ever been written, the theoretically oriented writings on the subject matter have become numerous, especially in recent decades. The discussions by I. M. Diakonoff, which go back to the 1940s, are crucial. Important contributions in English include, 1969; 1982; 1991: 27–66. Mario Liverani also has addressed the subject in the last three decades (e.g., 1976; 1984). The series of articles by Johannes Renger has increased the awareness of the need to see the Mesopotamian economy as fundamentally different from our own (e.g., 1984, 1988, 1989, 1994, 1995). The new book by

Daniel Snell (1997) provides an impressive collection of data on research in social and economic history.

Few comprehensive studies of agricultural practices in Mesopotamia are available. For Ur III Lagash the numerous articles by K. Maekawa are crucial. The journal *Bulletin on Sumerian Agriculture* (1984–95) has dealt with several aspects of agriculture in the various periods of Mesopotamian history.

The innumerable documents that can be used for the study of the Mesopotamian economy are mostly published in a format only accessible to Assyriologists. Most commonly, texts are rendered in a hand-drawn copy of the original cuneiform tablet, without a transliteration or translation. Publication series of all major tablet collections use this format, including *Cuneiform Texts from Babylonian Tablets in the British Museum* (58 volumes), *Musée du Louvre. Département des antiquités orientales. Textes cunéiformes* (31 volumes), *Yale Oriental Series: Babylonian Texts* (18 volumes), *Babylonian Inscriptions in the Collection of James B. Nies, Yale University* (10 volumes), *Texts in the Iraq Museum* (11 volumes), and others. Many of the excavation projects have their publication series of excavated texts (e.g. *Ur Excavations: Texts*, 9 volumes), and numerous articles of selected materials presented in similar fashion exist (e.g. in such periodicals as *Journal of Cuneiform Studies*). Many of the above listed publications also include non-economic texts published in hand-copies only. New technology will probably make this format of publication obsolete in the near future as scanning by computer is becoming less expensive. To the layman the simple rendering of an original cuneiform tablet is obviously uninformative, but it remains the fastest way of making large collections accessible to the scholar. There are few recent publications that attempt to translate large groups of economic documents and contracts. An early attempt at translating all Old Babylonian texts of this type is Kohler and Ungnad (1909–23). For neo-Assyrian imperial archival texts, see Fales and Postgate (1992 and 1995). Entire archives are sometimes published in transliteration and translation, e.g. Postgate (1988).

5 GENDER AND MESOPOTAMIAN HISTORY

For some representative examples of studies seeking to document the presence of women in particular historical periods, see Hallo (1976), Kramer (1976), Asher-Greve (1985), Durand (ed.)

(1987b), Cameron and Kuhrt (eds) (1983), Lesko (ed.) (1989). Most recent is Stol (1995b), who is preparing a book on the subject. A good critique of the preconceptions used in this type of scholarship can be found in J. Westenholz (1990). A recent programmatic statement, with abundant bibliography, is provided in Julia Asher-Greve, "Feminist Research and Ancient Mesopotamia: Problems and Prospects," in A. Brenner and C. Fontaine (eds) *A Feminist Companion to Reading the Bible*, Sheffield: Academic Press, 1997: 218–37. For a discussion of activities of queens in the Sumerian economy, see Van De Mieroop (1989).

Bibliography

Adams, Robert McC. (1984) "Mesopotamian Social Evolution: Old Outlooks, New Goals," in T. Earle (ed.) *On the Evolution of Complex Societies: Essays in Honor of Harry Hoijer 1982*, Malibu: Undena Publications: 79–129.

Al-Azmeh, Aziz (1981) *Ibn Khaldun in Modern Scholarship: A Study in Orientalism*, London: Third World Centre for Research and Publishing.

Al-Jadir, Walid (1987) "Une bibliothèque et ses tablettes," *Archéologia* 224: 127.

Alloula, Malek (1986) *The Colonial Harem*, Minneapolis: University of Minnesota Press.

Anderson, Perry (1974) *Lineages of the Absolutist State*, London: NLB.

Asher-Greve, J. M. (1985) *Frauen in altsumerischer Zeit*, Malibu: Undena Publications.

—— (1997a) "The Essential Body: Mesopotamian Conceptions of the Gendered Body," *Gender and History* 9: 432–61.

—— (1997b) "Feminist Research and Ancient Mesopotamia: Problems and Prospects," in A. Brenner and C. Fontaine (eds) *A Feminist Companion to Reading the Bible*, Sheffield: Academic Press: 218–37.

Astour, Michael C. (1992) "The Date of the Destruction of Palace G at Ebla," in M. W. Chavalas and J. L. Hayes (eds) *New Horizons in the Study of Ancient Syria*, Malibu: Undena Publications: 23–39.

Austin, M. M. and Vidal-Naquet, P. (1977) *Economic and Social History of Ancient Greece: An Introduction*, Berkeley and Los Angeles: University of California Press.

Bahrani, Zainab (1995) "Assault and Abduction: The Fate of the Royal Image in the Ancient Near East," *Art History* 18: 363–82.

—— (1998a) "Conjuring Mesopotamia: Imaginative Geography and a World Past," in L. Meskell (ed.) *Archaeology Under Fire*, London: Routledge: 159–74.

—— (1998b) "Review of M. T. Larsen, *The Conquest of Assyria*, London and New York, Routledge, 1996," *Journal of the American Oriental Society* 118: (in press).

Barnes, Harry Elmer (1963) *A History of Historical Writing*, 2nd edition, New York: Dover Publications.

Barré, Michael L. (1992) "Treaties in the ANE," in D. N. Freedman (ed.) *The Anchor Bible Dictionary*, vol. 6, New York: Doubleday: 653–6.

Barthes, Roland (1981) "The Discourse of History," in E. S. Shaffer (ed.) *Comparative Criticism: A Yearbook* 3, Cambridge: Cambridge University Press: 3–20.

—— (1988) *The Semiotic Challenge*, New York: Hill and Wang.

Batto, Bernard (1974) *Studies on Women at Mari*, Baltimore and London: Johns Hopkins University Press.

Beard, Mary and Henderson, John (1997) "With This Body I Thee Worship: Sacred Prostitution in Antiquity," *Gender and History* 9: 480–503.

Beckman, Gary M. (1996) *Hittite Diplomatic Texts*, Atlanta: Scholars Press.

Bhabha, Homi (1994) *The Location of Culture*, London and New York: Routledge.

Bilgic, Emin (1995) *Ankaraner Kultepe-Texte* III, *Texte der Grabungskampagne 1970*, Stuttgart: F. Steiner Verlag.

Birot, Maurice (1980) "Fragment de rituel de Mari rélatif au *kispum*," in B. Alster (ed.) *Death in Mesopotamia*, Copenhagen: Akademisk Forlag: 139–50.

Boone, Elizabeth Hill (1994) "Aztec Pictorial Histories: Records without Words," in E. H. Boone and W. D. Mignolo (eds) *Writing without Words*, Durham and London: Duke University Press: 50–74.

Borger, Riekele (1956) *Die Inschriften Asarhaddons Königs von Assyrien*, Archiv für Orientforschung, Beiheft 9, Graz.

—— (1979) *Babylonisch-Assyrische Lesestücke* I, 2nd edition, Rome: Pontificium Institutum Biblicum.

—— (1996) *Beiträge zum Inschriftenwerk Assurbanipals: die Prismenklassen A, B, C = K, D, E, F, G, H, J und T sowie andere Inschriften*, Wiesbaden: Harrassowitz Verlag.

Bottéro, Jean (1992) *Mesopotamia: Writing, Reasoning, and the Gods*, trans. Z. Bahrani and M. Van De Mieroop, Chicago and London: University of Chicago Press.

Briant, Pierre (1996) *Histoire de l'empire perse*, Paris: Fayard.

Brinkman, J. A. (1976) *Materials and Studies for Kassite History* vol. I, Chicago: The Oriental Institute of the University of Chicago.

Brinkman, J. A. and Kennedy, D. A. (1983) "Documentary Evidence for the Economic Base of Early Neo-Babylonian Society: A Survey of Dated Babylonian Economic Texts, 721–626 B.C.," *Journal of Cuneiform Studies* 35: 1–90.

Bryce, Trevor (1998) *The Kingdom of the Hittites*, Oxford: Oxford University Press.

Buccellati, Giorgio (1993) "Through a Tablet Darkly. A Reconstruction of Old Akkadian Monuments Described in Old Babylonian Copies," in M. E. Cohen, D. C. Snell and D. B. Weisberg (eds) *The Tablet and the Scroll: Near Eastern Studies in Honor of William W. Hallo*, Bethesda: CDL Press: 58–71.

Bücher, Karl (1906) *Die Entstehung der Volkswirtschaft*, Tübingen: H. Lauppsche Buchhandlung.

Butz, K. (1980–83) "Landwirtschaft," *Reallexikon der Assyriologie* 6, Berlin and New York: Walter de Gruyter: 470–86.

Cagni, Luigi (1977) *The Poem of Erra*, Malibu: Undena Publications.

Cameron, Averil and Kuhrt, Amélie (eds) (1983) *Images of Women in Antiquity*, Detroit: Wayne State University Press.

Capomacchia, Anna Maria G. (1986) *Semiramis: una femminilita ribaltata*, Rome: "L'Erma" di Bretschneider.

Carter, Elizabeth and Stolper, Matthew W. (1984) *Elam: Surveys of Political History and Archaeology*, Berkeley: University of California Press.

Charpin, Dominique (1986) "Transmission des titres de propriété et constitution des archives privées en Babylonie ancienne," in K. Veenhof (ed.) *Cuneiform Archives and Libraries*, Istanbul: Nederlands Historisch-Archaeologisch Instituut: 121–40.

—— (1990) "Une alliance contre l'Elam et le rituel du *lipit napištim*," in F. Vallat (ed.) *Contribution à l'histoire de l'Iran*, Paris: Éditions Recherche sur les Civilisations: 109–18.

—— (1991) "Un traité entre Zimri-Lim de Mari et Ibâl-pî-El II d'Eshnunna," in D. Charpin and F. Joannès (eds) *Marchands, Diplomates et Empereurs*, Paris: Éditions Recherche sur les Civilisations: 139–66.

—— (1995) "The History of Ancient Mesopotamia: An Overview," in Jack M. Sasson (ed.) *Civilizations of the Ancient Near East*, New York: Charles Scribner's Sons: 807–29.

Charpin, Dominique *et al.* (1988) *Archives épistolaires de Mari* I/2 (Archives royales de Mari XXVI), Paris: Éditions Recherche sur les Civilisations.

Chiera, Edward (1938) *They Wrote on Clay*, Chicago: University of Chicago Press.

Cifarelli, Megan (1998) "Gesture and Alterity in the Art of Ashurnasirpal II of Assyria," *The Art Bulletin* 80: 210–28.

Civil, Miguel (1980) "Les limites de l'information textuelle," in M.-T. Barrelet (ed.) *L'archéologie de l'Iraq du début de l'époque néolithique à 333 avant notre ère*, Paris: Éditions du CNRS: 225–32.

—— (1994) *The Farmer's Instructions: A Sumerian Agricultural Manual*, Barcelona: Editorial AUSA.

Clay, A. T. (1915) *Miscellaneous Inscriptions in the Yale Babylonian Collection*, New Haven: Yale University Press.

—— (1923) *Epics, Hymns, Omens, and Other Texts*, New Haven: Yale University Press.

—— (1927) *Letters and Transactions from Cappadocia*, New Haven: Yale University Press.

Cook, Scott (1968) "The Obsolete 'Anti-Market' Mentality," in E. E. Leclair and H. Schneider (eds) *Economic Anthropology: Readings in Theory and Analysis*, New York: Holt, Rinehart and Winston, Inc.: 208–28.

Cooper, Jerrold (1980) "Apodotic Death and the Historicity of 'Historical' Omens," in B. Alster (ed.) *Death in Mesopotamia*, Copenhagen: Akademisk Forlag: 99–105.

—— (1983) *The Curse of Agade*, Baltimore and London: Johns Hopkins University Press.

—— (1986) *Sumerian and Akkadian Royal Inscriptions, I. Presargonic Inscriptions*, New Haven: The American Oriental Society.

Cooper, Jerrold S. and Heimpel, Wolfgang (1983) "The Sumerian Sargon Legend," *Journal of the American Oriental Society* 103: 67–82.

Croce, Benedetto (1960) *History: Its Theory and Practice*, trans. D. Ainslie, New York: Russell & Russell.

Dalley, Stephanie (1989) *Myths from Mesopotamia*, Oxford and New York: Oxford University Press.

—— (1995) "Review of Foster 1993," *Bibliotheca Orientalis* 52: 83–7.

Damrosch, David (1987) *The Narrative Covenant*, San Francisco: Harper & Row.

Deimel, Anton (1931) *Sumerische Tempelwirtschaft zur Zeit Urukaginas und seiner Vorgänger*, Rome: Pontificio Instituto Biblico.

de Maaijer, R. (1997) "Land Tenure in Ur III Lagash," in B. Haring and R. de Maaijer (eds) *Landless and Hungry? Access to Land in Early and Traditional Societies*, Leiden: Research School (NWS School of Asian, African and Amerindian Studies): 43–61.

de Ste Croix, G. E. M. (1975) "Karl Marx and Classical Antiquity," *Arethusa* 8: 7–41.

—— (1981) *The Class Struggle in the Ancient Greek World*, London: Duckworth.

Diakonoff, Igor M. (ed.) (1969) *Ancient Mesopotamia*, Moscow: Nauka House.

—— (1971) "On the Structure of Old Babylonian Society," in H. Klengel (ed.) *Beiträge zur sozialen Struktur des alten Vorderasien*, Berlin: Akademie Verlag: 15–31.

—— (1982) "The Structure of Near Eastern Society Before the Middle of the 2nd Millennium BC," *Oekumene* (Budapest) 3: 7–100.

—— (1986) "Women in Old Babylonia Not Under Patriarchal Authority," *Journal of the Economic and Social History of the Orient* 29: 225–38.

—— (1991) *Early Antiquity*, Chicago and London: University of Chicago Press.

Donbaz, Veysel and Stolper, Matthew W. (1997) *Istanbul Murashû Texts*, Istanbul: Nederlands Historisch-Archaeologisch Instituut te Istanbul.

Dossin, G. (1950) *Correspondence de Šamši-Addu*, Paris: Imprimerie Nationale.

Durand, Jean-Marie (1986) "Fragments rejoints pour une histoire élamite," in L. de Meyer, H. Gasche, and F. Vallat (eds) *Fragmenta Historiae Elamicae*, Paris: Éditions Recherche sur les Civilisations: 111–28.

—— (1987a) "L'organisation de l'espace dans le palais de Mari: le témoignage des textes," in E. Lévy (ed.) *Le système palatial en orient, en Grèce et à Rome*, Leiden: E. J. Brill: 39–110.

—— (ed.) (1987b) *La femme dans le Proche-Orient antique: XXXIIIe Rencontre Assyriologique Internationale*, Paris: Éditions Recherche sur les Civilisations.

—— (1997) *Les Documents épistolaires du palais de Mari*, Paris: Éditions du Cerf.

Edzard, D. O. (1976–80) "Irra (Erra)-Epos," *Reallexikon der Assyriologie* 5, Berlin and New York: Walter de Gruyter: 166–70.

—— (1980–83a) "Königsinschriften. A. Sumerisch," *Reallexikon der Assyriologie* 6, Berlin and New York: Walter de Gruyter: 59–65.

—— (1980–83b) "Königslisten und Chroniken. A. Sumerisch," *Reallexikon der Assyriologie* 6, Berlin and New York: Walter de Gruyter: 77–86.

—— (1985) "Amarna und die Archive seiner Korrespondenten zwischen Ugarit und Gaza," *Biblical Archaeology Today*, Jerusalem: Israel Exploration Society: 248–59.

—— (1992) "Der Vertrag von Ebla mit A-bar-QA," in P. Fronzaroli (ed.) *Literature and Literary Language at Ebla*, Firenze: Instituto di linguistica e di lingue orientali, Università di Firenze: 187–217.

—— (1997) *Gudea and his Dynasty* (The Royal Inscriptions of Mesopotamia. Early Periods, vol. 3/1), Toronto, Buffalo, New York: University of Toronto Press.

Eidem, Jesper (1991) "An Old Assyrian Treaty from Tell Leilan," in D. Charpin and F. Joannès (eds) *Marchands, Diplomates et Empereurs*, Paris: Éditions Recherche sur les Civilisations: 185–207.

Engels, Friedrich (1884) *The Origin of the Family, Private Property and the State*, in R. C. Tucker (ed.) *The Marx–Engels Reader*, 2nd edition, New York: W. W. Norton, 1978: 734–59.

Fales, F. M. (ed.) (1981) *Assyrian Royal Inscriptions: New Horizons*, Rome, Instituto per l'Oriente.

—— (1987) "The Enemy in Assyrian Royal Inscriptions: The Moral Judgement," in H. J. Nissen and J. Renger (eds) *Mesopotamien und seine Nachbarn*, 2nd edition, Berlin: Dietrich Reimer Verlag: 425–35.

Fales, F. M. and Postgate, J. N. (1992) *Imperial Administrative Records*, Part I (State Archives of Assyria, vol. VII), Helsinki: Helsinki University Press.

—— (1995) *Imperial Administrative Records*, Part II (State Archives of Assyria, vol. XI), Helsinki: Helsinki University Press.

Finkelstein, J. J. (1963) "Mesopotamian Historiography," *Proceedings of the American Philosophical Society* 107: 461–72.

Finley, M. I. (1981) "Politics," in M. I. Finley (ed.) *The Legacy of Greece: A New Appraisal*, Oxford: Clarendon Press: 22–36.

—— (1985) *The Ancient Economy*, 2nd edition, Berkeley and Los Angeles: University of California Press.

Foster, Benjamin R. (1993) *Before the Muses: An Anthology of Akkadian Literature*, Bethesda: CDL Press.

Frahm, Eckart (1997) *Einleitung in die Sanherib-Inschriften*, Horn: Institut für Orientalistik der Universität Wien.

Frame, Grant (1995) *Rulers of Babylonia from the Second Dynasty of Isin to the End of the Assyrian Domination (1157–612 BC)* (The Royal Inscriptions of Mesopotamia. Babylonian Periods, vol. 2), Toronto, Buffalo, London: University of Toronto Press.

Frank, Sabina (1995) "Kings of Akkad: Sargon and Naram-Sin," in Jack M. Sasson (ed.) *Civilizations of the Ancient Near East*, New York: Charles Scribner's Sons: 831–41.

Frayne, Douglas R. (1990) *The Old Babylonian Period (2003–1595 BC)* (The Royal Inscriptions of Mesopotamia. Early Periods, vol. 4), Toronto, Buffalo, New York: University of Toronto Press.

—— (1993) *Sargonic and Gutian Period (2334–2113 BC)* (The Royal Inscriptions of Mesopotamia. Early Periods, vol. 2), Toronto, Buffalo, New York: University of Toronto Press.

—— (1997) *Ur III Period (2112–2004 BC)* (The Royal Inscriptions of Mesopotamia. Early Periods, vol. 3/2), Toronto, Buffalo, New York: University of Toronto Press.

Freedberg, David (1989) *The Power of Images: Studies in the History and Theory of Response*, Chicago: University of Chicago Press.

Frymer-Kensky, Tikva (1992) *In the Wake of the Goddesses*, New York: The Free Press.

Fuchs, Andreas (1993) *Die Inschriften Sargons II. aus Khorsabad*, Göttingen: Cuvillier Verlag.

Gadd, C. J. (1971) "The Dynasty of Agade and the Gutian Invasion," *The Cambridge Ancient History*, 3rd edn, vol. I/2, Cambridge: Cambridge University Press: 417–63.

Garelli, Paul (1969) *Le proche-orient asiatique. Des origines aux invasions des peuples de la mer*, Paris: Presses Universitaires de France.

Gasche, H. (1989) *La Babylonie au 17ᵉ siècle avant notre ère*, Ghent: University of Ghent.

Gelb, I. J. (1952) *A Study of Writing: The Foundations of Grammatology*, Chicago: University of Chicago Press.

—— (1965) "The Ancient Mesopotamian Ration System," *Journal of Near Eastern Studies*, 24: 230–43.

—— (1971) "On the Alleged Temple and State Economies in Ancient Mesopotamia," *Studi in onore di Edoardo Volterra* VI, Milan: 137–54.

—— (1979) "Household and Family in Early Mesopotamia," in E. Lipinski (ed.) *State and Temple Economy in the Ancient Near East*, Louvain: Departement Orientalistiek: 1–97.

—— (1986) "Ebla and Lagash: Environmental Contrasts," in H. Weiss (ed.) *The Origins of Cities in Dry-Farming Syria and Mesopotamia in the Third Millennium B. C.*, Guilford: Four Quarters Publishing Co.:157–67.

Gelb, I. J. and Kienast B. (1990) *Die altakkadischen Königsinschriften des Dritten Jahrtausends v. Chr.*, Stuttgart: Franz Steiner Verlag.

Gelb, I. J., Steinkeller, P. and Whiting, R. (1991) *Earliest Land Tenure Systems in the Near East*, Chicago: The Oriental Institute of the University of Chicago.

Gibson, McGuire (1972) *The City and Area of Kish*, Coconut Grove, Miami: Field Research Publication.

Glassner, Jean-Jacques (1985) "Sargon 'Roi du combat'," *Revue d'assyriologie* 79: 115–26.

—— (1986) *La chute d'Akkadé. L'événement et sa mémoire*, Berlin: Dietrich Reimer Verlag.

—— (1993) *Chroniques mésopotamiennes*, Paris: Les belles Lettres.

Gledhill, John and Larsen, Mogens (1982) "The Polanyi Paradigm and a Dynamic Analysis of Archaic States," in C. Renfrew, M. J. Rowlands, and B. A. Segraves (eds) *Theory and Explanation in Archaeology: The Southampton Conference*, New York: Academic Press: 197–229.

Goetze, Albrecht (1947a) "Historical Allusions in Old Babylonian Omen Texts," *Journal of Cuneiform Studies* 1: 253–66.

—— (1947b) *Old Babylonian Omen Texts*, New Haven and London: Yale University Press.

Gomi, Tohru (1982) *Wirtschaftstexte der Ur III-Zeit aus dem British Museum*

(Materiali per il Vocabolario Neosumerico, vol. XII), Rome: Multigrafica Editrice.

Grayson, A. K. (1965) "Problematic Battles in Mesopotamian History," *Studies in Honor of Benno Landsberger* (Oriental Institute Publications 16), Chicago: University of Chicago Press: 337–42.

——— (1974–77) "The Empire of Sargon of Akkad," *Archiv für Orientforschung* 25: 56–64.

——— (1975a) *Babylonian Historical-Literary Texts*, Toronto and Buffalo: University of Toronto Press.

——— (1975b) *Assyrian and Babylonian Chronicles*, Locust Valley, New York: J. J. Augustin Publisher.

——— (1980) "Assyria and Babylonia," *Orientalia* 49: 140–94.

——— (1980–83) "Königslisten und Chroniken. B. Akkadisch," *Reallexikon der Assyriologie* 6, Berlin and New York: Walter de Gruyter: 86–135.

——— (1987) *Assyrian Rulers of the Third and Second Millennia BC* (The Royal Inscriptions of Mesopotamia. Assyrian Periods, vol. 1), Toronto, Buffalo, London: University of Toronto Press.

——— (1991a) "Assyria: Sennacherib and Esarhaddon (704–669 B.C.)," *The Cambridge Ancient History* 2nd edn, vol. III/2, Cambridge: Cambridge University Press: 103–41.

——— (1991b) *Assyrian Rulers of the Early First Millennium BC* I (The Royal Inscriptions of Mesopotamia. Assyrian Periods, vol. 2), Toronto, Buffalo, London: University of Toronto Press.

——— (1996) *Assyrian Rulers of the Early First Millennium BC* II (The Royal Inscriptions of Mesopotamia. Assyrian Periods, vol. 3), Toronto, Buffalo, London: University of Toronto Press.

Greengus, Samuel (1979) *Old Babylonian Tablets from Ishchali and Vicinity*, Istanbul: Nederlands Historisch-Archaeologisch Instituut te Istanbul.

Grégoire, Jean-Pierre (1970) *Archives administratives sumériennes*, Paris: Librairie Orientaliste Paul Geuthner.

Guinan, Ann (1989) "The Peril of Living High: Divinatory Rhetoric in *Šumma Alu*," *Studies in Honor of Ake W. Sjöberg*, Philadelphia: Occasional Publications of the Samuel Noah Kramer Fund: 227–36.

Güterbock, Hans G. (1934) "Die historische Tradition und ihre literarische Gestaltung bei Babyloniern und Hethitern," *Zeitschrift für Assyrologie* 42: 1–91.

——— (1964) "Sargon of Akkad Mentioned by Hattushili I of Hatti," *Journal of Cuneiform Studies* 18: 1–6.

——— (1969) "Ein neues Bruchstück der Sargon-Erzählung 'König der Schlacht'," *Mitteilungen der Deutschen Orient-Gesellschaft zu Berlin* 101: 14–26.

Hallo, William W. (1976) "Women of Sumer," in D. Schmandt-Besserat (ed.) *The Legacy of Sumer*, Malibu: Undena Publications: 23–40.

——— (1978) "Simurrum and the Hurrian Frontier," *Revue Hittite et Asianique* 36: 71–83.

——— (1988) "The Nabonassar Era and other Epochs in Mesopotamian Chronology and Chronography," in E. Leichty, M. de J. Ellis and P. Gerardi (eds) *A Scientific Humanist: Studies in Memory of Abraham Sachs,*

Philadelphia: Occasional Publications of the Samuel Noah Kramer Fund: 175–90.

—— (1990) "Assyriology and the Canon," *The American Scholar,* Winter 1990: 105–8.

—— (1991a) "The Concept of Canonicity in Cuneiform and Biblical Literature. A Comparative Appraisal," in K. L. Younger, W. W. Hallo, and B. F. Batto (eds) *The Biblical Canon in Comparative Perspective,* Lewiston: The Edwin Mellen Press: 1–20.

—— (1991b) "The Death of Kings," *Studies . . . Presented to Hayim Tadmor,* Jerusalem: Magness Press: 148–65.

Hallo, William W. and Simpson, William (1998) *The Ancient Near East: A History,* 2nd edition, Fort Worth: Harcourt Brace College Publishers.

Halstead, Paul (1990) "Quantifying Sumerian Agriculture – Some Seeds of Doubt and Hope," *Bulletin on Sumerian Agriculture* 5: 187–95.

Harris, Rivkah (1977) "Notes on the Slave Names of Old Babylonian Sippar," *Journal of Cuneiform Studies* 29: 46–51.

—— (1989) "Independent Women in Ancient Mesopotamia?," in B. S. Lesko (ed.) *Women's Earliest Records from Ancient Egypt and Western Asia,* Atlanta: Scholars Press: 145–56.

—— (1992) "Women (Mesopotamia)," in D. N. Freedman (ed.) *The Anchor Bible Dictionary,* vol. 6, New York: Doubleday: 947–51.

Hegel, G. W. F. (1956) *The Philosophy of History,* trans. J. Sibree, New York: Dover Publications.

Heimpel, Wolfgang (1981) "Das Untere Meer," *Zeitschrift für Assyriologie* 77: 22–91.

—— (1995) "Plow Animal Inspection Records from Ur III Girsu and Umma," *Bulletin on Sumerian Agriculture* 8: 71–171.

Heinrich, Ernst (1984) *Die Paläste im alten Mesopotamien,* Berlin: W. de Gruyter.

Helly, Dorothy O. and Reverby, Susan M. (eds) (1992) *Gendered Domains: Rethinking Public and Private in Women's History,* Ithaca: Cornell University Press.

Herodotus (1954) *The Histories,* trans. Aubrey de Sélincourt, Harmondsworth: Penguin Books.

Hirsch, Hans (1963) "Die Inschriften der Könige von Agade," *Archiv für Orientforschung* 20: 1–82.

Hobsbawn, E. J. (1988) "History From Below – Some Reflections," in F. Krantz (ed.) *History From Below: Studies in Popular Protest and Popular Ideology,* Oxford: Blackwell: 13–27.

Horowitz, Wayne (1988) "The Babylonian Map of the World," *Iraq* 50: 147–65.

Hunger, Hermann and Sachs, Abraham J. (1988–96) *Astronomical Diaries and Related Texts from Babylonia,* 3 volumes, Vienna: Verlag der Österreichischen Akademie der Wissenschaften.

Ichisar, Metin (1981) *Les archives cappadociennes du marchand Imdilum,* Paris: Éditions A.D.P.E.

Jeyes, Ulla (1983) "The Nadītu Women of Sippar," in A. Cameron and A. Kuhrt (eds) *Images of Women in Antiquity,* Detroit: Wayne State University Press: 260–72.

Jones, Tom B. (1975) "Sumerian Administrative Documents: An Essay," in
    S. J. Lieberman (ed.) *Sumerological Studies in Honor of Thorkild Jacobsen*,
    Chicago: The Oriental Institute of the University of Chicago: 41–61.
Kabbani, Rana (1986) *Europe's Myths of Orient*, London: Macmillan.
Kandiyoti, Deniz (1996) "Contemporary Feminist Scholarship and Middle
    East Studies," in D. Kandiyoti (ed.) *Gendering the Middle East: Emerging
    Perspectives*, Syracuse: Syracuse University Press: 1–27.
Katz, Dina (1993) *Gilgamesh and Akka*, Groningen: Styx.
Kennedy, Douglas (1969) "Realia," *Revue d'Assyriologie* 63: 79–82.
King, L. W. (1899) *Cuneiform Texts from Babylonian Tablets in the British
    Museum*, 7, London.
—— (1900) *Cuneiform Texts from Babylonian Tablets in the British Museum*, 10,
    London.
—— (1907) *Chronicles Concerning Early Babylonian Kings*, vol. II, London:
    Luzac and Co.
Kinnier Wilson, J. V. (1972) *The Nimrud Wine Lists*, London: British School
    of Archaeology in Iraq.
Kohl, Philip L. (1987) "The Use and Abuse of World Systems Theory: The
    Case of the Pristine West Asian State," in M. B. Schiffer (ed.) *Advances in
    Archaeological Method and Theory*, 11, San Diego: Academic Press, Inc.:
    1–35.
Kohler, J. and Ungnad, A (1909–23) *Hammurabi's Gesetz*, III–VI, Leipzig.
Komoroczy, G. (1978) "Landed Property in Ancient Mesopotamia and the
    Theory of the So-called Asiatic Mode of Production," *Oekumene* 2: 9–26.
Kovacs, Maureen Gallery (1989) *The Epic of Gilgamesh*, Stanford: Stanford
    University Press.
Kramer, Samuel Noah (1959) *History Begins at Sumer*, New York: Anchor
    Books.
—— (1976) "Poets and Psalmists: Goddesses and Theologians," in
    D. Schmandt-Besserat (ed.) *The Legacy of Sumer*, Malibu: Undena
    Publications: 3–21.
Kraus, F. R. (1975) "Feldpachtverträge aus der Zeit der III. Dynastie von
    Ur," *Die Welt des Orients* 8: 185–205.
Kuhrt, Amélie (1987) "Usurpation, Conquest, and Ceremonial: From
    Babylon to Persia," in D. Cannadine and S. Price (eds) *Rituals of Royalty*,
    Cambridge: Cambridge University Press: 20–55.
—— (1995) *The Ancient Near East c. 3000–330 BC*, 2 volumes, London and
    New York: Routledge.
Kutscher, Raphael (1989) *The Brockmon Tablets at the University of Haifa.
    Royal Inscriptions*, Haifa: Haifa University Press.
Kwasman, Theodore and Parpola, Simo (1991) *Legal Transactions of the
    Royal Court of Nineveh*, Part I (State Archives of Assyria, vol. VI), Helsinki:
    Helsinki University Press.
Lambert, Wilfred G. (1992) "Prostitution," in V. Haas (ed.) *Außenseiter und
    Randgruppen* (*Xenia* 3), Konstanz: Universitätsverlag: 127–57.
Langdon, Stephen (1912) *Die neubabylonischen Königsinschriften*, Leipzig:
    Hinrichs'sche Buchhandlung.
Larsen, Mogens Trolle (1976) *The Old Assyrian City-State and Its Colonies*,
    Copenhagen: Akademisk Forlag.

—— (1982) "Your Money or Your Life! A Portrait of an Assyrian Businessman," *Societies and Languages of the Ancient Near East: Studies in Honour of I. M. Diakonoff*, Warminster: Aris & Phillips: 214–45.

—— (1987) "Commercial Networks in the Ancient Near East," in M. Rowlands, M. Larsen, and K. Kristiansen (eds) *Centre and Periphery in the Ancient World*, Cambridge: Cambridge University Press: 47–56.

Leemans, W. F. (1983) "Trouve-t-on des 'communautés rurales' dans l'ancienne Mésopotamie?," *Recueils de la société Jean Bodin pour l'histoire comparative des institutions*, XLI/2, Paris: Dessain et Tolra: 43–106.

Lerner, Gerda (1986) *The Creation of Patriarchy*, New York: Oxford University Press.

Le Roy Ladurie, Emmanuel (1979) *Montaillou: The Promised Land of Error*, New York: Vintage Books.

Lesko, Barbara S. (ed.) (1989) *Women's Earliest Records from Ancient Egypt and Western Asia*, Atlanta: Scholars Press.

Levine, Louis D. (1981) "Manuscripts, Texts and the Study of the Neo-Assyrian Royal Inscriptions," in F. M. Fales (ed.) *Assyrian Royal Inscriptions: New Horizons*, Rome: Instituto per l'Oriente: 49–70.

—— (1982) "Sennacherib's Southern Front: 704–689 B.C.," *Journal of Cuneiform Studies* 34: 28–58.

—— (1983) "Preliminary Remarks on the Historical Inscriptions of Sennacherib," in H. Tadmor and M. Weinfeld (eds) *History, Historiography, and Interpretation*, Jerusalem: Magness Press: 58–75.

Lewis, Brian (1980) *The Sargon Legend: A Study of the Akkadian Text and the Tale of the Hero who was exposed at Birth*, Cambridge, MA: American Schools of Oriental Research.

Liverani, Mario (1973) "Memorandum on the Approach to Historiographic Texts," *Orientalia* 42: 178–94.

—— (1976) "Il modo di produzione," in S. Moscati (ed.) *L'alba della civiltá*, vol. 2: *L'economia*, Turin: UTET: 1–126.

—— (1979) "The Ideology of the Assyrian Empire," in M. T. Larsen (ed.) *Power and Propaganda*, Copenhagen: Akademisk Forlag: 297–318.

—— (1981) "Critique of Variants and the Titulary of Sennacherib," in F. M. Fales (ed.) *Assyrian Royal Inscriptions: New Horizons*, Rome: Instituto per l'Oriente: 225–57.

—— (1984) "Land Tenure and Inheritance in the Ancient Near East: the Interaction between Palace and Family Sectors," in T. Khalidi (ed.) *Land Tenure and Social Transformation in the Middle East*, Beirut: American University of Beirut: 33–44.

—— (1992) "Nationality and Political Identity," in D. N. Freedman (ed.) *The Anchor Bible Dictionary*, vol. 4, New York: Doubleday: 1031–7.

—— (1993a) "Model and Actualization. The Kings of Akkad in the Historical Tradition," in M. Liverani (ed.) *Akkad: The First World Empire*, Padua: Sargon srl: 41–67.

—— (ed.) (1993b) *Akkad: The First World Empire*, Padua: Sargon srl.

—— (1995) "The Deeds of Ancient Mesopotamian Kings," in Jack M. Sasson (ed.) *Civilizations of the Ancient Near East*, New York: Charles Scribner's Sons: 2353–66.

Longman, Tremper, III (1991) *Fictional Akkadian Autobiography: A Generic and Comparative Study*, Winona Lake: Eisenbrauns.

Luckenbill, Daniel David (1924) *The Annals of Sennacherib*, Oriental Institute Publications, vol. 2, Chicago: The Oriental Institute.

—— (1926) *Ancient Records of Assyria and Babylonia*, vol. I, Chicago: University of Chicago Press.

—— (1927) *Ancient Records of Assyria and Babylonia*, vol. II, Chicago: University of Chicago Press.

Lutz, W. F. (1917) *Early Babylonian Letters from Larsa*, New Haven: Yale University Press.

Mabro, Judy (1991) *Veiled Half-truths: Western Travellers' Perceptions of Middle Eastern Women*, London and New York: I. B. Tauris.

Machinist, Peter (1983) "Assyria and its Image in the First Isaiah," *Journal of the American Oriental Society* 103: 719–37.

—— (1986) "On Self-Consciousness in Mesopotamia," in S. N. Eisenstadt (ed.) *The Origins and Diversity of Axial Age Civilizations*, New York: State University of New York Press: 183–202, 511–18.

—— (1993) "Assyrians on Assyria in the First Millennium B.C.," in K. Raaflaub (ed.) *Anfänge politischen Denkens in der Antike*, Munich: R. Oldenburg Verlag: 77–104.

—— (1997) "The Fall of Assyria in Comparative Ancient Perspective," in S. Parpola and R. M. Whiting (eds) *Assyria 1995*, Helsinki: The Neo-Assyrian Text Corpus Project: 179–95.

Maekawa, Kazuya (1973–4) "The Development of the É-Mí in Lagash during the Early Dynastic III," *Mesopotamia* 8–9: 77–144.

—— (1977) "The Rent of the Tenant Field (gán-APIN.LAL) in Lagash," *Zinbun* 14: 1–54.

—— (1981) "The Agricultural Texts of Ur III Lagash of the British Museum (I)," *Acta Sumerologica* 3: 37–61.

—— (1984) "Cereal Cultivation in the Ur III Period," *Bulletin on Sumerian Agriculture* 1: 73–96.

—— (1986a) "The Agricultural Texts of Ur III Lagash of the British Museum (IV)," *Zinbun* 21: 91–157.

—— (1986b) "Two Ur III Tablets in the British Collections," *Acta Sumerologica* 8: 345–7.

—— (1987) "The Agricultural Texts of Ur III Lagash of the British Museum (V)," *Acta Sumerologica* 9: 89–129.

Manitius, Walther (1910) "Das stehende Heer der Assyrerkönige," *Zeitschrift für Assyriologie* 24: 97–149, 185–224.

Mayer, Walter (1983) "Sargons Feldzug gegen Urartu – 714 v. Chr. Text und Übersetzung," *Mitteilungen der Deutschen Orient-Gesellschaft zu Berlin* 115: 65–132.

Merrill, Anne W. (1979) "Theoretical Explanations of the Change from Matriarchy to Patriarchy," *The Kroeber Anthropological Society Papers* 59/60: 13–18.

Meskell, Lynn (1995) "Goddesses, Gimbutas and 'New Age' Archaeology," *Antiquity* 69: 74–86.

—— (1996) "The Somatization of Archaeology: Institutions, Discourses, Corporeality," *Norwegian Archaeological Review* 29: 1–14.

Meyer, Eduard (1924) *Kleine Schriften*, 2 volumes, Halle: Niemeyer.

Michalowski, Piotr (1987) "Charisma and Control: On Continuity and Change in Early Mesopotamian Bureaucratic Systems," in McGuire Gibson and Robert D. Biggs (eds) *The Organization of Power*, Chicago: The Oriental Institute of the University of Chicago: 55–68.

—— (1993) "Memory and Deed: The Historiography of the Political Expansion of the Akkad State," in M. Liverani (ed.) *Akkad: The First World Empire*, Padua: Sargon srl: 69–90.

Michel, Cécile (1991) *Innāya dans les tablettes paléo-assyriennes*, Paris: Éditions Recherche sur les Civilisations.

Millard, Alan (1994) *The Eponyms of the Assyrian Empire, 910–612 BC*, State Archives of Assyria Studies, vol. II, Helsinki: The Neo-Assyrian Text Corpus Project.

Morgan, Lewis Henry (1985) *Ancient Society*, Tucson: University of Arizona Press (originally published 1877).

Murray, Oswyn (1991a) "Greek Historians," in J. Boardman, J. Griffin, and O. Murray (eds) *The Oxford History of Greece and the Hellenistic World*, Oxford and New York: Oxford University Press: 214–39.

—— (1991b) "Life and Society in Classical Greece," in J. Boardman *et al.* (eds) *The Oxford History of Greece and the Hellenistic World*, Oxford and New York: Oxford University Press: 240–76.

Neumann, Hans (1992) "Zur privaten Geschäftstätigkeit in Nippur in der Ur III-Zeit," in M. de J. Ellis (ed.) *Nippur at the Centennial*, Philadephia: Occasional Publications of the Samuel Noah Kramer Fund: 161–76.

—— (1993) "Zur Problem der privaten Feldpacht in neusumerischer Zeit," in J. Zablocka and S. Zawadzki (eds) *Shulmu IV: Everyday Life in Ancient Near East*, Poznan: Poznan University: 223–33.

Nissen, Hans (1995) "Western Asia Before the Age of Empires," in Jack M. Sasson (ed.) *Civilizations of the Ancient Near East*, New York: Charles Scribner's Sons: 791–806.

Novick, Peter (1988) *That Noble Dream: The 'Objectivity Question' and the American Historical Profession*, Cambridge: Cambridge University Press.

Nylander, Carl (1980) "Who Mutilated 'Sargon's' Head?," in B. Alster (ed.) *Death in Mesopotamia*, Copenhagen: Akademisk Forlag: 271–2.

Olmstead, Albert Ten Eyck (1916) *Assyrian Historiography: A Source Study*, Columbia, Missouri.

Oppenheim, Leo A. (1955) "'Siege Documents' from Nippur." *Iraq* 17: 69–89.

—— (1957) "A Bird's-Eye View of Mesopotamian Economic History," in K. Polanyi, C. M. Arensberg, and H. W. Pearson (eds) *Trade and Market in Early Empires*, Chicago: Free Press: 27–37.

—— (1973) "A Note on ša rēši," *Journal of the Ancient Near East Society* 5: 325–34.

—— (1967) *Letters from Mesopotamia*, Chicago and London: University of Chicago Press.

—— (1977) *Ancient Mesopotamia. Portrait of a Dead Civilization*, 2nd edition, Chicago: University of Chicago Press.

—— (1979) "Neo-Assyrian and Neo-Babylonian Empires," in H. D.

Laswell, D. Lerner, and H. Speier (eds) *Propaganda and Communication in World History*, I, Honolulu: University Press of Hawaii: 111–44.

Oppenheim, A. Leo *et al.* (1956–) *The Assyrian Dictionary*, Chicago: The Oriental Institute.

Parpola, Simo (1980) "The Murderer of Sennacherib," in B. Alster (ed.) *Death in Mesopotamia*, Copenhagen: Akademisk Forlag: 171–82.

Parpola, Simo and Watanabe, Kazuko (1988) *Neo-Assyrian Treaties and Loyalty Oaths*, State Archives of Assyria, vol. II, Helsinki: Helsinki University Press.

Pearson, Harry W. (1957) "The Secular Debate on Economic Primitivism," in K. Polanyi, C. M. Arensberg, and H. W. Pearson (eds) *Trade and Market in Early Empires*, Chicago: Free Press: 3–11.

Peirce, Leslie P. (1993) *The Imperial Harem: Women and Sovereignty in the Ottoman Empire*, New York: Oxford University Press.

Pettinato, Giovanni (1970–71) "Il Conflitto tra Lagash ed Umma per la 'Frontiera Divina' e la sua soluzione durante la terza dinastia di Ur," *Mesopotamia* 5/6: 281–320.

—— (1977) "Due testi inediti di agrimensura neosumerici e il problema delle qualità del suolo agricolo," *Atti della Accademia Nazionale dei Lincei. Serie ottava. Rendiconti. Classe di Scienze morale, storichi e filologiche* 32: 63–95.

Polanyi, Karl (1957) "Marketless Trading in Hammurabi's Time," in K. Polanyi, C. M. Arensberg, and H. W. Pearson (eds) *Trade and Market in Early Empires*, Chicago: Free Press: 12–26.

—— (1977) *The Livelihood of Man*, New York: Academic Press.

Pollock, Sheldon (1989) "Mīmāṃsā and the Problem of History in Traditional India," *Journal of the American Oriental Society* 109: 603–10.

Pollock, Susan (1991) "Women in a Men's World: Images of Sumerian Women," in J. M. Gero and M. W. Conkey (eds) *Engendering Archaeology: Women and Prehistory*, Oxford: Basil Blackwell: 366–87.

Polybius (1927) *The Histories*, trans. W. R. Paton, London: William Heinemann.

Pomeroy, Sarah B. (1975) *Goddesses, Whores, Wives, and Slaves: Women in Classical Antiquity*, New York: Schocken Books.

Porter, Barbara Nevling (1993) *Images, Power, and Politics: Figurative Aspects of Esarhaddon's Babylonian Policy*, Philadelphia: American Philosophical Society.

—— (1995) "Language, Audience and Impact in Imperial Assyria," *Israel Oriental Studies* 15: 51–72.

Postgate, J. N. (1988) *The Archive of Urad-Šerūa and his Family*, Rome: Editore Roberto Denicola.

—— (1992) *Early Mesopotamia: Society and Economy at the Dawn of History*, London and New York: Routledge.

Powell, Marvin A. (1978) "Götter, Könige, und 'Kapitalisten' im Mesopotamien des 3. Jahrtausends v.u.Z.," *Oekumene* 2: 127–44.

—— (1981) "Three Problems in the History of Cuneiform Writing: Origins, Direction of Script, Literacy," *Visible Language* XV/4: 419–40.

Reiner, Erica (1960) "Plague Amulets and House Blessings," *Journal of Near Eastern Studies* 29: 148–55.

—— (1969) "Akkadian Treaties from Syria and Assyria," in J. B. Pritchard (ed.) *Ancient Near Eastern Texts Relating to the Old Testament*, 3rd edition, Princeton, NJ: Princeton University Press: 531–41.

Renger, Johannes (1980–83) "Königsinschriften. B. Akkadisch," *Reallexikon der Assyriologie*, 6, Berlin and New York: Walter de Gruyter: 65–77.

—— (1984) "Patterns of Non-institutional Trade and Non-commercial Exchange in Ancient Mesopotamia at the Beginning of the Second Millennium B.C.," in A. Archi (ed.) *Circulation of Goods in Non-Palatial Context in the Ancient Near East*, Rome: Edizione dell'Ateneo: 31–123.

—— (1988) "Zu aktuellen Frage der Mesopotamische Wirtschafts-geschichte," in P. Vavrousek and V. Soucek (eds) *Shulmu*, Prague: Charles University: 301–17.

—— (1989) "Probleme und Perspektiven einer Wirtschaftsgeschichte Mesopotamiens," *Saeculum* 40: 166–78.

—— (1994) "On Economic Structures in Ancient Mesopotamia," *Orientalia* 63: 157–208.

—— (1995) "Institutional, Communal, and Individual Ownership or Possession of Arable Land in Ancient Mesopotamia from the End of the Fourth to the End of the First Millennium B.C.," *Chicago-Kent Law Review* 71: 269–319.

—— (1996) "Vergangenes Geschehen in der Textüberlieferung des alten Mesopotamien," in H.-J. Gehrke and A. Möller (eds) *Vergangenheit und Lebenswelt. Soziale Kommunikation, Traditionsbildung und historisches Bewußtsein*, Tübingen: Gunter Narr Verlag: 9–60.

Rohrlich, Ruby (1980) "State Formation in Sumer and the Subjugation of Women," *Feminist Studies* 6: 76–102.

Röllig, Wolfgang (1976) "Der altmesopotamische Markt," *Die Welt des Orients* 8: 286–95.

Roth, Martha T. (1995) *Law Collections from Mesopotamia and Asia Minor*, Atlanta: Scholars Press.

Russell, John Malcolm (1991) *Sennacherib's Palace Without Rival at Nineveh*, Chicago and London: University of Chicago Press.

Sahlins, Marshall D. (1972) *Stone-Age Economics*, Chicago: Aldine Publishing Co.

Sallaberger, Walther (1993) *Der kultische Kalender der Ur III-Zeit*, Berlin and New York: Walter de Gruyter.

Sasson, Jack M. (ed.) (1995) *Civilizations of the Ancient Near East*, 4 volumes, New York: Charles Scribner's Sons.

Schaps, David M. (1979) *Economic Rights of Women in Ancient Greece*, Edinburgh: Edinburgh University Press.

Schneider, Anna (1920) *Die Anfänge der Kulturwirtschaft. Die sumerische Tempelstadt*, Essen: G. D. Baedeker.

Schneider, Helmuth (1990) "Die Bücher-Meyer Kontroverse," in W. M. Calder and A. Demondt (eds) *Eduard Meyer. Leben und Leistung eines Universalhistoriker*, Leiden: Brill: 417–45.

Scholes, Robert and Kellogg, Robert (1966) *The Nature of Narrative*, Oxford and New York: Oxford University Press.

Seux, M.-J. (1980–83) "Königtum," *Reallexikon der Assyriologie* 6, Berlin and New York: Walter de Gruyter: 140–73.

Sigrist, Marcel (1985) "Mu Malgium basig," *Revue d'assyriologie* 79: 161–8.
—— (1992) *Drehem*, Bethesda: CDL Press.
Silver, Morris (1985) *Economic Structures of the Ancient Near East*, London and Sidney: Croom Helm.
Skaist, Aaron (1994) *The Old Babylonian Loan Contract*, Ramat Gan: Bar-llan University Press.
Smith, George (1875) *Assyrian Discoveries*, New York: Scribner, Armstrong & Co.
Smith, Sidney (1929) "Sennacherib and Esarhaddon," in J. B. Bury, S. A. Cook, and F. E. Adcock (eds) *The Cambridge Ancient History*, 1st edn, vol. III, Cambridge: Cambridge University Press: 61–87.
Snell, Daniel C. (1997) *Life in the Ancient Near East*, New Haven and London: Yale University Press.
Steible, H. (1982) *Die altsumerischen Bau- und Weihinschriften*, Stuttgart: Franz Steiner Verlag.
—— (1991) *Die neusumerischen Bau- und Weihinschriften*, Stuttgart: Franz Steiner Verlag.
Steiner, Gerd (1987) "Die *femme fatale* im alten Orient," in J.-M. Durand (ed.) *La femme dans le proche-orient antique*, Paris: Éditions Recherche sur les Civilisations: 147–53.
Steinkeller, Piotr (1987a) "The Foresters of Umma: Toward a Definition of Ur III Labor," in M. A. Powell (ed.) *Labor in the Ancient Near East*, New Haven: American Oriental Society: 73–115.
—— (1987b) "The Administrative and Economic Organization of the Ur III State: The Core and the Periphery," in McGuire Gibson and R. D. Biggs (eds) *The Organization of Power: Aspects of Bureaucracy in the Ancient Near East*, Chicago: The Oriental Institute of the University of Chicago: 19–41.
—— (1996) "The Organization of Crafts in Third Millennium Babylonia: The Case of Potters," *Altorientalische Forschungen* 23: 232–53.
Stol, Marten (1976) *Studies in Old Babylonian History*, Istanbul: Nederlands Historisch-Archaeologisch Instituut te Istanbul.
—— (1993–97) "mus̆kēnu," *Reallexikon der Assyriologie*, 8, Berlin and New York: Walter de Gruyter: 492–3.
—— (1995a) "Private Life in Ancient Mesopotamia," in Jack M. Sasson (ed.) *Civilizations of the Ancient Near East*, New York: Charles Scribner's Sons: 485–501.
—— (1995b) "Women in Mesopotamia," *Journal of the Economic and Social History of the Orient* 38: 123–44.
Stolper, Matthew W. (1985) *Entrepreneurs and Empire*, Istanbul: Nederlands Historisch-Archaeologisch Instituut te Istanbul.
Stone, Lawrence (1987) *The Past and Present Revisited*, London and New York: Routledge and Kegan Paul.
Streck, M. (1916) *Assurbanipal und die letzen assyrische Könige*, Leipzig: J. C. Hinrichs'sche Buchhandlung.
Tadmor, Hayim (1994) *The Inscriptions of Tiglath-Pileser III King of Assyria*, Jerusalem: Israel Academy of Sciences and Humanities.
Tadmor, Hayim and Weinfeld, Moshe (eds) (1983) *History, Historiography, and Interpretation*, Jerusalem: Magness Press.

Thompson, E. P. (1966) *The Making of the English Working Class*, New York: Vintage Books.

Thureau-Dangin, François (1903) *Recueil des tablettes Chaldéennes*, Paris: Leroux.

—— (1907) *Die sumerischen und akkadischen Königsinschriften*, Leipzig: J. C. Hinrichs'sche Buchhandlung.

Tringham, Ruth E. (1991) "Households with Faces: The Challenge of Gender in Prehistoric Architectural Remains," in J. M. Gero and M. W. Conkey (eds) *Engendering Archaeology: Women and Prehistory*, Oxford: Basil Blackwell: 93–131.

Uchitel, Alexander (1984) "Daily Work at Sagdana Millhouse," *Acta Sumerologica* 6: 75–98.

Ussishkin, David (1997) "Lachish," in E. Meyers (ed.) *The Oxford Encyclopedia of Archaeology in the Near East*, vol. 3, New York and Oxford: Oxford University Press: 317–23.

Van De Mieroop, Marc (1987a) *Sumerian Administrative Documents from the Reigns of Išbi-Erra and Šu-ilišu*, New Haven and London: Yale University Press.

—— (1987b) *Crafts in the Early Isin Period*, Louvain: Departement Orientalistiek.

—— (1989) "Women in the Economy of Sumer," in B. S. Lesko (ed.) *Women's Earliest Records from Ancient Egypt and Western Asia*, Atlanta: Scholars Press: 53–66.

—— (1992) *Society and Enterprise in Old Babylonian Ur*, Berlin: Dietrich Reimer Verlag.

—— (1997a) "On Writing a History of the Ancient Near East," *Bibliotheca Orientalis* 54: 285–305.

—— (1997b) "Why Did they Write on Clay?," *Klio* 79: 7–18.

—— (1997c) *The Ancient Mesopotamian City*, Oxford: Oxford University Press.

—— (forthcoming) "Ancient Near Eastern History in its Middle Eastern Setting," in H. Dabashi and T. Riccardi (eds) *The Postcolonial Word*.

van der Spek, R. J. (1993) "The Astronomical Diaries as a Source for Achaemenid and Seleucid History," *Bibliotheca Orientalis* 50: 91–101.

—— (1994) ". . . en hun machthebbers worden weldoeners genoemd," inaugural address at the Vrije Universiteit, Amsterdam, 28 April 1994.

van der Toorn, Karel (1995) "Review of Bottéro 1992," *Numen* 42: 83–90.

Van Driel, G. (1987) "Continuity or Decay in the Late Achaemenid Period: Evidence from Southern Mesopotamia," in H. Sancisi-Weerdenburg (ed.) *Achaemenid History I: Sources, Structures and Synthesis*, Leiden: Nederlands Instituut voor het Nabije Oosten: 159–81.

—— (1989) "The Murashûs in Context," *Journal of the Economic and Social History of the Orient* 32: 203–29.

Veenhof, Klaas R. (1977) "Some Social Aspects of Old Assyrian Trade," *Iraq* 39: 109–18.

—— (1995) "Kanesh: An Assyrian Colony in Anatolia," in Jack M. Sasson (ed.) *Civilizations of the Ancient Near East*, New York: Charles Scribner's Sons: 859–71.

—— (1997) "'Modern' Features in Old Assyrian Trade," *Journal of the Economic and Social History of the Orient* 40: 336–66.

Veyne, Paul (1984) *Writing History: Essay on Epistemology*, Middletown: Wesleyan University Press.

Von Soden, Wolfram (1965–) *Akkadisches Handwörterbuch*, Wiesbaden: Otto Harrassowitz.

Waetzoldt, Hartmut (1987) "Compensation of Craft Workers and Officials in the Ur III Period," in M. A. Powell (ed.) *Labor in the Ancient Near East*, New Haven: American Oriental Society: 117–41.

Walker, C. B. F. (1973) "Cuneiform Tablets in the County Museum and Art Gallery, Truro, Cornwall," *Archiv für Orientforschung* 24: 122–7.

—— (1987) *Cuneiform*, University of California Press/British Museum.

Wall-Romana, Christophe (1990) "An Areal Location of Agade," *Journal of Near Eastern Studies* 49: 205–45.

Weber, Max (1958) *The City*, trans. and ed. by Don Martindale and Gertrud Neuwirth, New York: Free Press.

—— (1976) *The Agrarian Sociology of Ancient Civilizations*, trans. R. I. Frank, London and New York: Verso.

Weidner, Ernst (1954–56) "Hof- und Harems-Erlasse assyrischer Könige aus dem 2. Jahrtausend v. Chr.," *Archiv für Orientforschung* 17: 257–93.

Weissbach, F. H. (1911) *Die Keilinschriften der Achämeniden*, Leipzig: J. C. Hinrichs'sche Buchhandlung.

Westenholz, Aage (1975) *Old Sumerian and Old Akkadian Texts in Philadelphia chiefly from Nippur*, Malibu: Undena Publications.

Westenholz, Joan (1983) "Heroes of Akkad," *Journal of the American Oriental Society* 103: 327–33.

—— (1990) "Towards a New Conceptualization of the Female Role in Mesopotamian Society," *Journal of the American Oriental Society* 110: 510–21.

—— (1997) *Legends of the Kings of Akkade*, Winona Lake: Eisenbrauns.

White, Hayden (1972) "The Structure of Historical Narrative," *Clio* 1/3, June 1972: 5–20.

—— (1973) *Metahistory: The Historical Imagination in Nineteenth-Century Europe*, Baltimore and London: Johns Hopkins University Press.

—— (1987) *The Content of the Form: Narrative Discourse and Historical Representation*, Baltimore and London: Johns Hopkins University Press.

Wilhelm, Gernot (1986) "Urartu als Region der Keilschrift-Kultur," in V. Haas (ed.) *Das Reich Urartu*, Konstanz: Universitäts Verlag Konstanz: 95–116.

—— (1990) "Marginalien zu Herodot Klio 199," in T. Abusch, J. Huehnergard, and P. Steinkeller (eds) *Lingering Over Words. Studies in Ancient Near Eastern Literature in Honor of William L. Moran*, Atlanta: Scholars Press: 505–24.

Will, Édouard (1954) "Trois quarts de siècle de recherches sur l'économie grecque antique," *Annales* 9: 7–22.

Winter, Irene (1987) "Women in Public: The Disk of Enheduanna, the Beginning of the Office of en-priestess, and the Weight of Visual Evidence," in J.-M. Durand (ed.) *La femme dans le proche-orient antique*, Paris: Éditions Recherche sur les Civilisations: 189–201.

—— (1996) "Sex, Rhetoric, and the Public Monument: The Alluring Body of Naram-Sîn of Agade," in N. B. Kampen (ed.) *Sexuality in Ancient Art,* Cambridge: Cambridge University Press: 11–26.

Wittfogel, Karl (1957) *Oriental Despotism,* New Haven: Yale University Press.

Wright, Rita P. (ed.) (1996) *Gender and Archaeology,* Philadelphia: University of Pennsylvania Press.

Zaccagnini, Carlo (1981a) "An Urartean Royal Inscription in the Report of Sargon's Eighth Campaign," in F. M. Fales (ed.) *Assyrian Royal Inscriptions: New Horizons,* Rome: Instituto per l'Oriente: 259–95.

—— (1981b) "Modi di produzione asiatico e Vicino Oriente antico. Appunti per una discussione," *Dialoghi di archeologia* NS 3/3: 3–65.

—— (ed.) (1989) *Production and Consumption in the Ancient Near East,* Budapest: University of Budapest.

Zarins, J. (1992) "The Early Settlement of Southern Mesopotamia: A Review of Recent Historical, Geological, and Archaeological Research," *Journal of the American Oriental Society* 112: 55–77.

Zettler, Richard L. (1996) "Written Documents as Excavated Artifacts and the Holistic Interpretation of the Mesopotamian Archaeological Record," in J. S. Cooper and G. M. Schwartz (eds) *The Study of the Ancient Near East in the Twenty-First Century,* Winona Lake: Eisenbrauns: 81–101.

Index

Note: the titles of ancient Mesopotamian texts are italicized.